*A Letter
Concerning Toleration
and Other Writings*

John Locke

THE THOMAS HOLLIS LIBRARY

David Womersley, General Editor

John Locke:
A Letter
Concerning Toleration
and Other Writings

Edited and with an Introduction
by Mark Goldie

LIBERTY FUND

Indianapolis

This book is published by Liberty Fund, Inc., a foundation established to encourage study of the ideal of a society of free and responsible individuals.

The cuneiform inscription that serves as our logo and as the design motif for our endpapers is the earliest-known written appearance of the word "freedom" (*amagi*), or "liberty." It is taken from a clay document written about 2300 B.C. in the Sumerian city-state of Lagash.

Introduction, editorial additions, and index
© 2010 by Liberty Fund, Inc.

Frontispiece: Engraved portrait of John Locke that prefaces Thomas Hollis's 1765 edition of *Letters Concerning Toleration.* Reproduced by courtesy of the Thomas Fisher Rare Book Library, University of Toronto.

Printed in the United States of America

C   10   9   8   7   6   5   4   3   2   1
P   10   9   8   7   6   5   4   3   2

Library of Congress Cataloging-in-Publication Data
Locke, John, 1632–1704.
[Epistola de tolerantia. English]
A letter concerning toleration and other writings/John Locke; edited by David Womersley and with an introduction by Mark Goldie.
p. cm.—(The Thomas Hollis Library)
Includes bibliographical references and index.
ISBN 978-0-86597-790-7 (hc: alk. paper)—
ISBN 978-0-86597-791-4 (pbk.: alk. paper)
1. Toleration—Early works to 1800.
I. Womersley, David.   II. Goldie, Mark.   III. Title.
BR1610.L823 2010
261.7'2—dc22   2010002621

LIBERTY FUND, INC.
8335 Allison Pointe Trail, Suite 300
Indianapolis, Indiana 46250-1684

CONTENTS

The Thomas Hollis Library, by David Womersley   vii

Introduction, by Mark Goldie   ix

Further Reading   xxv

Notes on the Texts   xxix

Chronology of Locke's Life   xli

Acknowledgments   xlvii

1. *A Letter Concerning Toleration*   1

2. Excerpts from *A Third Letter for Toleration*   69

3. *An Essay Concerning Toleration*   105

4. Fragments on Toleration   141

Index   191

THE THOMAS HOLLIS LIBRARY

Thomas Hollis (1720–74) was an eighteenth-century Englishman who devoted his energies, his fortune, and his life to the cause of liberty. Hollis was trained for a business career, but a series of inheritances allowed him to pursue instead a career of public service. He believed that citizenship demanded activity and that it was incumbent on citizens to put themselves in a position, by reflection and reading, in which they could hold their governments to account. To that end for many years he distributed books that he believed explained the nature of liberty and revealed how liberty might best be defended and promoted.

A particular beneficiary of Hollis's generosity was Harvard College. In the years preceding the Declaration of Independence, Hollis was assiduous in sending to America boxes of books, many of which he had had specially printed and bound, to encourage the colonists in their struggle against Great Britain. At the same time he took pains to explain the colonists' grievances and concerns to his fellow Englishmen.

The Thomas Hollis Library makes freshly available a selection of titles that, because of their intellectual power, or the influence they exerted on the public life of their own time, or the distinctiveness of their approach to the topic of liberty, comprise the cream of the books distributed by Hollis. Many of these works have been either out of print since the eighteenth century or available only in very expensive and scarce editions. The highest standards of scholarship and production ensure that these classic texts can be as salutary and influential today as they were two hundred and fifty years ago.

David Womersley

INTRODUCTION

The Context of Intolerance

Protestant Europe inherited a fundamental belief from the medieval Catholic Church: that membership of the church was coextensive with membership of the commonwealth and that it was the duty of a "godly prince" to promote and support the true religion. Protestants agreed with Catholics that "schism" and "heresy" were intolerable, though what counted as orthodoxy now depended on which side of the Alps one stood. There was therefore no intrinsic connection between religious freedom and the advent of Protestantism. Luther was ferocious against the Anabaptists, calling down the wrath of the German princes upon them. At Geneva, Calvin burned Servetus for heresy. In England, the regime of Elizabeth and the early Stuarts drove religious nonconformists to flee to the Netherlands and America; in the Netherlands, Calvinists harassed those who deviated into Arminianism; and in Massachusetts, separatists were punished. During the English Civil Wars, Presbyterians, who had suffered under the episcopal Church of England, were vociferous in demanding suppression of the radical Puritan sects. The Reformation and Counter-Reformation witnessed extraordinary savagery in the name of religious orthodoxy, in events such as the St. Bartholomew's Day Massacre in France and the Cromwellian annihilation of Irish "papists." Nor was there any cessation after the mid-seventeenth century. In 1685 Louis XIV revoked the Edict of Nantes, under which Protestant Huguenots had achieved a measure of toleration, causing thousands to flee, and introducing a new word, *refugee,* into the English language; thousands who were left behind faced torture, enslavement, and death. In England, the later Stuart era saw the final attempt in that country's history to coerce citizens to be of one church: the Anglican church restored after the Civil Wars. Hundreds of Quakers died in prison, the Baptist John Bunyan was incarcerated in Bedford jail, and William Penn resolved to create a safe haven, which he named Pennsylvania.

It is mistaken to suppose that the practice of intolerance betokened mere unthinking bigotry. On the contrary, a fully developed ideology of intolerance was articulated in countless treatises and sermons and was upheld by Protestants and Catholics alike. Religious minorities were castigated on three grounds. First, dissenters were seditious dangers to the state, and their claims of "conscience" were masks for rebellion and anarchy. Second, they were schismatic violators of the unity and catholicity of God's church, since Christian creeds taught that the church is "one." Third, they held erroneous beliefs that endangered their souls and polluted those of their neighbors, so that they should be obliged to harken to the truth. To these political, ecclesiastical, and theological objections could be added ethical suspicions that dissenters were closet libertines who concealed their depravity under outward piety. Scripturally, it was claimed that Christ himself had authorized religious coercion of the wayward, for, as St. Augustine had explained, Jesus' injunction in St. Luke's Gospel to "compel them to come in" must be understood in relation to the church (Luke 14:23). *Compelle intrare* became the cardinal text for Christian brutality and remained a pulpit staple. The Christian magistrate, guided by the Christian pastor, was duty bound to suppress error, for "he beareth not the sword in vain: he is the minister of God, a revenger to execute wrath upon him that doeth evil" (Romans 13:4).

Locke's *Letter* and Evangelical Tolerance

John Locke's *Letter Concerning Toleration* was one of the seventeenth century's most eloquent pleas to Christians to renounce religious persecution. It was also timely. It was written in Latin in Holland in 1685, just after the Revocation of the Edict of Nantes, and published in Latin and English in 1689, just after the English parliament conceded a statutory toleration for Protestant dissenters. Locke was certainly not the first writer to argue for toleration. The case can be traced to authors such as Sebastian Castellio and Jacopo Acontius in the late sixteenth century, to the radical Puritans of Civil War England, such as William Walwyn and Roger Williams, and to Locke's contemporaries, such as Penn and, in Holland, the Jew Baruch Spinoza, the Arminian Philip van Limborch, and the Huguenot Pierre Bayle, whose *Philosophical Commentary on the Words of Our Lord, "Compel Them to Come In"* (1686) is exactly contemporary with Locke's *Letter*.

Today Locke is regarded as the canonical philosopher of liberalism. Theorists continue to invoke Locke in addressing religious questions: the relationship between religion and civil society, and the boundaries of public tolerance of cultural pluralism, particularly in a West suddenly less convinced that secularism is an ineluctable characteristic of modernity. Locke's liberalism is not, however, the same as modern secular liberalism. His *Letter* can surprise and disconcert by the apparently limited basis and extent of its tolerance. It is not just that Locke excludes Roman Catholics and atheists from tolerance, but also that his very premises are rooted in Christian evangelism. His arguments are not as radical as those of Spinoza or Bayle, who were more inclusive and more skeptical. Crudely, Locke is not John Stuart Mill, for it is to *On Liberty* (1859) that we turn to find a celebration of pluralism and arguments for moral diversity. "Tolerance," after all, denotes forbearance, not approval, and Locke defends rather than applauds religious diversity. Moreover, he does not offer toleration in the ethical sphere; quite the contrary, he upholds godly living as a better aspiration for civil societies than the disciplining of doctrine and worship. The first thing to emphasize, therefore, about Locke's *Letter* is that it is limited to a case for toleration of religious conscience in matters of worship and speculative theology. Furthermore, its argument is grounded in the question: What are the legitimate means at the disposal of Christians to bring the wayward to the truth? While Locke is absolutely emphatic that coercion is not a legitimate means, the *Letter* remains an essay in *evangelical* tolerance, penned by a devout Christian, albeit one whom contemporaries suspected of theological heterodoxy and who thereby himself needed—or, in his enemies' eyes, did not deserve— the blessings of toleration.

Separating Church from State

Locke's *Letter* offers three principal arguments for toleration. He begins by asserting that peaceable means are of the essence of Christianity, and that Scripture does not authorize harshness. This point, however, is scarcely developed, and he does not explicitly discuss Jesus' exhortation to "compel." Rather, Locke's overriding case is for the separation of the church from the state. Religion is not the business of the magistrate, and the state is not a proper instrument for the saving of souls. Church and state are "perfectly distinct and infinitely different" (p. 24). A church is a voluntary association within civil society; it is not a department of government. In this respect, churches are no different from other associations, such as "merchants for commerce" (p. 16). Broadly, this is a teleological argument: each gathering of people has its own ends or purposes and is delimited in its remit and governance by those ends. The state is no exception, for it cannot make totalizing claims: it, too, is limited by its temporal and secular purposes: the protection of life, liberty, and property. Locke was scarcely the first to offer such an assertion, but it is not too much to claim that he had broken with the concept of the "confessional state" that had governed medieval and Reformation Europe. Shockingly to his contemporaries, he avers that "there is absolutely no such thing, under the Gospel, as a Christian commonwealth" (p. 42). Temporal governors may and should be Christians, but Locke's point is that their religious profession pertains to their private selves and not their public office.

Locke underpins the case for separation by showing that it is we who designate the purposes of our several communities. The state has its source in the "consent of the people." It is for the protection of "civil rights and worldly goods" that the people originally authorized the state.

People therefore have worldly purposes when they form states and spiritual purposes when they form churches. "The care of each man's soul" (p. 48) cannot be part of the "mutual compacts" (p. 47) that create the polity. Fundamentally this is because it would be irrational to consent to a government that claimed a right to enforce a particular path to heaven, since that path might prove abhorrent to our conscience. This aspect of Locke's argument firmly connects the *Letter* with his *Two Treatises of Government,* also published in 1689, and represents a crucial extrapolation of the latter's premises. While it may appear puzzling that Locke does not supply this deduction in the *Treatises* themselves, which are conspicuously silent on the problem of religious persecution, their relentless insistence on the state's purely secular purposes is so eloquent in its silence that Locke's strategy is surely deliberate. The *Treatises* are not about religion because the state is not about religion.

A momentous corollary of Locke's position is that toleration must be extended to non-Christians. Since the commonwealth is not, in its nature, Christian, then its ambit is extensive. Locke is quite clear that purely religious opinions of any sort cannot provide a ground for civil discrimination. "Neither pagan, nor Mahumetan, nor Jew, ought to be excluded from the civil rights of the commonwealth, because of his religion" (pp. 58–59). Furthermore, "not even [Native] Americans . . . are to be punished . . . for not embracing our faith and worship" (p. 39).

Locke's separation of church and state is problematic in relation to the circumstances of England after the passage of the Toleration Act in 1689. Though toleration of Protestant dissenters was now legal, the Anglican creed in the Thirty-Nine Articles, the rituals of the Book of Common Prayer, and episcopacy continued to constitute the "Established" Church of England, which in turn retained a panoply of legal jurisdictions over people's lives and a great body of landed and financial wealth. Citizens remained obliged to pay church taxes known as tithes; it was difficult to conduct marriage and burial outside the official church; and bishops were crown appointees who sat in the House of Lords. Furthermore, the Test Acts remained in place, by which citizens were disabled from holding public office unless they were communicant members of the Anglican Church. Although the Tests were often evaded in practice, they were not formally repealed until 1828. The separation of religion from public institutions proved a long, slow, and incomplete process, and in national schooling, for example, it has never fully occurred. Today, while religious schooling has been pluralized beyond Anglicanism, Britons remain wedded to tax-funded "faith schools," apparently believing that the saving of souls is one purpose of the state.

It is unclear if Locke was a categorical separationist. The logic of his position is abolition of the state church. Yet he does not categorically say so in the *Letter*, nor did he show any personal inclination to worship outside the established church. Some of his remarks point toward "comprehension," which would have entailed liberalizing the terms of membership of the national church so as to admit moderate dissenters. On the other hand, even if Locke favored comprehension, he clearly also upheld the rights of separatists. Moreover, he exhibited a strong streak of anticlericalism, criticizing the tendency of established religions to serve as engines of clerical "avarice and insatiable desire of dominion" (p. 60). In the *Constitutions of Carolina* (1669), which he helped to draft, the attitude toward churches is radically congregationalist: any group can register themselves as a church. If we assume that Locke was a categorical separationist, then it is not to Britain that one would look for a modern Lockean state, but to the United States, where the argument of Locke's *Letter* found fulfillment in Thomas Jefferson's *Virginia Statute for Religious Freedom* (1779), or to France, with its secular republican tradition of *laïcité*.

The Ineffectiveness of Intolerance

The second principal argument of the *Letter* in seeking to preclude coercion is Locke's insistence that persecution is radically ineffective. Coercion cannot, in principle, he argues, achieve its purported aim of bringing people to a conviction that a particular belief is true. This claim takes Locke into philosophical territory, for the argument depends upon an epistemological view about the etiology of human belief and the interiority of the mind. Belief is a matter of inward conviction, stemming from faith and persuasion, so that conscience cannot be forced. To punish somebody for believing an "error" is a non sequitur, since physical pressure, whether fines, imprisonment, torture, or death, cannot bring about genuine belief, any more than the rod can persuade a schoolchild of the truth of a mathematical equation. Admittedly, coercion can modify behavior, for people can be forced to make declarations, sign documents, or attend church; but they do so as compliant hypocrites rather than recovered souls. Moreover, some will resist pressure and opt for martyrdom, and these, too, have not changed their minds. Religious compulsion is therefore based on a misapprehension about the efficacy of coercion for its ostensible evangelical purpose. Locke consequently wonders whether churchmen and "godly" magistrates do not have some other motive in persecuting, and he returns to his critique of clerical domination.

This aspect of Locke's argument loomed large in his *Second, Third,* and unfinished *Fourth Letters* on toleration (1690, 1692, and, posthumously, 1706), which are many times the length of the original *Letter.* They were composed after Locke had been strenuously criticized by an Oxford high churchman, Jonas Proast, who resented the Toleration Act of 1689, and who echoed the Augustinian injunctions to "compel" that had been strongly voiced in Restoration England. Proast's case was subtle and there are modern interpreters who hold that Locke was unable to sustain his position convincingly. Proast conceded that coercion cannot directly convince the mind, but that, indirectly, it can encourage people to reconsider. Since Proast held that our beliefs are largely inherited and habitual, rather than rational, he claimed that we can be jolted into serious thought by discipline. Proast thought of dissenting sects rather as we might think of cults: people who have been brainwashed can be decontaminated, but they need to be physically removed from the cult. More generally, religious believers do often refer to some physical trauma as occasioning their conversion: St. Paul was shocked into Christianity on the road to Damascus. The disconnection between inner belief and the outer material self is, hence, not unbridgeable. As a good Augustinian, Proast insisted that the machinery of coercion must be accompanied by pastoral activity, the magistrate with a preacher at hand. Locke's *Second* and *Third Letters* offered laborious refutations of Proast and are not much read today, yet they offer valuable elaborations of ideas outlined in the original *Letter.*

Locke's argument from the disutility of intolerance had another and different aspect. This might be termed the "reciprocity" or "Alpine argument." Truth, Locke observed, is apt to be different on each side of the

Channel, the Alps, and the Bosphorus. "Every prince is orthodox to him-self" (p. 38). Protestantism is the state religion in England, Catholicism in France, and Islam in Turkey. He contrasts the fates of religions under different regimes: the dominant religion is apt to persecute the minor-ity. The pattern of persecution is thus an indicator of the distribution of power rather than of the provenance of religious truth. Persecution has no utility for advancing the cause of the real truth if the case for coer-cion can so easily be mobilized by *any* regime that believes it has the truth. Hence, it is foolish to license the state to enforce "truth," because the same argument will be used elsewhere against our co-religionists. In a world of divided religions and confessional states, those who suffer are not the erroneous but the weak. Protestants will suffer in France and Christians in Turkey. Locke offers the enforcer a calculus of prudence: if you wish to promote true belief, do not arm magistrates the world over with the sword of righteousness.

Skepticism

In keeping with Locke's evangelical premise in the *Letter,* there is a lim-ited role for skepticism. A nonbeliever would elevate doubt about reli-gious belief into a principal ground for tolerance: how can we be so sure of our "truth" as to inflict it violently on others? Locke's case for toleration is not that the claims of Christianity are doubtful, still less false. Arguably, however, his avoidance of a skeptical position is in part tactical. If he seeks to persuade the devout persecutor that force is improper, it makes more sense to dwell on reasons why force is inappropriate than on reasons why devoutness is ill-grounded. We may wish to bring people to Gospel truth, but compulsion is not Christlike, politic, or efficacious.

There is, nevertheless, a clear strand of skepticism in the *Letter,* in regard to the sphere of what theologians termed "things indifferent," as distinct from "things necessary," to salvation. Locke was among those lat-itudinarians who envisaged a wide ambit of "things indifferent": matters that were not prescribed by Scripture and hence were open to human choice and local convention. God requires that he be worshipped, but he is not unduly prescriptive about the manner of worship. Accordingly, to insist that worshippers stand or kneel, or that ministers wear particular garments, is to impose human preferences rather than divine precepts. Locke is likewise emphatic that the creedal content of Christianity is limited, and in his *Reasonableness of Christianity* (1695) he would be minimalist in asserting that the sole necessary truth was faith that Christ is the Messiah. He holds that much that has historically preoccupied theologians, and led to inquisitions and heresy-hunting, is merely speculation; Christian simplicity has been bemired in spiritual vanity and metaphysical pedantry. A constant theme of the *Letter* is Locke's insistence on freedom of "speculation," an emphasis alloyed with anxiety about his own position. Charges of Socinianism, denoting a denial of the Trinity and the divinity of Christ, would be leveled against both his *Essay Concerning Human Understanding* (1689) and the *Reasonableness*.

Locke was, however, aware that the argument for toleration drawn from the concept of "things indifferent" was problematic and had two drawbacks. The first was that consensus could not be reached regarding the boundary between "things necessary" and "things indifferent." For example, quarrels over the "popish" white surplice and the black "Geneva gown" had bedeviled Protestant debate since the Reformation: the sartorial became soteriological. A Puritan might agree that "things indifferent" should be tolerated but deny that a popish surplice was a thing indifferent, which thereby rendered it utterly intolerable. The second drawback was that the notion of "things indifferent" can just as easily lead to an argument for intolerance. If something is a "thing indifferent," then nobody has good reason to object to it on conscientious grounds. It was commonly held that "things indifferent" could be imposed by authority, not because God requires it, but rather for the sake of decency and good order. Shared practices should prevail for aesthetic and communal reasons. God requires "beauty in holiness" even if its specifics remain open to human ordinance. Hence it is not the rulers in church and state who are zealots but, on the contrary, nonconformists who pointlessly plead "conscience" and "indulgence" in matters indifferent. For this reason many latitudinarians, whose position is at first glance liberal, were in fact intolerant, for their intention was to embrace moderate nonconformists, by softening the rigidities of the church's "good order," before penalizing the recalcitrant minority who refused to accept such revised terms. At this point Locke departs from his fellow latitudinarians. For him, the comeliness and fellowship of conformity cannot trump the right of religious self-expression for those who have an unassuageable conviction, however misguided, that the terms of conformity are ungodly.

Here Locke stresses an elementary principle of respect. Conscientiously held beliefs are to be respected; or, rather, believers are to be respected, even if we regard their beliefs as ill-founded. We may agree that a sect is blighted by errant conscience, but freedom of conscience must take priority over (our own conception of) truth. Locke does not doubt his own version of Christian truth, but his argument is at its most apparently skeptical when he insists that we must tolerate error. What matters most is the sincere pursuit of truth, however tangled and tortuous the paths people take. In according a central place to sincerity, Locke bears the stamp of modern liberalism. To search sincerely after truth, even if failing to arrive, is held to be more valuable than to possess truth merely through happenstance or outward conformity. Locke is conscious that most people are full of mental clutter derived from upbringing, education, circumstance, culture. They are scarcely to be blamed for erroneous beliefs, though they are culpable if lacking in strenuous effort in sorting out their thoughts. Earnest endeavor must command our respect. A crucial caveat, however, remains. The duty of tolerance must not abridge our equal right to argue against error. "Every man has commission to admonish, exhort, convince another of error, and, by reasoning, to draw him into truth" (p. 14). Locke would thus have been dismayed by a society such as ours in which the onus on "respect" frequently produces a timid unwillingness to challenge the beliefs of others.

Antinomians

Given the powerful nature of Locke's case for religious tolerance, it comes as a shock that, near the close of the *Letter*, he excludes atheists and Catholics from toleration. There is no gainsaying that he rejects the possibility of tolerating atheists, whom he claims have no motive for keeping rules, since they lack fear of divine punishment. "Promises, covenants, and oaths, which are the bonds of human society, can have no hold upon an atheist" (pp. 52–53). Spinoza and Bayle disagreed. Locke's position on Catholicism, however, needs finessing, since he did not, in fact, exclude the theoretical possibility of tolerating Catholics. Although Catholics held absurd beliefs, such as transubstantiation, the absurdity of another's belief is not, in itself, a ground for coercion. What rendered Catholics unable to be tolerated was that they held political and moral positions that fundamentally threatened civil society. These were twofold: that the pope can depose heretic princes and authorize his followers to overthrow such princes; and that "faith need not be kept with heretics": in other words, that rules of honesty and promise-keeping need not apply when Catholics deal with heretics. The implication of Locke's position was that if Catholics could discard their uncivil beliefs, they could then be tolerated. Eighteenth-century Catholics took succor from this argument and strove to demonstrate that Catholicism was not committed to papal political dominion nor to breach of faith with heretics.

What Locke was precluding was not Catholicism as such, but antino-mianism. An *antinomian* is one who holds that ordinary moral laws are trumped by the superiority of religious "truth." This is to put religion in collision with reason and natural law, which are also the works of God and not in conflict with revelation. Antinomians hold either that they are divinely inspired to rule (the ultimate form of a godly commonwealth) or, on the contrary, that they are exempt from rule (the ultimate form of godly anarchy). Catholic claims that the pope had Christ's commission to dictate to all nations and Calvinist claims that the "elect" should rule ("the rule of the saints") were equally antinomian. There are hints that Locke had Puritan fanatics in mind as being also potentially intolerable. There are plenty of other varieties of antinomianism, then and now, such as the proposition that a particular territory belongs to a particular group because "God gave it to them," or that one state should fight a war against another because it deems it to be the "antichrist."

Locke was explicit that governments should concern themselves with religious behavior only insofar as it was dangerous to society's temporal interests. Eccentric behavior in places of worship is no more harmful to civil society than eccentric behavior in marketplaces. Conversely, terrorist behavior in a church was as legitimately subject to surveillance as in a marketplace. Locke readily accepted that the state might need to exercise vigilance with regard to some religious groups, though the state should be explicit about the grounds for its suspicion. Conversely, citizens had a parallel duty to be vigilant in ensuring that those in charge of the state were not framing policy in accordance with "godly" agendas. Antinomianism can manifest itself from above as well as from below.

Locke's Transition

Although this account has, thus far, dwelt on the *Letter*, Locke reflected and wrote about toleration across four decades. Conspicuously, he did not hold the same views in 1690 that he held in 1660. When monarchy and the Church of England were restored after the Civil Wars and republic, Locke had written in defense of the civil magistrate's authority to impose a uniform public worship. Locke composed these essays, now known as the *Two Tracts on Government* (1660–62), while a young scholar and teacher at Oxford University, although they remained unpublished until 1967. They reveal a Locke deeply fearful of civil anarchy driven by religious fanaticism. Like most of his compatriots, he thought the Civil Wars had opened a Pandora's box of wild "enthusiasm" and antinomian zealotry masquerading under the banner of conscience. He argued within the theological tradition of "things indifferent" and concluded that because most matters of worship and religious discipline are indifferent, the nonconformists had no conscientious ground for objecting to the imposition of order.

A striking feature of the *Tracts* is that they epitomize the argumentation that Locke would later come to oppose. For reasons that still remain unclear, by 1667 he had decisively changed his mind. Probably most important was his new association with Lord Ashley, the future Whig leader and Earl of Shaftesbury, and his consequent move from Oxford, the ideological home of Anglican churchmanship. Locke settled in the more cosmopolitan London, close to the court of Charles II, which had its own reasons for seeking toleration, as the king was either religiously indifferent or crypto-Catholic. Locke's visit to Cleves in Germany in 1666 was also an eye-opener, for he was agog, in that tolerant city, that it was possible for Lutherans, Calvinists, and even Catholics to worship openly and yet live in peace. Locke's conversion was signaled in his *Essay on Toleration* (1667), another piece that remained unpublished until long after his death. Containing arguments that would recur in the *Letter,* the *Essay* may have originated as a memorandum for Ashley and in turn for the royal court.

A large archive of Locke's private notebooks and memoranda survives today. In these documents he constantly returned to consider the case for toleration. These materials have been gathered together in this volume under the heading "Fragments on Toleration." Locke's papers explore a number of themes that are not always prominent in the *Letter.* They include polemical critiques of churchmen who, in essence, echoed the arguments of his own early *Tracts,* which he had now abandoned. Several of his memoranda relate to Catholicism, illustrating his vehement hostility to a church that insisted on its own infallibility. At the same time, Locke continued to be disturbed by the dangers of Protestant antinomianism, not only in the dissenting sects but also by all forms of "enthusiasts," whose mystical spirituality dangerously threatened to exceed the boundaries of Christian reasonableness.

Priestcraft

Catholics, antinomians, and "enthusiasts" do not exhaust the categories of the religious against whom Locke's animus was directed. There is a stridently anticlerical tone in Locke's *Letter* and in other writings, evincing his insistence that much that passes for Christian doctrine is merely priestly fabrication, supervening upon Gospel simplicity. Locke is constantly hostile to clergies. Those who persecute do so "upon pretence of religion"; they are bigots who seek personal power and wealth, rather than the salvation of others (p. 8). Such a charge had long been at the heart of the Protestant assault on medieval Catholicism. Yet, for Locke and increasingly for his contemporaries, priestly usurpation was not a Catholic monopoly. There are passages in Locke that prefigure the Enlightenment's critique of "priestcraft," a word that became fashionable in the 1690s and that Locke uses in *The Reasonableness of Christianity*. It denoted a general theory of the propensities of all priesthoods to pervert religion in pursuit of earthly domination. Religious creeds and clerically inspired political creeds are apt to be ideological in the strict sense of that term: they are doctrines that serve power rather than truth. Locke thought that the doctrine of the divine right of kings was a salient case: priests elevate princes so that princes will return the favor by awarding churches the trappings of temporal power. Over a longer historical span, it is possible to see that Locke's claim that religions are projections of temporal power and worldly aspirations is one of the high roads to atheism. Locke provided a signpost to that road but did not himself make the journey. After all, the charge that religion has been perverted by worldliness lies deep in the Christian tradition itself. In this sense, distinguishing the Enlightenment from the Reformation is far from straightforward.

Early Reception

By the end of the eighteenth century, Locke's *Letter Concerning Toleration* had been published in twenty-six editions, as well as being included in nine editions of his *Works* and in the *Œuvres diverses de Monsieur Jean Locke* (1710). It appeared in Latin, French, German, and Dutch and achieved its first American edition at Boston in 1743. Voltaire's edition of 1764 accompanied his own *Traité sur la tolérance,* provoked by the Calas affair, in which the *philosophe* sought and achieved a posthumous pardon for a Protestant merchant of Toulouse wrongly executed for murdering his son. In North America, Locke's arguments were appropriated in Elisha Williams's *Essential Rights and Liberties of Protestants,* subtitled "A Seasonable Plea for the Liberty of Conscience, and the Right of Private Judgment, in Matters of Religion, Without any Control from Human Authority" (1744), a protest against a Connecticut law that restricted itinerant preachers. Another conduit to North America was the English "commonwealthman" Thomas Hollis, who published a collected edition of all Locke's *Letters* and presented a copy to Harvard: "Thomas Hollis, an Englishman, Citizen of the World, is desirous of having the honor to present this Book to the library of Harvard College, at Cambridge in N. England. Pall Mall, Jan. 1, 1765." The book's frontispiece carries an engraved portrait of Locke: he is wreathed in oak leaves, and beneath his image is the cap of liberty.

Mark Goldie

FURTHER READING

On Tolerance and Intolerance

Coffey, John. *Persecution and Toleration in Protestant England, 1558–1689*. Harlow: Longman, 2000.

Grell, O. P., J. I. Israel, and N. Tyacke, eds. *From Persecution to Toleration: The Glorious Revolution and Religion in England*. Oxford: Oxford University Press, 1991.

Israel, Jonathan I. *Enlightenment Contested: Philosophy, Modernity, and the Emancipation of Man, 1670–1752*. Oxford: Oxford University Press, 2006.

Kaplan, Benjamin J. *Divided by Faith: Religious Conflict and the Practice of Toleration in Early Modern Europe*. Cambridge, Mass.: Harvard University Press, 2007.

Marshall, John. *John Locke, Toleration, and Early Enlightenment Culture*. Cambridge: Cambridge University Press, 2006.

Murphy, Andrew R. *Conscience and Community: Revisiting Toleration and Religious Dissent in Early Modern England and America*. Philadelphia: Pennsylvania State University Press, 2001.

Walsham, Alexandra. *Charitable Hatred: Tolerance and Intolerance in England, 1500–1700*. Manchester: Manchester University Press, 2006.

Zagorin, Perez. *How the Idea of Religious Toleration Came to the West*. Princeton: Princeton University Press, 2003.

By Locke

Epistola de Tolerantia: A Letter on Toleration. Edited by Raymond Klibansky and J. W. Gough. Oxford: Oxford University Press, 1968.

An Essay Concerning Human Understanding. Edited by Peter H. Nidditch. Oxford: Oxford University Press, 1975.

An Essay Concerning Toleration and Other Writings on Law and Politics, 1667–1675. Edited by J. R. Milton and Philip Milton. Oxford: Oxford University Press, 2006.

Political Essays. Edited by Mark Goldie. Cambridge: Cambridge University Press, 1997.

The Reasonableness of Christianity. Edited by John C. Higgins-Biddle. Oxford: Oxford University Press, 1999.

Selected Correspondence. Edited by Mark Goldie. Oxford: Oxford University Press, 2002.

Selected Political Writings. Edited by Paul E. Sigmund. New York: W. W. Norton, 2005.

Some Thoughts Concerning Education. Edited by John W. Yolton and Jean S. Yolton. Oxford: Oxford University Press, 1989.

Two Tracts on Government. Edited by Philip Abrams. Cambridge: Cambridge University Press, 1967.

Two Treatises of Government. Edited by Peter Laslett. Cambridge: Cambridge University Press, 1988.

Writings on Religion. Edited by Victor Nuovo. Oxford: Oxford University Press, 2002.

With Locke

Bayle, Pierre. *A Philosophical Commentary on These Words of the Gospel, Luke 14:23, "Compel Them to Come In"* (1686). Edited by John Kilcullen and Chandran Kukathas. Indianapolis: Liberty Fund, 2005.

Penn, William. "The Great Case of Liberty of Conscience" (1670). In *The Political Writings of William Penn.* Edited by Andrew Murphy. Indianapolis: Liberty Fund, 2002.

Pufendorf, Samuel. *Of the Nature and Qualification of Religion in Reference to Civil Society* (1687). Edited by Simone Zurbuchen. Indianapolis: Liberty Fund, 2002.

Spinoza, Baruch. *Theological-Political Treatise* (1670). Edited by Jonathan

Israel and Michael Silverthorne. Cambridge: Cambridge University Press, 2007.

Walwyn, William. *The Compassionate Samaritan* (1644). Excerpts in *Divine Right and Democracy*, edited by David Wootton. Harmondsworth: Penguin, 1986.

Williams, Elisha. *The Essential Rights and Liberties of Protestants* (1744). In *The Church, Dissent, and Religious Toleration, 1689–1773*. Vol. 5 of Mark Goldie, ed., *The Reception of Locke's Politics: From the 1690s to the 1830s*. 6 vols. London: Pickering and Chatto, 1999.

Williams, Roger. *The Bloudy Tenent of Persecution* (1644). Excerpts in *Divine Right and Democracy*, edited by David Wootton. Harmondsworth: Penguin, 1986.

Against Locke

Long, Thomas. *The Letter for Toleration Decipher'd* (1689). In *The Church, Dissent, and Religious Toleration, 1689–1773*. Vol. 5 of Mark Goldie, ed., *The Reception of Locke's Politics: From the 1690s to the 1830s*. 6 vols. London: Pickering and Chatto, 1999.

Proast, Jonas. *The Argument of the Letter Concerning Toleration Briefly Consider'd and Answer'd* (1690). In *The Church, Dissent, and Religious Toleration, 1689–1773*. Vol. 5 of Mark Goldie, ed., *The Reception of Locke's Politics: From the 1690s to the 1830s*. 6 vols. London: Pickering and Chatto, 1999.

On Locke

Anstey, Peter, ed. *John Locke: Critical Assessments*. 4 vols. London: Routledge, 2006.

Ashcraft, Richard. *Revolutionary Politics and Locke's Two Treatises of Government*. Princeton: Princeton University Press, 1986.

Dunn, John. *Locke*. Oxford: Oxford University Press, 1984.

———. *The Political Thought of John Locke*. Cambridge: Cambridge University Press, 1969.

Dunn, John, and Ian Harris, eds. *Locke*. 2 vols. Cheltenham: Edward Elgar, 1997.

Grant, Ruth. *John Locke's Liberalism*. Chicago: Chicago University Press, 1987.

Harris, Ian. *The Mind of John Locke*. Cambridge: Cambridge University Press, 1994.

Horton, John, and Susan Mendus, eds. *Locke: A Letter Concerning Toleration in Focus.* London: Routledge, 1991.

Marshall, John. *John Locke: Resistance, Religion, and Responsibility.* Cambridge: Cambridge University Press, 1994.

Milton, J. R., ed. *Locke's Moral, Political, and Legal Philosophy.* Aldershot: Ashgate, 1999.

Tuckness, Alex. *Locke and the Legislative Point of View: Toleration, Contested Principles, and the Law.* Princeton: Princeton University Press, 2002.

Vernon, Richard. *The Career of Toleration: John Locke, Jonas Proast, and After.* Montreal: McGill-Queen's University Press, 1997.

Waldron, Jeremy. *God, Locke, and Equality.* Cambridge: Cambridge University Press, 2002.

NOTES ON THE TEXTS

This volume opens with Locke's principal work on toleration, the *Letter Concerning Toleration*. It is followed by excerpts from *A Third Letter for Toleration*, his public defense of the *Letter*. Practically all of the other writings included here remained unpublished during his lifetime. Whereas this edition of the *Letter* and the *Third Letter* follows the spelling, punctuation, and capitalization of the early printed editions, the remaining texts, which are mostly derived from manuscripts, have been modernized, since an exact rendering of Locke's private drafts and memoranda would give the modern reader a tough time. I have, however, retained some verbal features that alert us to the fact we are reading seventeenth-century texts, such as "hath" and "'tis." Words in square brackets are editorial interpolations. All references in the following notes to "MS Locke" are to the Locke archive at the Bodleian Library in Oxford.

A Letter Concerning Toleration

Locke wrote the *Letter Concerning Toleration* in Latin, and it was first published as the *Epistola de Tolerantia* at Gouda in Holland in April 1689. In the three centuries since, the anglophone world has known the work from the translation made by William Popple and published in London about October of that year.

The text reproduced here is the second edition, which appeared about March 1690, the title page of which announced it to be "corrected." It contains some 475 amendments to the first. These mostly comprise changes to punctuation (generally strengthening it), capitalization (generally more capitals), italicization (usually more), and spelling. Just two typographical errors were corrected: both editions were prepared with care. More significantly, there were two dozen changes in wording, which clarify or finesse the meaning. They show Popple's hand at work, for these are not just printer's corrections. Some scholars have suggested that Locke was involved in these amendments, but this is unlikely. I have, however, noted a couple of occasions that may justify the claim.

Later editions of the *Letter* have been evenhanded in their preferences between the first and second editions. The *Works* (1714), Sherman (1937), Montuori (1963), Horton and Mendus (1991), and Sigmund (2005) follow the first edition; Gough (1946) and Wootton (1993) follow the second, as did most eighteenth-century editions; Hollis (1765), the *Works* (1777 and later), Tully (1983), and Shapiro (2003) are hybrids.

In reading the English *Letter*, it is important to realize that it is not of Locke's composing. Scholars have disputed the reliability of Popple's translation. In his will, Locke wrote that it was prepared "without my privity," meaning without his authorization. However, as early as June 1689 he did know a translation was being undertaken, and he was evidently content with the result, for it was the English version that he defended in his subsequent controversy with Jonas Proast. Moreover, in his *Second Letter* he remarked of one passage that, though it might have been rendered "more literally . . . yet the translator is not to be blamed, if he chose to express the sense of the author, in words that very lively represented" his meaning. Even so, the reader should be alert to Popple's style and not take the text for granted as unmediated Locke.

I have footnoted some passages to illustrate the more marked deviations from the Latin; generally I do not supply Locke's Latin but use the modern English translation published by Klibansky and Gough in 1968. Such notes are indicated by the phrases "alternatively," "Popple omits," or "added by Popple."

Some general characteristics of Popple's approach are worth noting, since I have made no attempt to footnote all the variants. He used intensifiers to heighten the emotional tone. For example, "vices" becomes "enormous vices," "superstition" becomes "credulous superstition," and "immutable right" becomes "fundamental and immutable right"; the cool "magistrate's favour" becomes the more pointed "Court favour." He gave literary variety to Locke's mechanical repetition of "You say" and "I answer" in stating and responding to his imaginary interlocutor's objections. He gave a topical spin to points that Locke stated more abstractly, and he anglicized some references that originally had a Dutch context. He sometimes omitted, but more often elaborated, a phrase. One (extreme) example may suffice: where the modern translation of Locke's Latin has "blindly accept the doctrines imposed by their prince, and worship God in the manner laid down by the laws of their country," Popple has "blindly to resign up themselves to the will of their governors, and to the religion, which either ignorance, ambition, or superstition had chanced to establish in the countries where they were born."

Popple wrote stylishly, and some of the more memorable phrases are entirely his. The likening of a church, as a voluntary society, to a "club for claret" has no authority in Locke's Latin. All translation involves interpretation, and Popple is not quite Locke. But Locke broadly approved, and, for us today, Popple's version has the supreme advantage of being a text that is at once an authentic seventeenth-century voice, both vivid and readable.

The English *Letter* has two further differences from the Latin *Epistola*. Popple added a preface of his own, "To the Reader," which does not make explicit that it is written by the translator rather than the author, so that many generations of readers assumed that the preface was Locke's own work. Many Enlightenment readers therefore attributed Popple's ringing phrase about "absolute liberty" to Locke. The other difference is that Popple deleted the perplexing cryptogram that appeared on the title page of the Latin edition: "Epistola de Tolerantia ad Clarissimum Virum T.A.R.P.T.O.L.A. Scripta à P.A.P.O.I.L.A."

There are two versions of what the abbreviations on the title page stand for. Phillip van Limborch, the Dutch Arminian theologian and friend of Locke who put the *Epistola* through the press, deciphered them as "Theologiae Apud Remonstrantes Professorem, Tyrannidis Osorem, Libertatis Amantem, a Pacis Amante, Persecutionis Osore, Ioanne Lockio

Anglo" (Professor of Theology among the Remonstrants, Enemy of Tyranny, Lover of Liberty, from a Friend of Peace, Enemy of Persecution, John Locke, Englishman). But Jean Le Clerc had a different reading of the medial "L. A.": "Limburgium Amstelodamensem" ("Limborch of Amsterdam" instead of "Lover of Liberty"). Although Limborch might be expected to know best, Le Clerc's version seems more plausible: the parallel between the two names of Limborch and Locke seems natural; and Limborch contradicts himself by also saying that Locke "wanted our names to be hidden by the letters of the title." In offering his explanation, Limborch was probably being modest.

When Locke's publisher Awnsham Churchill issued the first edition of the *Works* in 1714, he placed an epigraph (in Latin) on the title page of the *Letter*, from Cicero, *De Officiis*, ii.83, saluting Locke: "A wise and outstanding man, he thought that he should consult the interests of all; and it showed the wisdom and extreme reasonableness that befits a good citizen that he did not separate the interests of the citizens, but held everyone together under a single standard of fairness."

I have taken the opportunity of the present edition to provide a fair amount of information by way of explanatory notes. Oddly, scarcely any of the editions published in the past half-century provide notes, and yet the references and allusions in the text are not always perspicuous. I have also drawn attention to some of the clues that the *Letter* provides to Locke's secular politics and hence to connections with his *Two Treatises of Government*. Although Popple's text has been reproduced in its original form, the scriptural citations that were awkwardly placed have been moved to appropriate points in the text and the names of biblical books spelled out.

Excerpts from *A Third Letter for Toleration*

Of the three responses that Locke prepared against his critic Jonas Proast, much the longest is the *Third Letter for Toleration*, published by Awnsham Churchill in 1692. Anonymous, it is signed "Philanthropus, June 20, 1692," and fills 350 quarto pages. It is sadly neglected today, though readers can be forgiven for not pursuing Locke through all the thickets of his relentless contradiction of Proast.

The tract is too long to reprint in its entirety here, and I have selected passages that either illuminate themes in the original *Letter* or pursue new lines of inquiry. In the footnotes I indicate the location of the excerpts in the 1692 edition and in volume 6 of the *Works*, 1801 and 1823. The topical headings supplied to each excerpt are mine. The first excerpt usefully incorporates passages from Locke's *Second Letter* (1690). Locke's marginal citations have been transferred to notes, except that biblical citations are incorporated in the text.

Proast's principal claim was that compulsion can indirectly achieve religious conversion and that the function of laws for conformity was to make people reconsider their beliefs. State and church were obliged to ensure that civil penalties were accompanied by evangelizing effort. It is these arguments that Locke sets out to refute.

An Essay Concerning Toleration

The *Essay Concerning Toleration* was written in 1667, shortly after Locke joined the household of Lord Ashley, later Earl of Shaftesbury. It remained in manuscript during Locke's lifetime and was not published until the nineteenth century, though a number of its arguments later appeared in the *Letter:* the parallels are numerous and I have not sought to record them in the notes. The *Essay* registers Locke's conversion to the principle of toleration and his break with the position he took in his earlier *Two Tracts on Government* (1660–62).

There are four surviving manuscripts, whose interrelationship is complex, and no attempt has been made to record textual variants: there are over a thousand of them. The version printed here derives from the manuscript in the Huntington Library, San Marino, California (HM 584). With the generous permission of J. R. Milton and Philip Milton, I have used their authoritative transcription (2006) but have modernized the text. To clarify the structure, I have slightly adjusted Locke's numeration of paragraphs and introduced a few section breaks. Some of the more significant variants in the version in MS Locke c. 28 are recorded in notes, as are also a couple of variants within the Huntington MS. Some other modern editions have preferred to use MS Locke c. 28 as their copy-text. *An Essay Concerning Toleration* is Locke's own title, but in one part of the Huntington MS he gives an alternative: "The Question of Toleration Stated."

Additions to the *Essay.*

The version in MS Locke c. 28 contains three additional passages not found in any other: these are Additions A to C (fols. 22, 28). Another of the manuscripts contains two further additions, which also have no counterpart: D and E (the notebook called "Adversaria 1661," pp. 125, 270–71). A to C are probably contemporaneous with the *Essay;* D probably dates from ca. 1671–72, and E from ca. 1675. I have indicated in the notes the places where A to C belong; D and E have no placements, since they follow at the end of the main body of the manuscript.

In the final two additions Locke sketches the corruption of Christianity by the ambition of priests, and the rise of the persecution of heresy and dissent. He suggests there has often been an unholy alliance between priests and princes, the former preaching the divine right of kings, the latter persecuting those deemed unorthodox. Locke notes the propensity of all priesthoods to domineer over civil society.

Fragments on Toleration

This is a collection of Locke's essays, notes, and memoranda on topics relating to toleration, composed at various times between the 1660s and 1690s. With the exception of *The Constitutions of Carolina,* none was published in Locke's lifetime. Some items carry the title Locke gave them; other titles are editorially supplied.

Infallibility (1661).

Untitled. The National Archives: PRO 30/24/47/33. Written in Latin, with the title "An necesse sit dari in ecclesia infallibilem sacro sanctae scripturae interpretem? Negatur." (Is it necessary that an infallible interpreter of Holy Scripture be granted in the church? No.) The translation used here is from J. C. Biddle, "John Locke's Essay on Infallibility: Introduction, Text, and Translation," *Journal of Church and State* 19 (1977):

301–27. The format of this essay—a question posed for disputation—is similar to that of Locke's *Essays on the Law of Nature* (1663–64).

Locke addresses the topic of scriptural hermeneutics and evinces a conventional Protestant hostility to Catholicism. He perhaps borrows from William Chillingworth's *Religion of Protestants* (1638) and Jeremy Taylor's *Liberty of Prophesying* (1647). He affirms the principle of *sola scriptura* (the self-sufficiency of the Bible), in opposition to the Catholic claim that Scripture is often obscure and must be understood in the light of the church's tradition of authoritative teaching. Catholics believed that the church's authority to interpret the Bible was infallible (but did not necessarily place that infallibility in the pope). Locke warns against clogging the mysteries of faith with vain philosophy.

The Constitutions of Carolina (excerpt) (1669–70).

Published as *The Fundamental Constitutions of Carolina* (1670) and dated 1 March 1670. A manuscript (1669) in the National Archives, PRO 30/24/47/3, is almost identical, except for the absence of clause 96. There is uncertainty about Locke's role in drafting this document.[1] The manuscript opening and a number of corrections are in Locke's hand, and a colleague of his referred to "that excellent form of government in the composure of which you had so great a hand" (Sir Peter Colleton, October 1673). However, Locke cannot have been the sole author, for he was serving his masters, Lord Ashley and the other proprietors of Carolina. Only the clauses relating to religion are reproduced here.

Against Samuel Parker (1669–70).

MS Locke c. 39, fols. 5, 7, 9. Endorsed: "Q[uerie]s on S.P.'s discourse of toleration. 69." A commentary on Samuel Parker's *Discourse of Ecclesiastical Politie: wherein the authority of the civil magistrate over the consciences of*

---

1. James Farr has published a persuasive case for Locke's authorship of the discourse on Carolina, which appeared in John Ogilby's atlas, *America* (London, 1671). Promotional in nature, the discourse describes the manifold advantages of life in Carolina and summarizes the *Constitutions of Carolina*. See James Farr, "Locke, 'Some Americans,' and the Discourse on 'Carolina,'" *Locke Studies*, 9 (2009), 19–96.

subjects in matters of religion is asserted; the mischiefs and inconveniences of toleration are represented, and all pretences pleaded on behalf of liberty of conscience are fully answered ("1670," in fact 1669). This book was one of the most influential and virulent attacks on the dissenters (though its sentiments are not dissimilar from Locke's now abandoned position in his early *Tracts*). It was encouraged by Archbishop Gilbert Sheldon and was part of the inaptly styled "friendly debate" between churchmen and dissenters, which spanned the years 1666 to 1674. The Congregationalist John Owen and Andrew Marvell took part on the dissenters' side. Locke's patron, Lord Ashley, hoped to persuade the king to grant toleration, while Sheldon and Parker worked with the Anglican gentry in Parliament to implement further coercive legislation. Excerpts from Parker's book (pp. 11–12, 12, 21–22, 24, 25–26, 29, 144–47, 153) are supplied to make sense of Locke's comments and to indicate the contemporary case for intolerance. Locke's page citations are omitted.

Civil and Ecclesiastical Power (1674).

MS Locke c. 27, fol. 29. The title is a modern attribution: the manuscript is endorsed "Excommunication 73/4." Partly in Locke's hand. Locke is emphatic that the civil magistrate has no business to enforce religious conformity. He allows that churches have the right to discipline their members by excommunication, but without civil penalties attached.

Philanthropy (1675).

MS Locke c. 27, fol. 30. "Philanthropoy [*sic*] or The Christian Philosopher's" [*sic*]; endorsed "Philanthropy 75." A paper not certainly of Locke's authorship: the manuscript is in an unknown hand but has corrections by Locke and the endorsement is his. Possibly a statement of intent for a philosophical club. It is a reflection on the things that distort the pursuit of truth, a theme Locke pursued in the *Essay Concerning Human Understanding*, bk. 4. There is a strong anticlerical strain.

Infallibility Revisited (1675).

MS Locke c. 27, fols. 32–33. Headed "Queries"; endorsed "Queries Popery 75." Not in Locke's hand; the authorship is not certain. These notes again show Locke's distaste for the Catholic doctrine of infallibility. He believes that the intolerance of Rome is built on implausible claims. The topic of church councils is discussed. The Church of England accepted the authority of genuine councils of the Christian church but did not believe there had been any such councils since the fourth century; later councils were deemed partisan and papistical.

Religion in France (1676–79).

Excerpts from MS Locke f 1–3 (1676 78), and British Library, Add. MS 15642 (1679); omissions within the excerpts are marked [. . .]. These manuscripts are Locke's journals during his sojourn in France. They illustrate his observations on the pressures upon Protestants, which would culminate in savage persecution after the Revocation of the Edict of Nantes in 1685; also his comments on the Protestants' own system of discipline and his attitude to Catholicism. The transcriptions are taken from the edition by John Lough, *Locke's Travels in France, 1675–1679* (Cambridge: Cambridge University Press, 1953), pp. 15, 22–23, 29–30, 40, 43, 45, 85–86, 108, 130, 223, 229–30, 271. The journals contain many kinds of entry besides Locke's travelogue: the next three items below are also from these journals but are philosophical memoranda. Locke spent most of this period at Montpellier on the Mediterranean coast, in a region where many towns were predominantly Protestant.

The Obligation of Penal Laws (25 February 1676).

MS Locke f. 1, pp. 123–26. Marginal keywords: "Obligation of Penal Laws," "Lex Humana." This memorandum is an important measure of Locke's political opinions at this time. It is conservative in tone, showing no hint of a right of resistance, which suggests that the transition to the *Two Treatises of Government* came late. Locke does, however, stress that most human laws are purely regulatory and that divine authority cannot be invoked beyond the general duty of obeying those governments that uphold civil peace and mutual preservation. Similarly, no particular form of government has divine sanction.

Toleration and Error (23 August 1676).

MS Locke f. 1, pp. 412–15. Marginal keywords: "Toleration," "Peace." Written in shorthand: the transcription is from Wolfgang von Leyden's edition of Locke's *Essays on the Law of Nature* (Oxford: Oxford University Press, 1954), pp. 274–75. Locke answers objections to religious toleration and distinguishes between civil and ecclesiastical government.

Toleration in Israel (19 April 1678).

MS Locke f. 3, p. 107. Marginal keyword: "Toleration." A note concerning the ancient Jewish state.

Toleration and Sincerity (1679).

MS Locke d. 1, pp. 125–26. Heading: "Toleratio." Locke reiterates principles laid down in the *Essay Concerning Toleration*.

Latitude (1679).

MS Locke d. 1, p. 5. Headed "Conformitas." Locke recounts a story about Protestants at Constantinople, which implies a preference for the "comprehension" of dissenting Protestants within the fold of the national church.

The Origin of Religious Societies (1681).

An excerpt from Locke's critique of Edward Stillingfleet. MS Locke c. 34, fols. 75–79. This substantial manuscript is written in the hands of Locke, James Tyrrell, and Locke's amanuensis Sylvester Brounower. It is untitled, and the common designations, "Critical Notes on Stillingfleet" and "Defence of Nonconformity," are modern. The target is a sermon and treatise by Stillingfleet, *The Mischief of Separation* (1680) and *The Unreasonableness of Separation* (1681).

There is as yet no published edition, though short excerpts have appeared in various places, and there is a complete transcription in Timothy Stanton, "John Locke, Edward Stillingfleet, and Toleration" (Ph.D. thesis, Leicester, 2003), from which the present excerpt is derived, with his permission. I have not registered the innumerable alterations that occur in the manuscript. The sentence preceding this excerpt refers to examining "the original of religious societies."

Enthusiasm (19 February 1682).

MS Locke f. 6, pp. 20–25. Untitled. A commentary on *Select Discourses* (1660) by the Cambridge Platonist John Smith, concerning "The True Way or Method of Attaining to Divine Knowledge." "Enthusiasm" was a pejorative term for extravagant and dangerous forms of spirituality, involving claims for direct divine inspiration. Locke included some of this material in a letter he wrote to Damaris Masham in April. Later, he inserted a chapter on "Enthusiasm" in the *Essay Concerning Human Understanding:* bk. 4, chap. 19.

Ecclesia (1682).

MS Locke d. 10, p. 43. Locke's heading. A commentary on Richard Hooker, *The Laws of Ecclesiastical Polity* (1593–97). Locke bought a copy of Hooker in June 1681 and took extensive notes from it.

Tradition (1682).

MS Locke d. 10, p. 163. Headed "Traditio." A criticism of the role of clerical "tradition" in the teachings of Judaism, Catholicism, and Islam. Locke's implied position is the Protestant principle of *sola scriptura:* the sufficiency of Scripture alone, without the necessity of priestly interpretive authority. The quarrel between the sufficiency of Scripture and the necessity of tradition was known as the "Rule of Faith" controversy.

Pennsylvania Laws (1686).

MS Locke f. 9, fols. 33, 39. Excerpts from Locke's comments on William Penn's Frame of Government, headed "Pensilvania Laws." Only the comments on religious and moral matters are included. The first several items appear at the head of the document; the last item, on schools, appears later. Locke's final comment is comprehensively negative: "the whole is so far from a frame of government that it scarce contains a part of the materials."

Pacific Christians (1688).

MS Locke c. 27, fol. 80. Headed "Pacifick Christians." Apparently a set of guiding principles for a religious society. Compare "Rules of the Dry Club" (1692), whose members must declare that they believe "no person ought to be harmed in his body, name, or goods, for mere speculative opinions, or his external way of worship" (Locke, *Works*, 1801, vol. 10, pp. 312–14).

Sacerdos (1698).

In the notebook "Adversaria 1661," p. 93. Locke's heading. He begins with an account of ancient religion, out of Cicero, and then turns to stress the essential character of Christianity as holy living, not ritual performances. The passage is a commentary on Pierre Bayle's *Pensées diverses* (1683), §127.

Error (1698).

In the notebook "Adversaria 1661," pp. 320–21. Locke's heading. He attacks elaborate doctrinal confessions of faith, unquestioning belief, and the tyranny of orthodoxy. He affirms the priority of sincerity in belief and morality in conduct.

Scriptures for Toleration (undated, ca. 1676–90).

MS Locke c. 33, fol. 24. Headed "Tolerantia Pro." A series of biblical citations that Locke takes as favoring toleration.

CHRONOLOGY OF LOCKE'S LIFE

1632   Born at Wrington, Somerset, 29 August

1642   Outbreak of the Civil Wars

1643   Troops of Col. Popham, Locke's future patron, despoil Wells
        Cathedral

1645   Defeat of Charles I at Naseby by Oliver Cromwell

1647   Admitted to Westminster School, London

1648   Treaty of Westphalia ends European Thirty Years' War

1649   Execution of Charles I; England a republic

1651   Thomas Hobbes, *Leviathan*

1652   Elected a Student of Christ Church, Oxford

1652–67 Usually resident in Oxford

1655   Graduates as a bachelor of arts

1658   Graduates as a master of arts; death of Lord Protector Oliver
        Cromwell

1660   Restoration of monarchy under Charles II

1660–62 Writes *Two Tracts on Government,* against toleration
        (published 1967)

1661–64 Lecturer in Greek, rhetoric, and moral philosophy

1662   Act of Uniformity reimposes Anglicanism; dissenting worship illegal

1663   Attends chemical and medical lectures

1663–64   Writes *Essays on the Law of Nature* (published 1954)

1665–66   Embassy secretary sent to the Elector of Brandenburg at Cleves (Kleve)

1666   Licensed to practice medicine

    Granted dispensation to retain Studentship without taking holy orders

    Great Fire of London

1667   Joins Lord Ashley's household; usually resident in London until 1675.

    Writes *Essay Concerning Toleration* (published 1876)

1668   Oversees lifesaving operation on Ashley

    Elected a Fellow of the Royal Society

1669   Helps draft *The Fundamental Constitutions of Carolina*

1670   Baruch Spinoza, *Tractatus Theologico-Politicus*

1671   Secretary to the Lords Proprietors of Carolina (until 1675)

    First drafts of *An Essay Concerning Human Understanding*

1672   Ashley created Earl of Shaftesbury and Lord Chancellor

    Appointed secretary for ecclesiastical presentations (to 1673)

    First visit to France

    Samuel Pufendorf, *On the Law of Nature and Nations*

1673   Secretary to the Council of Trade and Plantations (to 1674)

    Charles II's brother and heir, James, Duke of York, converts to Catholicism

    Shaftesbury ousted from office; begins to lead opposition

1675   Shaftesburian manifesto, *A Letter from a Person of Quality*

    Graduates as a bachelor of medicine

    To France; chiefly resident at Montpellier until 1677; then mainly Paris

1676 Translates three of Pierre Nicole's *Essais de Morale*

1677 Repeal of writ *De haeretico comburendo,* abolishing burning for heresy

Andrew Marvell, *An Account of the Growth of Popery*

1678 Popish Plot revealed; executions of Catholics follow (to 1681)

1679 Returns to England

Habeas Corpus Act

1679–81 Exclusion Crisis; Whigs seek to exclude Catholic heir from the throne

Whig victory in three general elections, but Whigs outmaneuvered by the king

1680 Signs London's "monster petition," demanding sitting of Parliament

1679–83 Resides in London, Oxford, and Oakley (James Tyrrell's home)

Writes *Two Treatises of Government*

1681 Writes a defense of toleration against Edward Stillingfleet

Assists Shaftesbury at the Oxford Parliament

Oxford Parliament dismissed; Charles summons no more parliaments

Beginning of royal and Tory backlash against Whigs and dissenters

Shaftesbury accused of treason; charge dismissed by a Whig grand jury

1682 Court coup against Whigs in City of London; Shaftesbury flees to Holland

1683 Death of Shaftesbury in Holland; Locke attends funeral in Dorset

Whig Rye House Plot, to assassinate the king, exposed

Executions of Lord William Russell and Algernon Sidney

Earl of Essex's suicide in the Tower; Whigs suspect state murder

Judgment and Decree of Oxford University against seditious doctrines

1683–89 Exile in Holland; lives mainly in Utrecht, Amsterdam, and Rotterdam

1684 Expelled *in absentia* from Studentship of Christ Church

1685 Death of Charles II; accession of James II and VII

Abortive rebellion of the Whig Duke of Monmouth; his execution

Louis XIV revokes Edict of Nantes; persecution of Huguenots

Writes *Epistola de Tolerantia (Letter Concerning Toleration)*

1686 Pierre Bayle, *Philosophical Commentary* on religious persecution

1687 James II issues Declaration of Indulgence (edict of toleration)

1688 Reviews Newton's *Principia Mathematica* for *Bibliothèque universelle*

Culmination of resistance to James II's Catholicizing policies

"Glorious Revolution": invasion of England by William of Orange

James II overthrown and flees to France

1689 National Convention installs King William and Queen Mary

Nine Years' War against Louis XIV opens

Toleration Act: freedom of worship for Protestant dissenters

Returns to England; declines an ambassadorship

Appointed Commissioner of Appeals in Excise

Publication of *A Letter Concerning Toleration*

Publication of *Two Treatises of Government*

Publication of *An Essay Concerning Human Understanding*

1690 Battle of the Boyne: William defeats Jacobites in Ireland

Letter Concerning Toleration attacked by Jonas Proast

Publication of *A Second Letter Concerning Toleration*

1691 Publication of *Some Considerations of the . . . Lowering of Interest*

Settles at Oates in Essex in Damaris Masham's household

1692   Publication of *A Third Letter for Toleration*

Memorandum on the naturalization of immigrants

1693   Publication of *Some Thoughts Concerning Education*

1694   Founding of the Bank of England; invests £500

Triennial Act, requiring regular parliamentary elections

1695   Advises on the ending of press censorship and the recoinage

Publication of *The Reasonableness of Christianity*

The *Reasonableness* attacked by John Edwards; publishes *Vindication*

Publication of *Further Considerations Concerning . . . Money*

1696   Appointed a member of the Board of Trade and Plantations (to 1700)

The *Essay* attacked by Bishop Edward Stillingfleet

John Toland, *Christianity not Mysterious*

Pierre Bayle, *Historical and Critical Dictionary*

1697   Treaty of Ryswick: temporary peace with France

Publication of *Second Vindication of the Reasonableness of Christianity*

Publication of two replies to Stillingfleet in defense of the *Essay*

Composes *An Essay on the Poor Law*

Composes report on the government of Virginia

Composes *The Conduct of the Understanding*

Thomas Aikenhead hanged at Edinburgh, Britain's last heresy execution

1698   Molyneux's *Case of Ireland* cites *Two Treatises* in defense of Ireland

Algernon Sidney, *Discourses Concerning Government* (posthumous)

1701   Act of Settlement, ensuring Protestant (Hanoverian) succession

Renewal of war against France

1702 Final visit to London

Composes *A Discourse on Miracles*

Death of William III; accession of Queen Anne

World's first daily newspaper, in London

1703 First major critique of *Two Treatises,* by Charles Leslie

1704 Completes *A Paraphrase and Notes on the Epistles of St. Paul*

Battle of Blenheim: Duke of Marlborough's victory over France

Capture of Gibraltar begins Britain's Mediterranean naval dominance

Dies at Oates, 28 October; buried in High Laver churchyard, Essex

1705–7 Publication of *A Paraphrase and Notes on the Epistles of St. Paul*

1706 Publication of the unfinished *Fourth Letter for Toleration*

1710 First French and German editions of *A Letter Concerning Toleration*

1714 First edition of the *Works* of Locke

1743 First American edition of *A Letter Concerning Toleration*

1764 Voltaire's edition of *A Letter Concerning Toleration*

1765 Thomas Hollis's edition of the *Letters Concerning Toleration*

ACKNOWLEDGMENTS

In preparing this volume I am extremely grateful for the help of David Armitage, Clare Jackson, Dmitri Levitin, Joseph Loconte, John Marshall, John Milton, Philip Milton, Homyar Pahlan, Mark Parry, Delphine Soulard, Timothy Stanton, Stephen Thompson, and David Womersley. I also wish to thank most warmly Richard Fisher and Peter Momtchiloff, respectively of Cambridge and Oxford University Presses, for facilitating the availability of texts, earlier versions of which were published by their presses.

Many Lockeans have gone before me: I am particularly indebted to the editions of Locke's writings on toleration published by Raymond Klibansky and J. W. Gough in 1968, J. C. Biddle in 1977, Victor Nuovo in 2002, and J. R. Milton and Philip Milton in 2005. With characteristic generosity, David Armitage, the brothers Milton, Tim Stanton, and David Womersley made available transcriptions of Locke manuscripts.

I have benefited from the resources of the Bodleian Library in Oxford; the Cambridge University Library; the British Library, London; the Huntington Library, San Marino, California; and the National Archives, Kew, London.

The text of Locke's *Letter Concerning Toleration* is set from the copy in St. John's College Library, Cambridge.

A Letter
Concerning Toleration
and Other Writings

A
LETTER
Concerning
TOLERATION

LICENSED, *Octob.* 3. 1689.

The Second Edition Corrected

LONDON, Printed for Awnsham Churchill
at the Black Swan in Ave-Mary Lane.

MDCXC

TO THE READER[1]

The Ensuing Letter concerning Toleration, *first Printed in* Latin *this very Year, in* Holland, *has already been Translated both into* Dutch *and* French.[2] *So general and speedy an Approbation may therefore bespeak its favourable Reception in* England. *I think indeed there is no Nation under Heaven, in which so much has already been said upon that Subject, as Ours. But yet certainly there is no People that stand in more need of having something further both said and done amongst them, in this Point, than We do.*

Our Government has not only been partial in Matters of Religion; but those also who have suffered under that Partiality, and have therefore endeavoured by their Writings to vindicate their own Rights and Liberties, have for the most part done it upon narrow Principles, suited only to the Interests of their own Sects.

This narrowness of Spirit on all sides has undoubtedly been the principal

---

1. The preface was written by the translator, William Popple (1638–1708), a Unitarian merchant and religious writer. He had been a wine trader at Bordeaux before returning to England in 1688. He authored *A Rational Catechism* (1687) and *A Discourse of Humane Reason* (1690), reissued as *Two Treatises of Rational Religion* (1692).

2. A Dutch edition appeared in 1689 but no copy has survived; a French edition was planned but did not appear. The first French edition was published in 1710.

Occasion of our Miseries and Confusions. But whatever have been the Occasion, it is now high time to seek for a thorow Cure. We have need of more generous Remedies than what have yet been made use of in our Distemper. It is neither Declarations of Indulgence,[3] *nor* Acts of Comprehension,[4] *such as have yet been practised or projected amongst us, that can do the Work. The first will but palliate, the second encrease our Evil.*

Absolute Liberty,[5] *Just and True Liberty, Equal and Impartial Liberty, is the thing that we stand in need of. Now tho this has indeed been much talked of, I doubt it has not been much understood; I am sure not at all practised, either by our Governours towards the People, in general, or by any dissenting Parties of the People towards one another.*

I cannot therefore but hope that this Discourse, *which treats of that Subject, however briefly, yet more exactly than any we have yet seen, demonstrating both the Equitableness and Practicableness of the thing, will be esteemed highly*

3. Popple's reference to "Declarations of Indulgence" is puzzling. Charles II and James II had issued Declarations of Indulgence in 1672 and 1687, respectively. These granted toleration by prerogative edict, suspending the laws for Anglican uniformity. Yet, by the time Popple wrote, a statutory toleration had been achieved in the Toleration Act (May 1689). However, contemporaries sometimes referred to this as the Act of Indulgence: aptly enough, because, like earlier indulgences, it merely suspended the punishments for nonconformity but did not repeal the laws requiring conformity. It is possible, therefore, that Popple means the recent act. His general point is that all such indulgences are insufficient, for they leave the old laws in place, continue to exclude dissenters from public office, and (in the case of the act) exclude anti-Trinitarians. Despite the sobriquet it acquired, the Toleration Act nowhere used the word *toleration*. See note 41, p. 85.

4. In March 1689 a bill for comprehension was introduced, which aimed to modify the terms of church conformity in order to readmit moderate dissenters. The bill was withdrawn, but at the time Popple wrote, in autumn 1689, the matter was still expected to be reconsidered. Popple objects to comprehension schemes because, though based on a latitudinarian approach to church membership, they offered no guarantee of liberty for those who remained outside the church.

5. The ringing cry for "absolute liberty" was later used as a Lockean slogan by authors who did not realize that the preface was not by Locke. Some scholars point out that Locke rejects "absolute" liberty (e.g., *Essay*, 4.3.18), but the context here is religious toleration and Popple is stressing, with rhetorical exaggeration, the inadequacy of the Toleration Act. See Locke's use of *absolute*, p. 107.

seasonable, by all Men that have Souls large enough to prefer the true Interest of the Publick before that of a Party.

It is for the use of such as are already so spirited, or to inspire that Spirit into those that are not, that I have Translated it into our Language. But the thing it self is so short, that it will not bear a longer Preface. I leave it therefore to the Consideration of my Countrymen, and heartily wish they may make the use of it that it appears to be designed for.

A Letter Concerning Toleration.

Honoured Sir,

Since you are pleased to inquire what are my Thoughts about the mutual Toleration of Christians in their different Professions of Religion, I must needs answer you freely, That I esteem that Toleration to be the chief Characteristical Mark of the True Church.[6] For whatsoever some People boast of the Antiquity of Places and Names, or of the Pomp of their Outward Worship; Others, of the Reformation of their Discipline; All, of the Orthodoxy of their Faith; (for every one is Orthodox to himself): these things, and all others of this nature, are much rather Marks of Men

6. "the True Church": arguably, the indefinite article would better represent Locke's view of churches. That toleration is a "mark" of the church is a strong claim. The Reformation saw extensive theological debate over which "marks" or "notes" were the defining characteristics of the (or a) true church.

striving for Power and Empire over one another, than of the Church of Christ. Let any one have never so true a Claim to all these things, yet if he be destitute of Charity, Meekness, and Good-will in general towards all Mankind; even to those that are not Christians, he is certainly yet short of being a true Christian himself. *The Kings of the Gentiles exercise Lordship over them,* said our Saviour to his Disciples, *but ye shall not be so,* Luke 22:25. The Business of True Religion is quite another thing. It is not instituted in order to the erecting of an external Pomp, nor to the obtaining of Ecclesiastical Dominion, nor to the exercising of Compulsive Force; but to the regulating of Mens Lives according to the Rules of Vertue and Piety. Whosoever will list himself under the Banner of Christ, must in the first place, and above all things, make War upon his own Lusts and Vices.[7] It is in vain for any Man to usurp the Name of Christian, without Holiness of Life, Purity of Manners, and Benignity and Meekness of Spirit.[8]

Thou when thou art converted, strengthen thy Brethren, said our Lord to *Peter,* Luke 22:32. It would indeed be very hard for one that appears careless about his own Salvation, to perswade me that he were extreamly concern'd for mine. For it is impossible that those should sincerely and heartily apply themselves to make other People Christians, who have not really embraced the Christian Religion in their own Hearts. If the Gospel and the Apostles may be credited, no Man can be a Christian without *Charity,* and without *that Faith which works,* not by Force, but by *Love.*[9] Now I appeal to the Consciences of those that persecute, torment, destroy, and kill other Men upon pretence of Religion, whether they do it out of Friendship and Kindness towards them, or no: And I shall then indeed, and not till then, believe they do so, when I shall see those fiery Zealots

7. "Vices": alternatively, "pride." The appearance of "alternatively," "added by Popple," and "Popple omits" in these footnotes indicates places where Popple deviates from Locke's Latin. See pp. xxx–xxxi.

8. The first edition had included a further scriptural quotation, absent in Locke's *Epistola:* "Let every one that nameth the name of Christ depart from iniquity" (2 Timothy 2:19). If its inclusion in the first edition was inauthentic, what led Popple to be more scrupulous in the second? It has been suggested that this is one of two amendments that point to Locke's own hand in the second edition. See note 69, p. 30.

9. Galatians 5:6.

correcting, in the same manner, their Friends and familiar Acquaintance, for the manifest Sins they commit against the Precepts of the Gospel; when I shall see them prosecute with Fire and Sword the Members of their own Communion that are tainted with enormous Vices, and without Amendment are in danger of eternal Perdition; and when I shall see them thus express their Love and Desire of the Salvation of their Souls, by the infliction of Torments, and exercise of all manner of Cruelties. For if it be out of a Principle of Charity, as they pretend, and Love to Mens Souls, that they deprive them of their Estates, maim them with corporal Punishments, starve and torment them in noisom Prisons, and in the end even take away their Lives;[10] I say, if all this be done meerly to make Men Christians, and procure their Salvation, Why then do they suffer *Whoredom, Fraud, Malice, and such like enormities*, Romans 1; which (according to the Apostle) manifestly rellish[11] of Heathenish Corruption, to predominate so much and abound amongst their Flocks and People? These, and such like things, are certainly more contrary to the Glory of God, to the Purity of the Church, and to the Salvation of Souls, than any conscientious Dissent[12] from Ecclesiastical Decisions, or Separation from Publick Worship, whilst accompanied with Innocency of Life. Why then does this burning Zeal for God, for the Church, and for the Salvation of Souls; burning, I say, literally, with Fire and Faggot; pass by those moral Vices and Wickednesses, without any Chastisement, which are acknowledged by all Men to be diametrically opposite to the Profession of Christianity; and bend all its Nerves either to the introducing of Ceremonies, or to the establishment of Opinions, which for the most part are about nice[13] and intricate Matters, that exceed the Capacity of ordinary Understandings? Which of the Parties contending about these things is in the right, which of them is guilty of Schism or Heresie; whether those that domineer or those that suffer; will then at last be manifest, when the Cause of their Separation comes to be judged of. He certainly that follows Christ,

---

10. The savagery described here points to Louis XIV's persecution of the Huguenots. See note 17, p. 11, and note 146, p. 55.
11. *rellish:* smell.
12. Popple omits: "however erroneous."
13. *nice:* subtle.

embraces his Doctrine, and bears his Yoke, tho he forsake both Father and Mother, separate from the Publick Assembly and Ceremonies of his Country, or whomsoever, or whatsoever else he relinquishes, will not then be judged an Heretick.

Now, tho' the Divisions that are amongst Sects should be allowed to be never so obstructive of the Salvation of Souls; yet nevertheless *Adultery, Fornication, Uncleanness, Lasciviousness, Idolatry, and such like things, cannot be denied to be Works of the Flesh;* concerning which the Apostle has expresly declared, that *they who do them shall not inherit the Kingdom of God,* Galatians 5. Whosoever therefore is sincerely sollicitous about the Kingdom of God, and thinks it his Duty to endeavour the Enlargement of it amongst Men, ought to apply himself with no less care and industry to the rooting out of these Immoralities, than to the Extirpation of Sects.[14] But if any one do otherwise, and whilst he is cruel and implacable towards those that differ from him in Opinion, he be indulgent to such Iniquities and Immoralities as are unbecoming the Name of a Christian, let such a one talk never so much of the Church, he plainly demonstrates by his Actions, that 'tis another Kingdom[15] he aims at, and not the Advancement of the Kingdom of God.

That any Man should think fit to cause another Man, whose Salvation he heartily desires, to expire in Torments, and that even in an unconverted estate; would, I confess, seem very strange to me; and, I think, to any other also. But no body, surely, will ever believe that such a Carriage can proceed from Charity, Love, or Good-will. If any one maintain that Men ought to be compelled by Fire and Sword to profess certain Doctrines, and conform to this or that exteriour Worship, without any regard had unto their Morals; if any one endeavour to convert those that are Erroneous unto the Faith, by forcing them to profess things that they do not believe, and allowing them to practise things that the Gospel does not permit; it cannot be doubted indeed but such a one is desirous to have a numerous

14. This passage, with its insistence that it is a false priority to discipline worship rather than immoral behavior, is characteristic of the Reformation of Manners movement that dominated the 1690s.

15. "another Kingdom": i.e., earthly dominion by priests.

Assembly joyned in the same Profession with himself: But that he principally intends by those means to compose a truly Christian Church, is altogether incredible. It is not therefore to be wondred at, if those who do not really contend for the Advancement of the true Religion, and of the Church of Christ, make use of Arms that do not belong to the Christian Warfare.[16] If, like the Captain of our Salvation, they sincerely desired the Good of Souls, they would tread in the Steps, and follow the perfect Example of that Prince of Peace; who sent out his Soldiers to the subduing of Nations, and gathering them into his Church, not armed with the Sword, or other Instruments of Force, but prepared with the Gospel of Peace, and with the Exemplary Holiness of their Conversation. This was his Method. Tho' if Infidels were to be converted by force, if those that are either blind or obstinate were to be drawn off from their Errors by Armed Soldiers, we know very well that it was much more easie for Him to do it, with Armies of Heavenly Legions, than for any Son of the Church, how potent soever, with all his Dragoons.[17]

The Toleration of those that differ from others in Matters of Religion, is so agreeable to the Gospel of Jesus Christ, and to the genuine Reason of Mankind, that it seems monstrous for Men to be so blind, as not to perceive the Necessity and Advantage of it,[18] in so clear a Light. I will not here tax the Pride and Ambition of some, the Passion and uncharitable Zeal of others. These are Faults from which Humane Affairs can perhaps scarce ever be perfectly freed; but yet such as no body will bear the plain Imputation of, without covering them with some specious Colour; and so pretend to Commendation, whilst they are carried away by their own irregular Passions.[19] But however, that some may not colour their spirit of Persecution and unchristian Cruelty, with a Pretence of Care of the Publick Weal, and Observation of the Laws; and that others, under pretence

16. 2 Corinthians 10:4.

17. *Dragoons:* an allusion to the French *dragonnades,* the quartering of soldiers on Huguenot households to terrorize them into conversion. The Latin has *cohortes.*

18. "as not . . . it": added by Popple, where Locke has just "blind in so clear a light."

19. "whilst they . . . Passions": added by Popple.

of Religion, may not seek Impunity for their Libertinism and Licentiousness;[20] in a word, that none may impose either upon himself or others, by
the Pretences of Loyalty and Obedience to the Prince, or of Tenderness
and Sincerity in the Worship of God; I esteem it above all things necessary to distinguish exactly the Business of Civil Government from that of
Religion, and to settle the just Bounds that lie between the one and the
other. If this be not done, there can be no end put to the Controversies
that will be always arising, between those that have, or at least pretend to
have, on the one side, a Concernment for the Interest of Mens Souls, and
on the other side, a Care of the Commonwealth.

The Commonwealth seems to me to be a Society of Men constituted
only for the procuring, preserving, and advancing of their own *Civil
Interests.*[21]

Civil Interests I call Life, Liberty, Health, and Indolency of Body;[22] and
the Possession of outward things, such as Money, Lands, Houses, Furniture, and the like.

It is the Duty of the Civil Magistrate, by the impartial Execution of
equal Laws, to secure unto all the People in general, and to every one of
his Subjects in particular, the just Possession of these things belonging to
this Life. If any one presume to violate the Laws of Publick Justice and
Equity, established for the Preservation of these things,[23] his Presump-
tion is to be check'd by the fear of Punishment, consisting in the Deprivation or Diminution of those Civil Interests, or Goods, which otherwise
he might and ought to enjoy. But seeing no Man does willingly suffer
himself to be punished by the Deprivation of any part of his Goods, and
much less of his Liberty or Life, therefore is the Magistrate armed with
the Force and Strength of all his Subjects, in order to the punishment of
those that violate any other Man's Rights.

Now that the whole Jurisdiction of the Magistrate reaches only to
these civil Concernments; and that all Civil Power, Right, and Dominion,

---

20. "Impunity . . . Licentiousness": alternatively, "licence for their immorality and
impunity for their misdeeds."

21. "Civil Interests": alternatively, "civil goods" (*bona civilia*).

22. "Indolency of Body": alternatively, "freedom from pain."

23. "established . . . things": added by Popple.

is bounded and confined to the only care of promoting these things; and that it neither can nor ought in any manner to be extended to the Salvation of Souls; these following Considerations seem unto me abundantly to demonstrate.

First, Because the Care of Souls is not committed to the Civil Magistrate any more than to other Men. It is not committed unto him, I say, by God; because it appears not that God has ever given any such Authority to one Man over another, as to compell any one to his Religion. Nor can any such Power be vested in the Magistrate by the *Consent of the People*;[24] because no man can so far abandon the care of his own Salvation, as blindly to leave it to the choice of any other, whether Prince or Subject, to prescribe to him what Faith or Worship he shall embrace. For no Man can, if he would, conform his Faith to the Dictates of another. All the Life and Power of true Religion consists in the inward and full perswasion of the mind: And Faith is not Faith without believing.[25] Whatever Profession we make, to whatever outward Worship we conform, if we are not fully satisfied in our mind that the one is true, and the other well pleasing unto God; such Profession and such Practice, far from being any furtherance, are indeed great Obstacles to our Salvation. For in this manner, instead of expiating other Sins by the exercise of Religion; I say, in offering thus unto God Almighty such a Worship as we esteem to be displeasing unto him, we add unto the number of our other sins those also of Hypocrisie, and Contempt of his Divine Majesty.

In the second place. The care of Souls cannot belong to the Civil Magistrate, because his Power consists only in outward force: But true and saving Religion consists in the inward perswasion of the Mind; without which nothing can be acceptable to God. And such is the nature of the Understanding, that it cannot be compell'd to the belief of any thing by outward Force. Confiscation of Estate, Imprisonment, Torments, nothing of that Nature can have any such Efficacy as to make Men change the inward Judgment that they have framed of things.

It may indeed be alledged, that the Magistrate may make use of Argu-

---

24. "by the Consent of the People": alternatively, "by men" (*ab hominibus*).

25. "All the Life . . . believing": alternatively, "It is faith that gives force and efficacy to the true religion that brings salvation."

ments, and thereby draw the Heterodox into the way of Truth, and procure their Salvation. I grant it. But this is common to him with other Men. In teaching, instructing, and redressing the Erroneous by Reason, he may certainly do what becomes any good Man to do. Magistracy does not oblige him to put off either Humanity or Christianity. But it is one thing to perswade, another to command: One thing to press with Arguments, another with Penalties. This the Civil Power alone has a Right to do: to the other Good-will is Authority enough. Every Man has Commission to admonish, exhort, convince another of Error; and by reasoning to draw him into Truth. But to give Laws, receive Obedience, and compel with the Sword, belongs to none but the Magistrate. And upon this ground I affirm, that the Magistrate's Power extends not to the establishing of any Articles of Faith, or Forms of Worship, by the force of his Laws. For Laws are of no force at all without Penalties, and Penalties in this case are absolutely impertinent; because they are not proper[26] to convince the mind. Neither the Profession of any Articles of Faith, nor the Conformity to any outward Form of Worship (as has already been said) can be available to the Salvation of Souls; unless the Truth of the one, and the acceptableness of the other unto God, be thoroughly believed by those that so profess and practise. But Penalties are no ways capable to produce such Belief. It is only Light and Evidence that can work a change in Mens Opinions. And that Light can in no manner proceed from corporal Sufferings, or any other outward Penalties.[27]

In the third place. The care of the Salvation of Mens Souls cannot belong to the Magistrate; because, though the rigour of Laws and the force of Penalties were capable to convince and change Mens minds, yet would not that help at all to the Salvation of their Souls. For there being but one Truth, one way to heaven; what hopes is there that more Men would be led into it, if they had no other Rule to follow but the Religion of the Court; and were put under a necessity to quit the Light of their own Reason; to oppose the Dictates of their own Consciences; and blindly to resign up themselves to the Will of their Governors, and to the

26. "and Penalties . . . proper": alternatively, "while if penalties are applied they are obviously futile and inappropriate."

27. "or any . . . Penalties": added by Popple.

Religion, which either Ignorance, Ambition, or Superstition had chanced to[28] establish in the Countries where they were born? In the variety and contradiction of Opinions in Religion, wherein the Princes of the World are as much divided as in their Secular Interests, the narrow way would be much straitned.[29] One Country alone would be in the right, and all the rest of the World would be put under an Obligation of following their Princes in the ways that lead to Destruction.[30] And that which heightens the absurdity, and very ill suits the Notion of a Deity, Men would owe their eternal Happiness or Misery to the places of their Nativity.

These Considerations, to omit many others that might have been urged to the same purpose, seem unto me sufficient to conclude that all the Power of Civil Government relates only to Mens Civil Interests; is confined to the care of the things of this World; and hath nothing to do with the World to come.

Let us now consider what a Church is. A Church then I take to be a voluntary Society[31] of Men, joining themselves together of their own accord, in order to the publick worshipping of God, in such a manner as they judge acceptable to him, and effectual to the Salvation of their Souls.

I say it is a free and voluntary Society. No body is born a Member of any Church. Otherwise the Religion of Parents would descend unto Children, by the same right of Inheritance as their Temporal Estates, and every one would hold his Faith by the same Tenure he does his Lands; than which nothing can be imagined more absurd. Thus therefore that matter stands. No Man by nature is bound unto any particular Church or Sect, but every one joins himself voluntarily to that Society in which he believes he has found that Profession and Worship which is truly acceptable unto God. The hopes of Salvation, as it was the only cause of his entrance into that Communion, so it can be the only reason of his stay there. For if afterwards he discover any thing either erroneous in the Doc-

---

28. "which either . . . chanced to": added by Popple.

29. Matthew 7:14.

30. "and all . . . Destruction": added by Popple.

31. "voluntary Society": alternatively, "free society" (*societas libera*); the next paragraph has "free and voluntary Society" (*societatem liberam et voluntariam*). Locke's definition is striking; historically, since the fourth century, the Christian churches had scarcely been "voluntary" societies.

trine, or incongruous in the Worship of that Society to which he has join'd himself; Why should it not be as free for him to go out, as it was to enter? No Member of a Religious Society can be tied with any other Bonds but what proceed from the certain expectation of eternal Life. A Church then is a Society of Members voluntarily uniting to this end.

It follows now that we consider what is the Power of this Church, and unto what Laws it is subject.

Forasmuch as no Society, how free soever, or upon whatsoever slight occasion instituted, (whether of Philosophers for Learning, of Merchants for Commerce, or of men of leisure for mutual Conversation and Discourse), No Church or Company, I say, can in the least subsist and hold together, but will presently dissolve and break to pieces, unless it be regulated by some Laws, and the Members all consent to observe some Order. Place, and time of meeting must be agreed on. Rules for admitting and excluding Members must be establisht. Distinction of Officers, and putting things into a regular Course, and such like, cannot be omitted. But since the joyning together of several Members into this Church-Society, as has already been demonstrated, is absolutely free and spontaneous, it necessarily follows, that the Right of making its Laws can belong to none but the Society it self; or at least (which is the same thing) to those whom the Society by common consent has authorised thereunto.

Some perhaps may object, that no such Society can be said to be a true Church, unless it have in it a Bishop, or Presbyter,[32] with Ruling Authority derived from the very Apostles, and continued down unto the present times by an uninterrupted Succession.

To these I answer. *In the first place,* Let them shew me the Edict by which Christ has imposed that Law upon his Church.[33] And let not any man think me impertinent, if in a thing of this consequence, I require that the Terms of that Edict be very express and positive. For the Promise he

---

32. *Presbyter:* Locke means the Calvinist system of church government by consistories of ministers and elders.

33. Locke ignores the *locus classicus* for precisely this "Edict," Matthew 16:18–19: "Thou art Peter, and upon this rock I will build my church. . . . And I will give unto thee the keys of the kingdom of heaven: and whatsoever thou shalt bind on earth shall be bound in heaven." See next note.

has made us, that *wheresoever two or three are gathered together in his Name, he will be in the midst of them,* Matthew 18:20, seems to imply the contrary. Whether such an Assembly want any thing necessary to a true Church, pray do you consider. Certain I am, that nothing can be there wanting unto the Salvation of Souls; Which is sufficient to our purpose.

Next, Pray observe how great have always been the Divisions amongst even those who lay so much stress upon the Divine Institution, and continued Succession of a certain Order of Rulers in the Church.[34] Now their very Dissention unavoidably puts us upon a necessity of deliberating, and consequently allows a Liberty of choosing that which upon consideration we prefer.

And in the last place, I consent that these men have a Ruler of their Church, established by such a long Series of Succession as they judge necessary; provided I may have liberty at the same time to join my self to that Society, in which I am perswaded those things are to be found which are necessary to the Salvation of my Soul. In this manner Ecclesiastical Liberty will be preserved on all sides, and no man will have a Legislator imposed upon him, but whom himself has chosen.

But since men are so sollicitous about the true Church, I would only ask them, here by the way, if it be not more agreeable to the Church of Christ, to make the Conditions of her Communion consist in such things, and such things only, as the Holy Spirit has in the Holy Scriptures declared, in express Words, to be necessary to Salvation; I ask, I say, whether this be not more agreeable to the Church of Christ, than for men to impose their own Inventions and Interpretations upon others, as if they were of Divine Authority; and to establish by Ecclesiastical Laws, as absolutely necessary to the Profession of Christianity, such things as the Holy Scriptures do either not mention, or at least not expresly com-

---

34. Episcopalians believed in the *apostolic succession,* namely that authority was conveyed to them because there was an unbroken succession of bishops from the apostles. In its strongest form, this was the doctrine of the divine right of episcopacy. Catholics additionally believed in a Petrine succession of the papacy from the first pope, St. Peter. Given Locke's recent reference to "presbyters," his targets here also include the further claim that presbyters have exclusive succession from the apostles.

mand. Whosoever requires those things in order to[35] Ecclesiastical Communion, which Christ does not require in order to life Eternal; he may perhaps indeed constitute a Society accommodated to his own Opinion, and his own Advantage; but how that can be called the Church of Christ, which is established upon Laws that are not his, and which excludes such Persons from its Communion as he will one day receive into the Kingdom of Heaven, I understand not. But this being not a proper place to enquire into the marks of the true Church,[36] I will only mind[37] those that contend so earnestly for the Decrees of their own Society, and that cry out continually the Church, the Church, with as much noise, and perhaps upon the same Principle, as the *Ephesian* Silversmiths did for their *Diana;*[38] this, I say, I desire to mind them of, That the Gospel frequently declares that the true Disciples of Christ must suffer Persecution; but that the Church of Christ should persecute others, and force others by Fire and Sword, to embrace her Faith and Doctrine, I could never yet find in any of the Books of the New Testament.

The end of a Religious Society (as has already been said) is the Publick Worship of God, and by means thereof the acquisition of Eternal Life. All Discipline ought therefore to tend to that End, and all Ecclesiastical Laws to be thereunto confined. Nothing ought, nor can be transacted in this Society, relating to the Possession of Civil and Worldly Goods. No Force is here to be made use of, upon any occasion whatsoever. For Force belongs wholly to the Civil Magistrate, and the Possession of all outward Goods is subject to his Jurisdiction.

But it may be asked, By what means then shall Ecclesiastical Laws be established, if they must be thus destitute of all compulsive Power. I answer, They must be established by means suitable to the Nature of such Things, whereof the external Profession and Observation, if not proceeding from a thorow Conviction and Approbation of the Mind, is alto-

---

35. *in order to:* "for."
36. See note 6, p. 7.
37. *mind:* remind.
38. Acts 19. The silversmiths' livelihood depended on the cult of Diana, and accordingly they were angry at the arrival of Christianity. The cry "Great is Diana" was commonly taken to epitomize self-interest masquerading as godliness. Charles Blount's deistic tract of 1680 is titled *Great is Diana of the Ephesians.*

gether useless and unprofitable. The Arms by which the Members of this Society are to be kept within their Duty, are Exhortations, Admonitions, and Advices. If by these means the Offenders will not be reclaimed, and the Erroneous convinced, there remains nothing farther to be done, but that such stubborn and obstinate Persons, who give no ground to hope for their Reformation, should be cast out and separated from the Society.[39] This is the last and utmost Force of Ecclesiastical Authority. No other Punishment can thereby be inflicted, than that the relation ceasing between the Body and the Member which is cut off, the Person so condemned ceases to be a part of that Church.

These things being thus determined, let us inquire in the next place, how far the Duty of Toleration extends; and what is required from every one by it.

And first, I hold, That no Church is bound by the Duty of Toleration to retain any such Person in her Bosom, as, after Admonition, continues obstinately to offend against the Laws of the Society. For these being the Condition of Communion, and the Bond of the Society; If the Breach of them were permitted without any Animadversion, the Society would immediately be thereby dissolved. But nevertheless, in all such Cases, care is to be taken that the Sentence of Excommunication, and the Execution thereof, carry with it no rough usage of Word or Action, whereby the ejected Person may any wise be damnified[40] in Body or Estate. For all Force (as has often been said) belongs only to the Magistrate; nor ought any private Persons, at any time, to use Force, unless it be in Self-defence against unjust Violence. Excommunication neither does, nor can deprive the excommunicated Person of any of those Civil Goods that he formerly possessed. All those things belong to the Civil Government, and are under the Magistrate's Protection. The whole Force of Excommunication consists only in this, that the Resolution of the Society in that respect being declared, the Union that was between the Body and some

39. This is what churches call excommunication. Historically, and in Locke's time, excommunication by the established church carried civil penalties. Locke argues that while churches have a right to control their membership, no civil penalties should be attached to excommunication.

40. *damnified:* injured.

Member comes thereby to be dissolved; and that Relation ceasing; the participation of some certain things, which the Society communicated to its Members, and unto which no Man has any Civil Right, comes also to cease. For there is no Civil Injury done unto the excommunicated Person, by the Church-Minister's refusing him that Bread and Wine, in the Celebration of the Lord's Supper, which was not bought with his, but other mens Money.

Secondly, No private Person has any Right, in any manner, to prejudice another Person in his Civil Enjoyments, because he is of another Church or Religion. All the Rights and Franchises [41] that belong to him as a Man, or as a Denison, [42] are inviolably to be Preserved to him. These are not the Business of Religion. No Violence nor Injury is to be offered him, whether he be Christian or Pagan. Nay, we must not content our selves with the narrow Measures of bare Justice. Charity, Bounty, and Liberality must be added to it. This the Gospel enjoyns; this Reason directs; and this that natural Fellowship we are born into requires of us. If any man err from the right way, it is his own Misfortune, no Injury to thee: Nor therefore art thou to punish him in the things of this Life, because thou supposest he will be miserable in that which is to come.

What I say concerning the mutual Toleration of private Persons differing from one another in Religion, I understand also of particular Churches; which stand as it were in the same relation to each other as private Persons among themselves; nor has any one of them any manner of Jurisdiction over any other, no not even when the Civil Magistrate (as it sometimes happens) comes to be of this or the other Communion. For the Civil Government can give no new Right to the Church, nor the Church to the Civil Government. So that whether the Magistrate joyn himself to any Church, or separate from it, the Church remains always as it was before, a free and voluntary Society. It neither acquires the Power of the Sword by the Magistrate's coming to it, nor does it lose the Right of Instruction and Excommunication by his going from it. This is the fundamental and immutable Right of a spontaneous Society; that it has

41. *Franchises:* liberties.
42. "Denison": alternatively, "citizen."

power to remove any of its Members who transgress the Rules of its Institution. But it cannot, by the accession of any new Members, acquire any Right of Jurisdiction over those that are not joyned with it. And therefore Peace, Equity and Friendship, are always mutually to be observed by particular Churches, in the same manner as by private Persons, without any pretence of Superiority or Jurisdiction over one another.

That the thing may be made yet clearer by an Example; Let us suppose two Churches, the one of *Arminians,* the other of *Calvinists,* [43] residing in the City of *Constantinople;* Will any one say, that either of these Churches has Right to deprive the Members of the other of their Estates and Liberty, [44] (as we see practised elsewhere) because of their differing from it in some Doctrines or Ceremonies; whilst the *Turks* in the mean while silently stand by, and laugh to see with what inhumane Cruelty Christians thus rage against Christians? But if one of these Churches hath this Power of treating the other ill, I ask which of them it is to whom that Power belongs, and by what Right? It will be answered undoubtedly, That it is the Orthodox Church which has the Right of Authority over the Erroneous or Heretical. This is, in great and specious words, to say just nothing at all. For every Church is Orthodox to it self; to others, Erroneous or Heretical. Whatsoever any Church believes, it believes to be true; and the contrary thereunto it pronounces to be Error. So that the Controversie between these Churches about the Truth of their Doctrines, and the Purity of their Worship, is on both sides equal; nor is there any Judg, either at *Constantinople,* or elsewhere upon Earth, by whose Sentence it can be determined. The Decision of that Question belongs only to the Supream Judge of all men, to whom also alone belongs the Punishment of the Erroneous. In the mean while, let those men consider how hainously

43. "Arminians" and "Calvinists": alternatively "Remonstrants" and "Anti-Remonstrants." Popple here anglicizes Locke's text. Arminians derived their name from the Dutch theologian Jacob Arminius (1560–1609), who broke with the Calvinist doctrine of divine predestination to eternal life. By Locke's time, Arminians were called Remonstrants. The term *Arminian* was also regularly used in England for those who departed from Calvinism. A few lines later in this same paragraph, Locke's parenthetical comment "as we see practised elsewhere" hints at the persecution of Arminians by Calvinists in Holland.

44. Popple omits: "or punish them with exile or death."

they sin; Who, adding Injustice, if not to their Error, yet certainly to their Pride, do rashly and arrogantly take upon them to misuse the Servants of another Master, who are not at all accountable to them.

Nay further: If it could be manifest which of these two dissenting Churches were in the right way, there would not accrue thereby to the Orthodox any Right of destroying the other. For Churches have neither any Jurisdiction in worldly Matters, nor are Fire and Sword any proper Instruments wherewith to convince mens Minds of Error, and inform them of the Truth. Let us suppose, nevertheless, that the Civil Magistrate inclined to favour one of them, and to put his Sword into their Hands; that (by his consent) they might chastise the Dissenters as they pleased. Will any man say, that any Right can be derived unto a Christian Church over its Brethren, from a Turkish Emperor? An Infidel, who has himself no Authority to punish Christians for the Articles of their Faith, cannot confer such an Authority upon any Society of Christians, nor give unto them a Right, which he has not himself. This would be the Case at *Constantinople*.[45] And the Reason of the thing is the same in any Christian Kingdom. The Civil Power is the same in every place; nor can that Power, in the Hands of a Christian Prince, confer any greater Authority upon the Church, than in the Hands of a Heathen; which is to say, just none at all.

Nevertheless, it is worthy to be observed, and lamented, that the most violent of these Defenders of the Truth, the Opposers of Errors, the Exclaimers against Schism, do hardly ever let loose this their Zeal for God, with which they are so warmed and inflamed, unless where they have the Civil Magistrate on their side. But so soon as ever Court favour has given them the better end of the Staff, and they begin to feel themselves the stronger,[46] then presently Peace and Charity are to be laid aside; otherwise, they are religiously to be observed. Where they have not the Power to carry on Persecution, and to become Masters, there they desire

45. "This would . . . *Constantinople*": added by Popple.
46. "But so soon . . . stronger": alternatively, "But as soon as ever the magistrate's favour makes them the stronger." The colloquial phrase "the better end of the Staff" is Popple's addition. Locke here attacks the alliance between persecuting priests and authoritarian governments.

to live upon fair Terms, and preach up Toleration.[47] When they are not strengthened with the Civil Power, then they can bear most patiently and unmovedly the Contagion of Idolatry, Superstition and Heresie in their Neighbourhood; of which, in other Occasions, the Interest of Religion makes them to be extreamly apprehensive. They do not forwardly attack those Errors which are in fashion at Court, or are countenanced by the Government. Here they can be content to spare their Arguments; which yet (with their leave) is the only right Method of propagating Truth; which has no such way of prevailing, as when strong Arguments and good Reason are joyned with the softness of Civility and good Usage.[48]

No body therefore, in fine,[49] neither single Persons, nor Churches, nay, nor even Commonwealths, have any just Title to invade the Civil Rights and Worldly Goods of each other upon pretence of Religion. Those that are of another Opinion, would do well to consider with themselves how pernicious a Seed of Discord and War, how powerful a Provocation to endless Hatreds, Rapines, and Slaughters, they thereby furnish unto Mankind. No Peace and Security, no not so much as common Friendship, can ever be established or preserved amongst Men, so long as this Opinion prevails, That *Dominion is founded in Grace,*[50] and that Religion is to be propagated by force of Arms.

In the third Place, Let us see what the *Duty of Toleration requires* from those who are distinguished from the rest of Mankind, (from the Laity, as

47. "Where they ... Toleration": added by Popple. While this passage has a general application, it had particular resonance in 1689, since the Church of England had in recent years blown hot and cold about tolerating dissenters, depending on its own circumstances. Under the shock of James II's Catholicizing policies, the church had offered to settle with dissenters, which resulted in the begrudging passage of the Toleration Act.

48. "Civility and good Usage": alternatively, "humanity and benevolence."

49. *in fine:* to conclude.

50. *Dominion is founded in Grace:* the doctrine that the authority of governors depends upon their adherence to true religion. When citing (and deploring) this dictum, Locke's contemporaries sometimes had radical Puritan zealots in mind, the "rule of the saints." But the doctrine was also attributed to Catholics. The papacy claimed the power to depose heretical princes, and Catholic princes claimed the power to coerce heretical minorities. Locke regards this doctrine as antinomian. See notes 127 and 128, p. 50.

they please to call us) by some *Ecclesiastical Character and Office;* whether they be Bishops, Priests, Presbyters, Ministers, or however else dignified or distinguished. It is not my Business to enquire here into the Original of the Power or Dignity of the Clergy. This only I say, That whencesoever their Authority be sprung, since it is Ecclesiastical, it ought to be confined within the Bounds of the Church, nor can it in any manner be extended to Civil Affairs; because the Church it self is a thing absolutely separate and distinct from the Commonwealth. The Boundaries on both sides are fixed and immovable. He jumbles Heaven and Earth together, the things most remote and opposite, who mixes these Societies; which are in their Original, End, Business, and in every thing, perfectly distinct, and infinitely different from each other. No man therefore, with whatsoever Ecclesiastical Office he be dignified, can deprive another man, that is not of his Church and Faith, either of Liberty, or of any part of his Worldly Goods, upon the account of that difference which is between them in Religion. For whatever is not lawful to the whole Church, cannot, by any Ecclesiastical Right, become lawful to any of its Members.

But this is not all. It is not enough that Ecclesiastical Men abstain from Violence and Rapine, and all manner of Persecution. He that pretends to be a Successor of the Apostles, and takes upon him the Office of Teaching, is obliged also to admonish his Hearers of the Duties of Peace and Good-will towards all men; as well towards the Erroneous, as the Orthodox; towards those that differ from them in Faith and Worship, as well as towards those that agree with them therein. And he ought industriously to exhort all men, whether private Persons or Magistrates, (if any such there be in his Church) to Charity, Meekness, and Toleration; and diligently endeavour to allay and temper all that Heat and unreasonable Averseness of Mind, which either any man's fiery Zeal for his own Sect, or the Craft[51] of others, has kindled against Dissenters. I will not undertake to represent how happy and how great would be the Fruit, both in Church and State, if the Pulpits every where sounded with this Doctrine of Peace and Toleration; lest I should seem to reflect too severely upon

---

51. "Craft": The word *priestcraft* became fashionable in the 1690s. Locke uses it in his *Reasonableness of Christianity* (1695).

those Men whose Dignity I desire not to detract from, nor would have it diminished either by others or themselves. But this I say, That thus it ought to be. And if any one that professes himself to be a Minister of the Word of God, a Preacher of the Gospel of Peace, teach otherwise; he either understands not, or neglects the Business of his Calling, and shall one day give account thereof unto the Prince of Peace. If Christians are to be admonished that they abstain from all manner of Revenge, even after repeated Provocations and multiplied Injuries;[52] how much more ought they who suffer nothing, who have had no harm done them, forbear Violence, and abstain from all manner of ill usage towards those from whom they have received none. This Caution and Temper they ought certainly to use towards those who mind only their own Business, and are sollicitous for nothing but that (whatever men think of them) they may worship God in that manner which they are persuaded is acceptable to him, and in which they have the strongest hopes of Eternal Salvation. In private domestick Affairs, in the management of Estates, in the conservation of Bodily Health, every man may consider what suits his own conveniency, and follow what course he likes best. No man complains of the ill management of his Neighbour's Affairs. No man is angry with another for an Error committed in sowing his Land, or in marrying his Daughter.[53] No body corrects a Spend-thrift for consuming his Substance in Taverns. Let any man pull down, or build, or make whatsoever Expences he pleases; no body murmurs, no body controuls him; he has his Liberty. But if any man do not frequent the Church; if he do not there conform his Behaviour exactly to the accustomed Ceremonies, or if he brings not his Children to be initiated in the Sacred Mysteries of this or the other Congregation; this immediately causes an Uproar; and the Neighbourhood is filled with noise and clamour. Every one is ready to be the Avenger of so great a Crime. And the Zealots hardly have patience to refrain from Violence and Rapine so long till the Cause be heard, and the poor man be, according to Form, condemned to the loss of Liberty, Goods, or Life. Oh that

52. Popple omits: "even until seventy times seven," a quotation from Matthew 18:22.

53. "marrying his Daughter": note Locke's patriarchal assumption in respect of a daughter's marriage and his placement of this matter in the private sphere.

our Ecclesiastical Orators, of every Sect, would apply themselves with all the strength of Arguments that they are able, to the confounding of mens Errors! But let them spare their Persons. Let them not supply their want of Reasons with the Instruments of Force, which belong to another Jurisdiction, and do ill become a Church man's Hands. Let them not call in the Magistrate's Authority to the aid of their Eloquence or Learning; lest, perhaps, whilst they pretend only Love for the Truth, this their intemperate Zeal, breathing nothing but Fire and Sword, betray their Ambition; and shew that what they desire is Temporal Dominion. For it will be very difficult to persuade men of Sence, that he, who with dry Eyes, and satisfaction of Mind, can deliver his Brother unto the Executioner, to be burnt alive, does sincerely and heartily concern himself to save that Brother from the Flames of Hell in the world to come.

In the last place. Let us now consider *what is the Magistrate's Duty* in the Business of Toleration; which certainly is very considerable.

We have already proved, That the Care of Souls does not belong to the Magistrate. Not a Magisterial Care, I mean, (if I may so call it) which consists in prescribing by Laws, and compelling by Punishments. But a charitable Care,[54] which consists in teaching, admonishing, and persuading, cannot be denied unto any man. The Care therefore of every man's Soul belongs unto himself, and is to be left unto himself. But what if he neglect the Care of his Soul? I answer, What if he neglect the Care of his Health, or of his Estate; which things are nearlier related to the Government of the Magistrate than the other? Will the Magistrate provide by an express Law, That such a one shall not become poor or sick?[55] Laws provide, as much as is possible: That the Goods and Health of Subjects be not injured by the Fraud or Violence of others; they do not guard them from the Negligence or ill husbandry of the Possessors themselves. No man can be forced to be Rich or Healthful whether he will or no. Nay, God himself will not save men against their wills. Let us suppose, however, that some Prince were desirous to force his Subjects to accumulate

54. Note the distinction between magisterial and charitable care. Locke does not exclude the use of nonpenal proselytizing.

55. Locke's discussion here suggests a limited role for government in managing the well-being of citizens.

Riches, or to preserve the Health and Strength of their Bodies. Shall it be provided by Law, that they must consult none but *Roman* Physicians; and shall every one be bound to live according to their Prescriptions? What, shall no Potion, no Broth be taken, but what is prepared either in the *Vatican,* suppose, or in a *Geneva* Shop?[56] Or, to make these Subjects rich, shall they all be obliged by Law to become Merchants, or Musicians?[57] Or, shall every one turn Victualler, or Smith; because there are some that maintain their Families plentifully, and grow rich in those Professions? But it may be said, There are a thousand ways to Wealth, but only one way to Heaven. 'Tis well said indeed, especially by those that plead for compelling men into this or the other Way. For if there were several ways that lead thither, there would not be so much as a pretence left for Compulsion. But now if I be marching on with my utmost vigor, in that way which, according to the Sacred Geography, leads streight to *Jerusalem;* Why am I beaten and ill used by others, because, perhaps, I wear not Buskins;[58] because my Hair is not of the right Cut; because perhaps I have not been dipt[59] in the right Fashion; because I eat Flesh upon the Road, or some other Food which agrees with my stomach; because I avoid certain By-ways, which seem unto me to lead into Briars or Precipices; because amongst the several Paths that are in the same Road,[60] I chuse that to walk in which seems to be the streightest and cleanest; because I avoid to keep company with some Travellers that are less grave, and others that are more sowr than they ought to be; or in fine, because I follow a Guide that either is, or is not, cloathed in White, and crowned with a Mitre?[61] Certainly, if we consider right, we shall find that for the most part they are such frivolous things as these, that (without any prejudice to Religion, or the Salvation of Souls, if not accompanied with Superstition

56. *Geneva:* references to Geneva refer to Calvinism.

57. The reference to musicians makes sense when we note that the sentence should open, "Or, to provide his subjects with wealth and comfort at home."

58. *Buskins:* fashionable or outlandish footwear.

59. *dipt:* baptized.

60. Popple omits: "and lead in the same direction."

61. *cloathed in White:* signifying the surplice, to which Puritans objected as popish, preferring the black "Geneva gown"; *crowned with a Mitre:* signifying episcopacy. See note 75, p. 33.

or Hypocrisie) might either be observed or omitted; I say they are such like things as these, which breed implacable Enmities amongst Christian Brethren, who are all agreed in the substantial and truly fundamental part of Religion.

But let us grant unto these Zealots; who condemn all things that are not of their Mode, that from these Circumstances arise different Ends. What shall we conclude from thence? There is only one of these which is the true way to Eternal Happiness. But in this great variety of ways that men follow, it is still doubted which is this right one. Now neither the care of the Commonwealth, nor the Right of enacting Laws, does discover[62] this way that leads to Heaven more certainly to the Magistrate, than every private mans Search and Study discovers it unto himself. I have a weak Body, sunk under a languishing Disease, for which (I suppose) there is one only Remedy, but that unknown: Does it therefore belong unto the Magistrate to prescribe me a Remedy; because there is but one, and because it is unknown? Because there is but one way for me to escape Death, will it therefore be safe for me to do whatsoever the Magistrate ordains? Those things that every man ought sincerely to enquire into himself, and by Meditation, Study, Search, and his own Endeavours, attain the knowledge of, cannot be looked upon as the peculiar Possession of any one sort of Men. Princes indeed are born superior unto other Men in Power, but in Nature equal. Neither the Right, nor the Art of Ruling, does necessarily carry along with it the certain Knowledge of other things; and least of all of the true Religion. For if it were so, how could it come to pass that the Lords of the Earth should differ so vastly as they do in Religious Matters? But let us grant that it is probable the way to Eternal Life may be better known by a Prince than by his Subjects; or at least, that in this incertitude of things, the safest and most commodious way for private Persons is to follow his Dictates. You will say, what then? If he should bid you follow Merchandise for your Livelihood, would you decline that Course for fear it should not succeed? I answer: I would turn Merchant upon the Princes Command, because in case I should have ill success in Trade, he is abundantly able to make up my Loss some other way. If it be true, as

62. *discover:* reveal.

he pretends, that he desires I should thrive and grow rich, he can set me up again when unsuccessful Voyages[63] have broke me. But this is not the Case in the things that regard the Life to come. If there I take a wrong Course, if in that respect I am once undone; it is not in the Magistrates Power to repair my Loss, to ease my Suffering; or to restore me in any measure, much less entirely, to a good Estate. What Security can be given for the Kingdom of Heaven?

Perhaps some will say that they do not suppose this *infallible Judgment,* that all Men are bound to follow in the Affairs of Religion to be in the Civil Magistrate, but *in the Church.* What the Church has determined, that the Civil Magistrate orders to be observed; and he provides by his Authority that no body shall either act or believe in the business of Religion, otherwise than the Church teaches. So that the Judgment of those things is in the Church. The Magistrate himself yields Obedience thereunto, and requires the like Obedience from others. I answer; Who sees not how frequently the Name of the Church, which was so venerable in the time of the Apostles, has been made use of to throw Dust in Peoples Eyes, in following Ages? But however, in the present case it helps us not. The one only narrow way which leads to Heaven is not better known to the Magistrate than to private persons; and therefore I cannot safely take him for my Guide, who may probably be as ignorant of the way as my self, and who certainly is less concerned for my Salvation than I my self am. Amongst so many Kings of the *Jews,* how many of them were there whom any *Israelite,* thus blindly following, had not fallen into Idolatry, and thereby into Destruction? Yet nevertheless, you bid me be of good courage, and tell me that all is now safe and secure, because the Magistrate does not now enjoyn the observance of his own Decrees in matters of Religion, but only the Decrees of the Church. Of what Church I beseech you? Of that certainly which likes him best. As if he that compels me by Laws and Penalties to enter into this or the other Church, did not interpose his own Judgment in the matter. What difference is there whether he lead me himself, or deliver me over to be led by others? I depend both

---

63. "unsuccessful Voyages": alternatively, "ill fortune in trade." Popple, the former wine merchant, thinks in terms of high-risk investment in overseas trade.

ways upon his Will: and it is he that determines both ways of my eternal State. Would an *Israelite,* that had worshipped *Baal*[64] upon the Command of his King, have been in any better condition, because some body had told him that the King ordered nothing in Religion upon his own Head, nor commanded any thing to be done by his Subjects in Divine Worship, but what was approved by the Counsel of Priests, and declared to be of Divine Right by the Doctors of their Church? If the Religion of any Church become therefore true and saving, because the Heads of that Sect, the Prelates and Priests, and those of that Tribe,[65] do all of them, with all their might, extol and praise it; what Religion can ever be accounted erroneous, false and destructive? I am doubtful concerning the Doctrine of the *Socinians,*[66] I am suspicious of the way of Worship practised by the *Papists,* or *Lutherans?* Will it be ever a jot the safer for me to joyn either unto the one or the other of those Churches, upon the Magistrates Command; because he commands nothing in Religion but by the Authority and Counsel of the Doctors of that Church?

But to speak the truth, we must acknowledge that the Church (if a Convention of Clergy-men, making Canons, must be called by that Name)[67] is for the most part more apt to be influenced by the Court, than the Court by the Church. How the Church was under the Vicissitude of Orthodox and Arrian Emperors,[68] is very well known. Or if those things be too remote; The *English* History[69] affords us fresher Examples, in the

---

64. *Baal:* a Canaanite deity, often referred to in the Old Testament.

65. *Tribe:* a disparaging term for priests; Locke has "followers," pejorative also in the Latin (*asseclae*).

66. *Socinians:* those who deny the doctrine of the Trinity. Named after the Italian theologian Fausto Sozzini (Faustus Socinus) (1539–1604).

67. A strikingly anticlerical remark, questioning that "the church" is to be equated with the clergy. Canon law is church law.

68. *Arrian Emperors:* in the fourth century large parts of Christendom followed the teachings of Arius (d. 336), whose doctrine, if not entirely anti-Trinitarian, compromised the divinity of Christ; such emperors as Constantine II and Valens were Arians.

69. "The *English* History": the first edition has "our modern *English* History." The second edition is less felicitous but removes the word *our,* which identifies the author as English. It has been suggested that this amendment indicates Locke's own intervention in correcting the second edition.

Reigns of *Henry* the 8*th, Edward* the 6*th, Mary,* and *Elizabeth,* how easily and smoothly the Clergy changed their Decrees, their Articles of Faith, their Form of Worship, every thing, according to the inclination of those Kings and Queens.[70] Yet were those Kings and Queens of such different minds, in point of Religion, and enjoyned thereupon such different things, that no man in his Wits (I had almost said none but an Atheist) will presume to say that any sincere and upright Worshipper of God could, with a safe Conscience, obey their several Decrees. To conclude. It is the same thing whether a King that prescribes Laws to another mans Religion, pretend to do it by his own Judgment, or by the Ecclesiastical Authority and Advice of others. The Decisions of Churchmen, whose Differences and Disputes are sufficiently known, cannot be any sounder, or safer, than his. Nor can all their Suffrages joyned together add any new strength unto the Civil Power. Tho' this also must be taken notice of, that Princes seldom have any regard to the Suffrages of Ecclesiastics that are not Favourers of their own Faith and way of Worship.

But after all, The *Principal Consideration,* and which absolutely determines this Controversie, is this. Although the Magistrates Opinion in Religion be sound, and the way that he appoints be truly Evangelical, yet if I be not thoroughly perswaded thereof in my own mind, there will be no safety for me in following it. No way whatsoever that I shall walk in, against the Dictates of my Conscience, will ever bring me to the Mansions of the Blessed.[71] I may grow rich by an Art that I take not delight in; I may be cured of some Disease by Remedies that I have not Faith in; but I cannot be saved by a Religion that I distrust, and by a Worship that I abhor. It is in vain for an Unbeliever to take up the outward shew of another Mans Profession. Faith only, and inward Sincerity, are the things that procure acceptance with God. The most likely and most approved

70. Henry VIII (r. 1509–47) enforced a Reformation in church governance, expelling the papacy, but regarded himself as an orthodox Catholic in theology; Edward VI (r. 1547–53) was a thoroughgoing Protestant; Mary (r. 1553–58) instituted a Counter-Reformation to restore Catholicism; and Elizabeth (r. 1558–1603) settled a "middle way" Reformation. Many clergy conformed to these religious revolutions, though Locke is scarcely fair in overlooking those who endured martyrdom for their beliefs.

71. "Mansions of the Blessed": proverb, associated with John 14:2.

Remedy can have no effect upon the Patient, if his Stomach reject it as soon as taken. And you will in vain cram a Medicine down a sick Mans Throat, which his particular Constitution will be sure to turn into Poison. In a word. Whatsoever may be doubtful[72] in Religion, yet this at least is certain, that no Religion, which I believe not to be true, can be either true or profitable unto me. In vain therefore do Princes compel their Subjects to come into their Church-communion, under pretence of saving their Souls. If they believe, they will come of their own accord; if they believe not, their coming will nothing avail them. How great soever, in fine, may be the pretence of Good-will and Charity, and concern for the Salvation of Mens Souls; Men cannot be forced to be saved whether they will or no. And therefore, when all is done, they must be left to their own Consciences.

Having thus at length freed Men from all Dominion over one another in matters of Religion, let us now consider *what they are to do.* All men know and acknowledge that God ought to be publickly worshipped. Why otherwise do they compel one another unto the publick Assemblies? Men therefore constituted in this liberty are to enter into some Religious Society; that they may meet together, not only for mutual Edification, but to own to the World that they worship God, and offer unto his divine Majesty such service as they themselves are not ashamed of, and such as they think not unworthy of him, nor unacceptable to him; and finally that by the purity of Doctrine, Holiness of Life, and decent Form of Worship, they may draw others unto the love of the true Religion; and perform such other things in Religion as cannot be done by each private Man apart.

These Religious Societies I call Churches: and these I say the Magistrate ought to tolerate. For the business of these Assemblies of the People is nothing but what is lawful for every Man in particular to take care of; I mean the Salvation of their Souls. Nor in this case is there any difference between the National Church,[73] and other separated Congregations.

But as in every Church there are two things especially to be consid-

---

72. "doubtful": in quoting this in the *Second Letter,* Locke amends to "doubted."
73. "National Church": the term "Established Church" was not yet in use.

ered; *The outward Form and Rites of Worship; And the Doctrines and Articles of Faith;* These things must be handled each distinctly; that so the whole matter of Toleration may the more clearly be understood.

Concerning outward Worship, I say (in the first place) that the Magistrate has no Power to enforce by Law, either in his own Church, or much less in another, the use of any Rites or Ceremonies whatsoever in the Worship of God. And this, not only because these Churches are free Societies; but because whatsoever is practiced in the Worship of God, is only so far justifiable as it is believed by those that practise it to be acceptable unto him. Whatsoever is not done with that Assurance of Faith, is neither well in it self,[74] nor can it be acceptable to God. To impose such things therefore upon any People, contrary to their own Judgment, is in effect to command them to offend God; Which, considering that the end of all Religion is to please him, and that Liberty is essentially necessary to that End, appears to be absurd beyond expression.

But perhaps it may be concluded from hence, that I deny unto the Magistrate all manner of Power about *Indifferent things;*[75] which if it be not granted, the whole Subject matter of Law-making is taken away. No, I readily grant that Indifferent Things, and perhaps none but such, are subjected to the Legislative Power. But it does not therefore follow, that the Magistrate may ordain whatsoever he pleases concerning any thing

74. "well in it self": alternatively, "lawful" (*licitum*).

75. "Indifferent things": The concept of "things indifferent" (to salvation), also called *adiaphora,* was central to theological discussion, and was distinguished from "things necessary" (to salvation). Whereas the latter were prescribed by God in Scripture and hence could not be altered by man, the former were open to human variation and local ordinance. Thus, it might be held that while God requires to be worshipped, he is indifferent as to whether it is done standing or kneeling, or wearing black or white garments. Two problems arose: what things in fact came under the heading "things indifferent"; and, in the sphere of "things indifferent," are we obliged to accept magisterial ordinances? Some held that, even in the sphere of "things indifferent," magistrates could impose conformity, for the sake of good order and concord. An adiaphorist was theologically liberal (a "latitudinarian") in stressing the broad ambit of "things indifferent" but might nonetheless be politically illiberal in expecting obedience to human ordinances. This was Locke's own initial position in his *Tracts on Government* (1660–62); he had changed his mind by 1667. In the present passage, Locke makes clear that public safety (and not decency or aesthetic considerations) is the sole criterion for magisterial interference in worship.

that is indifferent. The Publick Good is the Rule and Measure of all Law-making.[76] If a thing be not useful to the Commonwealth, tho it be never so indifferent, it may not presently be established by Law.

But further: Things never so indifferent in their own nature, when they are brought into the Church and Worship of God, are removed out of the reach of the Magistrate's Jurisdiction; because in that use they have no connexion at all with Civil Affairs. The only business of the Church is the Salvation of Souls: And it no ways concerns the Commonwealth, or any Member of it, that this, or the other Ceremony be there made use of. Neither the Use, nor the Omission of any Ceremonies, in those Religious Assemblies, does either advantage or prejudice the Life, Liberty, or Estate of any Man. For Example: Let it be granted, that the washing of an Infant with Water is in it self an indifferent thing. Let it be granted also, that if the Magistrate understand such washing to be profitable to the curing or preventing of any Disease that Children are subject unto, and esteem the matter weighty enough to be taken care of by a Law, in that case he may order it to be done. But will any one therefore say, that a Magistrate has the same Right to ordain, by Law, that all Children shall be baptized by Priests, in the sacred Font, in order to the Purification of their Souls?[77] The extream difference of these two Cases is visible to every one at first sight. Or let us apply the last Case to the Child of a *Jew,* and the thing will speak it self. For what hinders but a Christian Magistrate may have Subjects that are *Jews?*[78] Now if we acknowledge that such an Injury may not be done unto a *Jew,* as to compel him, against his own Opinion, to practice in his Religion a thing that is in its nature indifferent; how can we maintain that any thing of this kind may be done to a Christian?

Again: Things in their own nature indifferent cannot, by any human Authority, be made any part of the Worship of God; for this very reason; because they are indifferent. For since indifferent things are not capable, by any Virtue of their own, to propitiate the Deity; no human Power or

---

76. See *Two Treatises of Government,* II, §3.

77. Popple omits: "Or that they shall be initiated by any sacred rites at all?"

78. The Jews were readmitted to England by Oliver Cromwell in 1656, and their protection was confirmed by Charles II in 1664. In Holland, Jewish communities were tolerated in a number of towns. See p. 59.

Authority can confer on them so much Dignity, and Excellency, as to enable them to do it. In the common Affairs of Life, that use of indifferent things which God has not forbidden, is free and lawful: And therefore in those things human Authority has place. But it is not so in matters of Religion. Things indifferent are not otherwise lawful in the Worship of God than as they are instituted by God himself; and as he, by some positive command, has ordain'd them to be made a part of that Worship which he will vouchsafe to accept of at the hands of poor sinful Men. Nor when an incensed Deity shall ask us, (*Who has required these, or such like, things at your hands?*)[79] will it be enough to answer him, that the Magistrate commanded them. If Civil Jurisdiction extended thus far, what might not lawfully be introduced into Religion? What hodgepodge of Ceremonies, what superstitious inventions, built upon the Magistrate's Authority, might not (against Conscience) be Imposed upon the Worshippers of God? For the greatest part of these Ceremonies and Superstitions consists in the Religious Use of such things as are in their own nature indifferent: Nor are they sinful upon any other account than because God is not the Author of them. The sprinkling of Water, and the use of Bread and Wine, are both in their own nature, and in the ordinary occasions of Life, altogether indifferent. Will any Man therefore say that these things could have been introduced into Religion, and made a part of Divine Worship, if not by Divine Institution? If any Human Authority or Civil Power could have done this; why might it not also injoyn the eating of Fish, and drinking of Ale, in the Holy Banquet, as a part of Divine Worship? Why not the sprinkling of the Blood of Beasts in Churches, and Expiations by Water or Fire, and abundance more of this kind? But these things, how indifferent soever they be in common uses, when they come to be annexed unto Divine Worship, without Divine Authority, they are as abominable to God, as the Sacrifice of a Dog. And why a Dog so abominable? What difference is there between a Dog and a Goat, in respect of the Divine Nature, equally and infinitely distant from all Affinity with Matter; unless it be that God required the use of the one in his Worship, and not of the other? We see therefore that indifferent things, how much soever they

---

79. Isaiah 1:12. Note that the parentheses are in the original.

be under the Power of the Civil Magistrate, yet cannot upon that pretence be introduced into Religion, and imposed upon Religious Assemblies; because in the Worship of God they wholly cease to be indifferent. He that Worships God does it with design to please him, and procure his Favour. But that cannot be done by him, Who, upon the command of another, offers unto God that which he knows will be displeasing to him, because not commanded by himself. This is not to please God, or appease his Wrath, but willingly and knowingly to provoke him, by a manifest Contempt; Which is a thing absolutely repugnant to the nature and end of Worship.

But it will here be asked: *If nothing belonging to Divine Worship be left to human Discretion, how is it then that Churches themselves have the Power of ordering any thing about the Time and Place of Worship, and the like?* To this I answer; That in Religious Worship we must distinguish between what is part of the Worship it self, and what is but a Circumstance. That is a part of the Worship which is believed to be appointed by God, and to be well-pleasing to him; and therefore that is necessary. Circumstances are such things which, tho' in general they cannot be separated from Worship, yet the particular instances or modifications of them are not determined; and therefore they are indifferent. Of this sort are the Time and Place of Worship, the Habit[80] and Posture of him that worships. These are Circumstances, and perfectly indifferent, where God has not given any express Command about them. For example: Amongst the *Jews*, the Time and Place of their Worship, and the Habits of those that officiated in it, were not meer Circumstances, but a part of the Worship it self; in which if any thing were defective, or different from the Institution, they could not hope that it would be accepted by God.[81] But these, to Christians under the liberty of the Gospel, are meer Circumstances of Worship, which the Prudence of every Church may bring into such use as shall be judged most subservient to the end of Order, Decency, and Edification.[82] Tho' even under the Gospel also, those who believe the First, or the Sev-

80. *Habit:* attire.
81. Locke implies that Christian intolerance is pharisaical in its formalistic preoccupation with ceremony.
82. "Order, Decency, and Edification": 1 Corinthians 14:26, 40.

enth Day,[83] to be set apart by God, and consecrated still to his Worship; to them that portion of Time is not a simple Circumstance, but a real Part of Divine Worship, which can neither be changed nor neglected.

In the next place: As the Magistrate has no Power to *impose* by his Laws, the use of any Rites and Ceremonies in any Church; so neither has he any Power[84] to *forbid* the use of such Rites and Ceremonies as are already received, approved, and practised by any Church. Because if he did so, he would destroy the Church it self; the end of whose Institution is only to worship God with freedom, after its own manner.

You will say, by this Rule, if some Congregations should have a mind to *sacrifice Infants,* or (as the Primitive Christians were falsly accused) *lust-fully pollute themselves in promiscuous Uncleanness,* or practise any other such heinous Enormities,[85] *is the Magistrate obliged to tolerate them,* because they are committed in a Religious Assembly? I answer, No. These things are not lawful in the ordinary course of life, nor in any private house; and therefore neither are they so in the Worship of God, or in any Religious Meeting.[86] But indeed if any People congregated upon account of Religion, should be desirous to sacrifice a Calf, I deny that That ought to be prohibited by a Law. *Melibaeus,* whose Calf it is,[87] may lawfully kill his own Calf at home, and burn any part of it that he thinks fit. For no Injury is thereby done to any one, no Prejudice to another man's Goods. And for the same reason he may kill his Calf also in a Religious Meeting. Whether the doing so be well-pleasing to God, or no, it is their part to consider that do it. The part of the Magistrate is only to take care that the Common-wealth receive no prejudice,[88] and that there be no Injury done to any man, either in Life or Estate. And thus what may be spent on a Feast, may be spent on a Sacrifice. But if peradventure such were the state

83. Some sabbatarians held that Saturday and not Sunday should be observed as the Sabbath.

84. "to *impose* . . . Power": added by Popple.

85. "such heinous Enormities": alternatively, "other such practices." "Primitive Christians": those of the early church.

86. Locke takes for granted that forbidding sexual immorality is a proper role for civil governments.

87. Virgil, *Eclogues,* iii.1.

88. Cicero, *Catiline,* i.2; *Milo,* 70; Caesar, *Civil Wars,* i.5.

of things, that the Interest of the Common-wealth required all slaughter of Beasts should be forborn for some while, in order to the increasing of the Stock of Cattel, that had been destroyed by some extraordinary Murrain;[89] Who sees not that the Magistrate, in such a case, may forbid all his Subjects to kill any Calves for any use whatsoever? Only 'tis to be observed, that in this case the Law is not made about a Religious, but a Political matter; nor is the Sacrifice, but the Slaughter of Calves thereby prohibited.

By this we see what difference there is between the Church and the Common-wealth. Whatsoever is lawful in the Common-wealth, cannot be prohibited by the Magistrate in the Church. Whatsoever is permitted unto any one of his Subjects for their ordinary use, neither can, nor ought to be forbidden by him to any Sect of People for their Religious Uses. If any man may lawfully take Bread or Wine, either sitting or kneeling,[90] in his own house, the Law ought not to abridge him of the same Liberty in his Religious Worship; though in the Church the use of Bread and Wine be very different, and be there applied to the Mysteries of Faith, and Rites of Divine Worship. But those things that are prejudicial to the Common weal of a People in their ordinary use, and are therefore forbidden by Laws, those things ought not to be permitted to Churches in their Sacred Rites. Only the Magistrate ought always to be very careful, that he do not misuse his Authority, to the oppression of any Church, under pretence of publick Good.[91]

It may be said; *What if a Church be* Idolatrous, *is that also to be tolerated by the Magistrate?* In answer, I ask; What Power can be given to the Magistrate for the suppression of an Idolatrous Church, which may not, in time and place, be made use of to the ruine of an Orthodox one? For it must be remembered that the Civil Power is the same every where, and the Religion of every Prince is Orthodox to himself. If therefore such a Power

89. *Murrain:* foot-and-mouth disease.

90. "sitting or kneeling": Puritans objected to kneeling to receive the Eucharist, for it involved excessive veneration and thereby implied the Catholic doctrine of transubstantiation.

91. Popple omits: "What is lawful in ordinary life, and outside the worship of God, cannot by civil law be forbidden in divine worship or in sacred places."

be granted unto the Civil Magistrate in Spirituals, as that at *Geneva* (for Example) he may extirpate, by Violence and Blood, the Religion which is there reputed Idolatrous;[92] by the same Rule another Magistrate, in some neighbouring Country, may oppress the Reformed Religion; and, in *India*,[93] the Christian. The Civil Power can either change every thing in Religion, according to the Prince's pleasure, or it can change nothing. If it be once permitted to introduce any thing into Religion, by the means of Laws and Penalties, there can be no bounds put to it; but it will in the same manner be lawful to alter every thing, according to that Rule of Truth which the Magistrate has framed unto himself. No man whatsoever ought therefore to be deprived of his Terrestrial Enjoyments, upon account of his Religion. Not even *Americans*,[94] subjected unto a Christian Prince, are to be punished either in Body or Goods, for not imbracing our Faith and Worship.[95] If they are perswaded that they please God in observing the Rites of their own Country, and that they shall obtain Happiness by that means, they are to be left unto God and themselves. Let us trace this matter to the bottom.[96]

Thus it is. An inconsiderable and weak number of Christians, destitute of every thing, arrive in a Pagan Countrey. These Foreigners beseech the Inhabitants, by the bowels of Humanity,[97] that they would succour them

92. Calvin's Geneva was a theocracy, and hence could be seen as parallel to Catholicism in its fusion of civil and ecclesiastical authority. This passage indicates Locke's hostility as much to full-blown Calvinist or Presbyterian ecclesiology as to papist or episcopalian. Calvin's burning of Michael Servetus for heresy in 1553 was notorious.

93. Locke was aware of persecutions by the Mughal emperor Aurangzeb (1618–1707).

94. *Americans:* Native Americans.

95. See *The Constitutions of Carolina*, pp. 146–48.

96. "Let us trace this matter to the bottom": alternatively, "This is how it began" (*Rem ab origine retexam*). The significance of the following passage is not quite clear. It echoes a conventional Protestant denunciation of the cruelty of the Spanish (Catholic) conquest of South and Central America, but this message is apparently conveyed analogically in a hypothetical narrative about the English in North America, who initially had been dependent on the good will of the natives. The account may indeed not be hypothetical but reflect John Smith's experiences in the earliest settlement at Jamestown, Virginia, 1607–9. See note 100 in this selection.

97. "bowels of Humanity": alternatively, "in the name of common humanity."

with the necessaries of Life. Those necessaries are given them; Habitations are granted; and they all joyn together, and grow up into one Body of People. The Christian Religion by this means takes root in that Countrey, and spreads it self; but does not suddenly grow the strongest. While things are in this condition, Peace, Friendship, Faith, and equal Justice, are preserved amongst them. At length the Magistrate becomes a Christian, and by that means their Party becomes the most powerful. Then immediately all Compacts are to be broken, all Civil Rights to be violated, that Idolatry may be extirpated; And unless these innocent Pagans, strict Observers of the Rules of Equity and of the Law of Nature, & no ways offending against the Laws of the Society,[98] I say unless they will forsake their ancient Religion, and embrace a new and strange one, they are to be turned out of the Lands and Possessions of their Forefathers, and perhaps deprived of Life it self. Then at last it appears what Zeal for the Church, joyned with the desire of Dominion, is capable to produce; and how easily the pretence of Religion, and of the care of Souls, serves for a Cloak to Covetousness, Rapine, and Ambition.

Now whosoever maintains that Idolatry is to be rooted out of any place by Laws, Punishments, Fire, and Sword, may apply this Story to himself.[99] For the reason of the thing is equal, both in *America* and *Europe*. And neither Pagans there, nor any Dissenting Christians here, can with any right be deprived of their worldly Goods, by the predominating Faction of a Court-Church: nor are any Civil Rights to be either changed or violated upon account of Religion in one place more than another.[100]

98. "strict Observers ... Society": alternatively, "strict observers of what is right, and in no way offending against good morals and the civil law."

99. Horace, *Satires,* i.69–70.

100. Locke's remarks about America are important for understanding his position regarding the legitimacy of European colonial settlement and the expropriation of native land. Locke denies any religious ground for interfering with property (a rule he elsewhere applies also to dealings with Jews and Muslims), for that would be a version of the iniquitous doctrine that "dominion is founded in grace" (see note 50, p. 23): being a Christian gives no right of dominion. It is commonly argued that while the *Two Treatises of Government* does seek to justify the superior property claims of European settlers, it does so on agriculturalist and not missionary grounds, namely that, whereas settlers cultivate the land industriously and render it fruitful, natives do not.

But *Idolatry* (say some) *is a Sin,* and therefore not to be tolerated. If they said, it were therefore to be avoided, the Inference were good. But it does not follow, that because it is a Sin, it ought therefore to be punished by the Magistrate. For it does not belong unto the Magistrate to make use of his Sword in Punishing every thing, indifferently, that he takes to be a Sin against God. Covetousness, Uncharitableness, Idleness, and many other things are sins, by the consent of all men, which yet no man ever said were to be punished by the Magistrate. The reason is, because they are not prejudicial to other mens Rights, nor do they break the publick Peace of Societies. Nay, even the Sins of Lying, and Perjury, are no where punishable by Laws; unless in certain cases in which the real Turpitude of the thing, and the Offence against God, are not considered, but only the Injury done unto mens Neighbours, and to the Commonwealth. And what if in another Country, to a Mahumetan, or a Pagan Prince, the Christian Religion seem false and offensive to God; may not the Christians, for the same reason, and after the same manner, be extirpated there?

But it may be urged further, *That by the Law of* Moses, *Idolaters were to be rooted out.*[101] True indeed, by the Law of *Moses:* But that is not obligatory to us Christians. No body pretends that every thing, generally, enjoyed by the Law of *Moses,* ought to be practised by Christians. But there is nothing more frivolous than that common distinction of Moral, Judicial, and Ceremonial Law,[102] which men ordinarily make use of. For no positive Law, whatsoever, can oblige any People, but those to whom it is given. *Hear O Israel;*[103] sufficiently restrains the Obligation of the Law of *Moses* only to that People: And this Consideration alone is Answer enough unto those that urge the Authority of the Law of *Moses;* for the inflicting of Capital Punishments upon Idolaters. But however, I will examine this Argument a little more particularly.

101. Locke here embarks on a proof that Christians are not bound by the Jewish law that idolaters be killed (Exodus 22:20–21). He may have found helpful John Spencer's *De legibus Hebraeorum* (1685), which supports the answer he gives.

102. Thomas Aquinas and Richard Hooker were among those who drew this tripartite distinction. Some held that while Christians were exempt from Jewish ceremonial law, they remained bound by the other parts. Locke held that Mosaic law in toto applied only to the Israelites.

103. Deuteronomy 5:1.

The Case of Idolaters, in respect of the *Jewish* Common-wealth, falls under a double Consideration. The first is, of those, Who, being initiated in the *Mosaical* Rites, and made Citizens of that Common-wealth, did afterwards apostatize from the Worship of the God of *Israel.* These were proceeded against as Traytors and Rebels, guilty of no less than High Treason. For the Common-wealth of the *Jews,* different in that from all others, was an absolute *Theocracy;* nor was there, or could there be, any difference between that Commonwealth and the Church. The Laws established there concerning the Worship of One Invisible Deity, were the Civil Laws of that People, and a part of their Political Government; in which God himself was the Legislator. Now if any one can shew me where there is a Commonwealth, at this time, constituted upon that Foundation, I will acknowledg that the Ecclesiastical Laws do there unavoidably become a part of the Civil; and that the Subjects of that Government both may, and ought to be kept in strict conformity with that Church, by the Civil Power. But there is absolutely no such thing, under the Gospel, as a Christian Commonwealth. There are, indeed, many Cities and Kingdoms that have embraced the Faith of Christ; but they have retained their ancient Form of Government; with which the Law of Christ hath not at all medled. He, indeed, hath taught men how, by Faith and good Works, they may attain Eternal Life. But he instituted no Commonwealth. He prescribed unto his Followers no new and peculiar Form of Government; Nor put he the Sword into any Magistrate's Hand, with Commission to make use of it in forcing men to forsake their former Religion, and receive his.

Secondly, Foreigners, and such as were Strangers to the *Commonwealth* of *Israel,* were not compell'd by force to observe the Rites of the *Mosaical* Law. But, on the contrary, in the very same place, where it is ordered, that *an Israelite, that was an Idolater, should be put to death,* there it is provided, that *Strangers should not be vexed nor oppressed,* Exodus 22:20–21.[104]

---

104. Locke puts a biblical case for toleration of "stranger" (foreign) communities. He shares a contemporary "reason of state" argument for toleration: that it encouraged inward migration and hence demographic and economic growth. In spite of English laws for conformity, there was a strong tradition since the Reformation of allowing "stranger" communities of Huguenots to have their own independent worship.

I confess, that the Seven Nations, that possest the Land which was promised to the *Israelites*, were utterly to be cut off. But this was not singly because they were Idolaters. For, if that had been the Reason; Why were the *Moabites*, and other Nations to be spared?[105] No, the Reason is this. God being in a peculiar manner the King of the *Jews*, he could not suffer the Adoration of any other Deity, (which was properly an Act of High Treason against himself) in the Land of *Canaan*, which was his Kingdom. For such a manifest Revolt could no ways consist with his Dominion, which was perfectly Political, in that Country. All Idolatry was therefore to be rooted out of the Bounds of his Kingdom; because it was an acknowledgment of another God; that is to say, another King; against the Laws of Empire.[106] The Inhabitants were also to be driven out, that the entire possession of the Land might be given to the *Israelites*. And for the like Reason, the *Emims*, and the *Horims* were driven out of their Countries, by the Children of *Esau* and *Lot*; and their Lands, upon the same grounds, given by God to the Invaders, Deuteronomy 2. But though all Idolatry was thus rooted out of the Land of *Canaan*, yet every Idolater was not brought to Execution. The whole Family of *Rahab*, the whole Nation of the *Gibeonites*, articled[107] with *Joshuah*, and were allowed[108] by Treaty: and there were many Captives amongst the *Jews*, who were Idolaters. *David* and *Solomon* subdued many Countries without[109] the Confines of the Land of Promise, and carried their Conquests as far as *Euphrates*. Amongst so many Captives taken, so many Nations reduced under their Obedience, we find not one man forced into the Jewish Religion, and the Worship of the True God; and punished for Idolatry; though all of them were certainly guilty of it. If any one indeed, becoming a Proselyte, desired to be made a Denison of their Commonwealth, he was obliged to submit unto their Laws; that is, to embrace their Religion. But this he did willingly, on his own accord, not by constraint. He did not unwillingly submit, to shew his Obedience; But he sought and sollicited for it, as a Privilege; And as soon as he was admitted, he became subject to the Laws of the

---

105. Numbers 33:50–52; Deuteronomy 7:1, 2:9.
106. "Laws of Empire": alternatively, "right of dominion" (*jus imperii*).
107. "articled": alternatively, "made a pact." Joshua 2:9.
108. *allowed*: reprieved.
109. *without*: outside.

Commonwealth; by which all Idolatry was forbidden within the Borders of the Land of *Canaan.* But that Law (as I have said) did not reach to any of those Regions, however subjected unto the *Jews,* that were situated without those Bounds.

Thus far concerning outward Worship. Let us now consider *Articles of Faith.*

The *Articles* of Religion[110] are some of them *Practical,* and some *Speculative.* Now, tho' both sorts consist in the Knowledge of Truth, yet these terminate simply in the Understanding, Those influence the Will and Manners. Speculative Opinions, therefore, and *Articles of Faith* (as they are called) which are required only to be believed, cannot be imposed on any Church by the Law of the Land. For it is absurd that things should be enjoyned by Laws, which are not in mens power to perform. And to believe this or that to be true, does not depend upon our Will. But of this enough has been said already. But (will some say) let men at least profess that they believe. A sweet Religion indeed, that obliges men to dissemble, and tell Lyes both to God and Man, for the Salvation of their Souls! If the Magistrate thinks to save men thus, he seems to understand little of the way of Salvation. And if he does it not in order to save them; Why is he so sollicitous about the Articles of Faith as to enact them by a Law?

Further, The Magistrate ought not to forbid the Preaching or Professing of any Speculative Opinions in any Church; because they have no manner of relation to the Civil Rights of the Subjects. If a *Roman Catholick*[111] believe that to be really the Body of Christ, which another man calls Bread, he does no injury thereby to his Neighbour. If a *Jew* do not believe the New Testament to be the Word of God, he does not thereby alter any thing in mens Civil Rights. If a Heathen doubt of both Testaments, he is not therefore to be punished as a pernicious Citizen. The Power of the Magistrate, and the Estates of the People, may be equally secure, whether any man believe these things or no. I readily grant, that these Opinions are false and absurd. But the business of Laws is not to provide for the Truth of Opinions, but for the Safety and Security of the

---

110. "Articles of Religion": alternatively, "doctrines of churches."
111. "Roman Catholick": alternatively, "papist" (*pontificius*).

Commonwealth, and of every particular mans Goods and Person. And so it ought to be. For Truth certainly would do well enough, if she were once left to shift for her Self. She seldom has received, and I fear never will receive, much Assistance from the Power of Great men; to whom she is but rarely known, and more rarely welcome. She is not taught by Laws, nor has she any need of Force to procure her entrance into the minds of men. Errors indeed prevail by the assistance of forreign and borrowed Succours. But if Truth makes not her way into the Understanding by her own Light, she will be but the weaker for any borrowed force Violence can add to her. Thus much for Speculative Opinions. Let us now proceed to *Practical* ones.

A Good Life,[112] in which consists not the least part of Religion and true Piety, concerns also the Civil Government; and in it lies the safety both of Mens Souls, and of the Commonwealth. *Moral Actions* belong therefore to the Jurisdiction both of the outward and inward Court;[113] both of the Civil and Domestick Governor; I mean, both of the Magistrate and Conscience. Here therefore is great danger, least[114] one of these Jurisdictions intrench upon the other, and Discord arise between the Keeper of the publick Peace, and the Overseers of Souls. But if what has been already said concerning the Limits of both these Governments be rightly considered, it will easily remove all difficulty in this matter.

Every man has an Immortal Soul, capable of Eternal Happiness or Misery; whose Happiness depending upon his believing and doing those things in this Life, which are necessary to the obtaining of Gods Favour, and are prescribed by God to that end; it follows from thence, 1*st,* That the observance of these things is the highest Obligation that lies upon Mankind, and that our utmost Care, Application, and Diligence, ought to be exercised in the Search and Performance of them; Because there is nothing in this World that is of any consideration in comparison with Eternity. 2*dly,* That seeing one Man does not violate the Right of another, by his Erroneous Opinions, and undue manner of Worship, nor is his Per-

---

112. "A Good Life": alternatively, "moral rectitude" (*morum rectitudo*).

113. *outward and inward Court:* public jurisdiction and private conscience (*forum externum* and *forum internum*).

114. *least:* lest.

dition any prejudice to another Mans Affairs; therefore the care of each Mans Salvation belongs only to himself. But I would not have this understood, as if I meant hereby to condemn all charitable Admonitions, and affectionate Endeavours to reduce Men from Errors; which are indeed the greatest Duty of a Christian. Any one may employ as many Exhortations and Arguments as he pleases, towards the promoting of another man's Salvation. But all Force and Compulsion are to be forborn. Nothing is to be done imperiously. No body is obliged in that matter to yield Obedience unto the Admonitions or Injunctions of another, further than he himself is perswaded. Every man, in that, has the supreme and absolute Authority of judging for himself. And the Reason is, because no body else is concerned in it, nor can receive any prejudice from his Conduct therein.

But besides their Souls, which are Immortal, Men have also their Temporal Lives here upon Earth; the State whereof being frail and fleeting, and the duration uncertain; they have need of several outward Conveniences to the support thereof, which are to be procured or preserved by Pains and Industry. For those things that are necessary to the comfortable support of our Lives, are not the spontaneous Products of Nature, nor do offer themselves fit and prepared for our use. This part therefore draws on another care, and necessarily gives another Imployment.[115] But the pravity[116] of Mankind being such, that they had rather injuriously prey upon the Fruits of other Mens Labours, than take pains to provide for themselves; the necessity of preserving Men in the Possession of what honest industry has already acquired; and also of preserving their Liberty and Strength, whereby they may acquire what they further want; obliges Men to enter into Society with one another; that by mutual Assistance, and joint Force, they may secure unto each other their Proprieties, in the things that contribute to the Comfort and Happiness of this Life;[117] leav-

115. "and necessarily gives another Imployment": added by Popple.
116. *pravity:* depravity.
117. "the necessity . . . Life": alternatively, "to protect their possessions, their wealth and property, and also their liberty and bodily strength, which are their means of livelihood, they are obliged to enter into society with one another, so that by mutual assistance and combined forces each man may have secure the private possession of

ing in the mean while to every Man the care of his own Eternal Happi-ness, the attainment whereof can neither be facilitated by another Mans Industry, nor can the loss of it turn to another Mans Prejudice, nor the hope of it be forced from him by any external Violence. But forasmuch as Men thus entring into Societies, grounded upon their mutual Compacts of Assistance, for the Defence of their Temporal Goods, may neverthe-less be deprived of them, either by the Rapine and Fraud of their Fellow-Citizens, or by the hostile Violence of Forreigners; the Remedy of this Evil consists in Arms, Riches, and Multitude of Citizens;[118] the Remedy of the other in Laws; and the Care of all things relating both to the one and the other, is committed by the Society to the Civil Magistrate. This is the Original, this is the Use, and these are the Bounds of the Legislative (which is the Supreme) Power, in every Commonwealth.[119] I mean, that Provision may be made for the Security of each Mans private Possessions; for the Peace, Riches, and publick Commodities[120] of the whole People; and, as much as possible, for the Increase of their inward Strength, against Forreign Invasions.

These things being thus explain'd, it is easie to understand to what end the Legislative Power ought to be directed, and by what Measures regu-lated;[121] and that is the Temporal Good and outward Prosperity of the Society; which is the sole Reason of Mens entring into Society, and the only thing they seek and aim at in it. And it is also evident what Liberty remains to Men in reference to their eternal Salvation; and that is, that every one should do what he in his Conscience is perswaded to be accept-

---

the things that are useful for life." This passage mirrors the argument of the *Two Treatises of Government:* e.g., II, §95. For Popple's phrases "honest industry" and "mutual assistance," see *Two Treatises,* II, §§19, 42. *Proprieties:* properties (amended thus in later editions).

118. "Arms, Riches, and Multitude of Citizens": the phrase reflects Locke's interest in the prudent enhancement of national power, a theme occasionally glimpsed in the *Two Treatises of Government:* see II, §42. He was especially anxious for demo-graphic growth. See note 104, p. 42.

119. See *Two Treatises of Government,* II, §134.

120. "Commodities": alternatively, "interests."

121. "to what end . . . regulated": alternatively, "the ends that determine the mag-istrate's prerogative of making laws."

able to the Almighty, on whose good pleasure and acceptance depends his eternal Happiness. For Obedience is due in the first place to God, and afterwards to the Laws.

But some may ask, *What if the Magistrate should enjoyn any thing by his Authority that appears unlawful to the Conscience of a private Person?* I answer, That if Government be faithfully administred, and the Counsels of the Magistrate be indeed directed to the publick Good, this will seldom happen. But if perhaps it do so fall out; I say, that such a private Person is to abstain from the Action that he judges unlawful; and he is to undergo the Punishment, which it is not unlawful for him to bear. For the private Judgment of any Person concerning a Law enacted in Political Matters, for the publick Good, does not take away the Obligation of that Law, nor deserve a Dispensation. But if the Law indeed be concerning things that lie not within the Verge of the Magistrate's Authority; (as for Example, that the People, or any Party amongst them, should be compell'd to embrace a strange Religion, and join in the Worship and Ceremonies of another Church), men are not in these cases obliged by that Law, against their Consciences. For the Political Society is instituted for no other end but only to secure every mans Possession of the things of this life. The care of each mans Soul, and of the things of Heaven, which neither does belong to the Commonwealth, nor can be subjected to it, is left entirely to every mans self. Thus the safeguard of mens lives, and of the things that belong unto this life, is the business of the Commonwealth; and the preserving of those things unto their Owners is the Duty of the Magistrate. And therefore the Magistrate cannot take away these worldly things from this man, or party, and give them to that; nor change Propriety amongst Fellow-Subjects, (no not even by a Law) for a cause that has no relation to the end of Civil Government; I mean, for their Religion; which whether it be true or false, does no prejudice to the worldly concerns of their Fellow-Subjects,[122] which are the things that only belong unto the care of the Commonwealth.

But what if the Magistrate believe such a Law as this to be for the publick Good? I answer: As the private Judgment of any particular Person,

---

122. "Fellow-Subjects": alternatively, "citizens" (*civibus*).

if erroneous, does not exempt him from the obligation of Law, so the private Judgment (as I may call it) of the Magistrate does not give him any new Right of imposing Laws upon his Subjects; which neither was in the Constitution of the Government granted him, nor ever was in the power of the People to grant; and least of all, if he make it his business to enrich and advance his Followers and Fellow-sectaries, with the Spoils of others. *But what if the Magistrate believe that he has a Right to make such Laws, and that they are for the publick Good; and his Subjects believe the contrary? Who shall be Judge between them?* I answer, God alone. For there is no Judge upon earth between the Supreme Magistrate and the People.[123] God, I say, is the only Judge in this case, who will retribute unto every one at the last day according to his Deserts; that is, according to his sincerity and uprightness, in endeavouring to promote Piety, and the publick Weal and Peace of Mankind. *But what shall be done in the mean while?* I answer: The principal and chief care of every one ought to be of his own Soul first, and in the next place of the publick Peace: tho' yet there are very few will think 'tis Peace there, where they see all laid waste.[124]

There are two sorts of Contests amongst Men, the one manag'd by Law, the other by Force: and these are of that nature, that where the one ends, the other always begins.[125] But it is not my business to inquire into the Power of the Magistrate in the different Constitutions of Nations. I only know what usually happens where Controversies arise, without a Judge to determine them. You will say then the Magistrate being the stronger will have his Will, and carry his point. Without doubt. But the Question is not here concerning the doubtfulness of the Event, but the Rule of Right.

[126]But to come to particulars. I say, *First*, No Opinions contrary to human Society, or to those moral Rules which are necessary to the preser-

---

123. See *Two Treatises of Government*, II, §§21, 168, 241.

124. "where they see all laid waste": alternatively, "where they see a desert made." Tacitus, *Agricola*, xxx.5: "They make a desolation and they call it peace."

125. See *Two Treatises of Government*, II, §202.

126. The edition of the *Letter* published at York in 1788 suppressed the following four paragraphs, in order to tone down Locke's objections against Roman Catholics. By that time public opinion was more supportive of toleration for Catholics, which was legislated in 1791.

vation of Civil Society, are to be tolerated by the Magistrate. But of these indeed Examples in any Church are rare. For no Sect can easily arrive to such a degree of madness, as that it should think fit to teach, for Doctrines of Religion, such things as manifestly undermine the Foundations of Society, and are therefore condemned by the Judgment of all Mankind: because their own Interest, Peace, Reputation, every Thing, would be thereby endangered.

Another more secret Evil, but more dangerous to the Commonwealth, is, when men arrogate to themselves, and to those of their own Sect, some peculiar Prerogative, covered over with a specious shew of deceitful words, but in effect opposite to the Civil Right of the Community. For Example: We cannot find any Sect that teaches expresly, and openly, that Men are not obliged to keep their Promise; that Princes may be dethroned by those that differ from them in Religion; or that the Dominion of all things belongs only to themselves. For these things, proposed thus nakedly and plainly, would soon draw on them the Eye and Hand of the Magistrate, and awaken all the care of the Commonwealth to a watchfulness against the spreading of so dangerous an Evil. But nevertheless, we find those that say the same things, in other words. What else do they mean, who teach *that Faith is not to be kept with Hereticks?*[127] Their meaning, forsooth, is that the priviledge of breaking Faith belongs unto themselves: For they declare all that are not of their Communion to be Hereticks, or at least may declare them so whensoever they think fit. What can be the meaning of their asserting that *Kings excommunicated forfeit their Crowns and Kingdoms?*[128] It is evident that they thereby arrogate unto themselves the

127. Protestants held that Catholics believed that "faith need not be kept with heretics"; in other words (to use a phrase a few lines earlier), "men are not obliged to keep their promise" (if made to a heretic). The classically cited instance was that of Jan Hus, promised a safe passage to the Council of Constance to put his case, but then arrested and burnt for heresy (1415). If such doctrine were indeed Catholic teaching, then Catholics were radically antinomian.

128. Protestants held that this doctrine was fundamental to Catholicism and iniquitous. Compare Hobbes, *Leviathan*, chap. 42 (against the Counter-Reformation theologian Robert Bellarmine). In 1570 Pope Pius V excommunicated and deposed Queen Elizabeth. The Spanish Armada, and the Gunpowder Plot against her successor, were Catholic attempts to give effect to the papal deposition. However, some

Power of deposing Kings: because they challenge[129] the Power of Excommunication, as the peculiar Right of their Hierarchy. That *Dominion is founded in Grace,*[130] is also an Assertion by which those that maintain it do plainly lay claim to the possession of all things. For they are not so wanting to themselves as not to believe, or at least as not to profess, themselves to be the truly pious and faithful. These therefore, and the like, who attribute unto the Faithful, Religious and Orthodox; that is, in plain terms, unto themselves; any peculiar Priviledge or Power above other Mortals, in Civil Concernments; or who, upon pretence of Religion, do challenge any manner of Authority over such as are not associated with them in their Ecclesiastical Communion; I say these have no right to be tolerated by the Magistrate; as neither those that will not own and teach the Duty of tolerating All men in matters of meer Religion.[131] For what do all these and the like Doctrines signifie, but that those Men may, and are ready upon any occasion to seise the Government, and possess themselves of the Estates and Fortunes of their Fellow-Subjects; and that they only ask leave to be tolerated by the Magistrate so long, until they find themselves strong enough to effect it?[132]

Catholics argued that the doctrine was not essential to their faith. The Oath of Allegiance (1606) required the taker to swear "that I do from my heart abhor, detest, and abjure as impious and heretical this damnable doctrine and position that princes which be excommunicated or deprived by the pope may be deposed or murdered by their subjects or any other whatsoever." Pope Sixtus V excommunicated Henry of Navarre, the future Henry IV of France; and the Calvinist theorist François Hotman published a famous retort, *Brutum Fulmen* (1585).

129. *challenge:* claim.

130. See note 50, p. 23.

131. *of meer Religion:* purely of religion. Note that Locke excludes from toleration those who do not themselves concede the principle of toleration.

132. Locke alludes to pleas by Catholics that they merit toleration because they are loyal subjects. Protestants commonly believed that this was a ruse, buying time until they had the power to turn the tables on their enemies. The point applied to religious minorities generally, who were apt to call for toleration when they were weak but deny it when strong. Thus, after the destruction of Anglicanism in the Civil War, the Anglican Jeremy Taylor called for toleration in his *Liberty of Prophesying* (1647); and, after the Restoration, Presbyterians called for toleration, whereas in the 1640s they had spoken ferociously against the radical sects. In Holland in the 1690s the exiled Huguenot Pierre Jurieu denounced French Catholic repression yet also upheld Calvinist coercive discipline.

Again; That Church can have no right to be tolerated by the Magistrate, which is constituted upon such a bottom, that all those who enter into it, do thereby, *ipso facto,* deliver themselves up to the Protection[133] and Service of another Prince. For by this means the Magistrate would give way to the settling of a foreign Jurisdiction in his own Country, and suffer his own People to be listed, as it were, for Soldiers against his own Government. Nor does the frivolous and fallacious distinction between the Court and the Church[134] afford any remedy to this Inconvenience; especially when both the one and the other are equally subject to the absolute Authority of the same Person; who has not only power to perswade the Members of his Church to whatsoever he lists, (either as purely Religious, or as in order thereunto) but can also enjoyn it them on pain of Eternal Fire. It is ridiculous for any one to profess himself to be a *Mahumetan*[135] only in his Religion, but in every thing else a faithful Subject to a Christian Magistrate, whilst at the same time he acknowledges himself bound to yield blind obedience to the *Mufti*[136] of *Constantinople;* who himself is intirely obedient to the *Ottoman* Emperor, and frames the feigned Oracles of that Religion according to his pleasure. But this Mahumetan living amongst Christians, would yet more apparently renounce their Government, if he acknowledged the same Person to be Head of his Church who is the Supreme Magistrate in the State.[137]

Lastly, Those are not at all to be tolerated who *deny the Being of a God.* Promises, Covenants, and Oaths, which are the Bonds of Humane

133. "Protection": alternatively, "allegiance" (*obedientiam*). See *Two Treatises of Government,* II, §217.

134. It was fashionable among English Catholics to distinguish between the "Church" and the "Court" of Rome, in an effort to show that moderate Catholicism could be detached from the aggrandizing politics of the papacy and the Jesuits.

135. It is unclear whether the following discussion of "Mahumetans" is to be taken literally, or as an allegory for Catholicism, or both.

136. *Mufti:* a Muslim teacher, but here specifically the Grand Mufti, the head of the religion of the Ottoman state.

137. "But this . . . State": alternatively, "But this Turk among Christians would even more obviously repudiate Christian government if he acknowledged the same person to be the head of his church and also the supreme magistrate." Note the conditional *if.* As in the case of Catholics, Muslims could be good citizens provided they did not hold such a doctrine.

Society, can have no hold upon an Atheist.[138] The taking away of God, though but even in thought, dissolves all. Besides also, those that by their Atheism undermine and destroy all Religion, can have no pretence of Religion whereupon to challenge the Privilege of a Toleration. As for other Practical Opinions, though not absolutely free from all Error, yet if they do not tend to establish Domination over others, or Civil Impunity to the Church in which they are taught, there can be no Reason why they should not be tolerated.[139]

It remains that I say something concerning those Assemblies, which being vulgarly called, and perhaps having sometimes been *Conventicles*,[140] and Nurseries of Factions and Seditions, are thought to afford the strongest matter of Objection against this Doctrine of Toleration. But this has not hapned by any thing peculiar unto the Genius of such Assemblies, but by the unhappy Circumstances of an oppressed or ill-setled Liberty. These Accusations would soon cease, if the Law of Toleration were once so setled, that all Churches were obliged to lay down Toleration as the Foundation of their own Liberty; and teach that Liberty of Conscience is every mans natural Right,[141] equally belonging to Dissenters as to themselves; and that no body ought to be compelled in matters of Religion, either by Law or Force. The Establishment of this one thing would take away all ground of Complaints and Tumults upon account of Conscience.

138. Locke holds that atheists are antinomians. His contemporaries Baruch Spinoza and Pierre Bayle did not share his view that atheists were intolerable.

139. "there can ... tolerated": alternatively, "there can be no reason why the churches in which they are taught should not be tolerated." Popple gives a more individualist twist to the sentiment. See note 141, below.

140. *Conventicles:* a term given wide currency by the Conventicle Acts (1664, 1670), which made any gathering of five or more people, other than a family, for non-Anglican worship a criminal offense. That conventicles were "Nurseries of Factions and Seditions" was common parlance in Anglican polemic. Locke's admission that some sects might indeed have been seditious echoes his own earlier view in his antitolerationist *Tracts*, but is negated by his following remark that it is only oppression that makes dissenters seditious. Popple's "conventicles" adds topical pertinence: Locke has "assemblies" (*coetibus*).

141. "and teach that Liberty of Conscience is every man's natural Right": Locke has only "the principle of toleration for others," where "others" refers to "other churches." There is no mention of "natural right," so Popple turns Locke's claim about churches into a claim about individual conscience.

And these Causes of Discontents and Animosities being once removed, there would remain nothing in these Assemblies that were not more peaceable, and less apt to produce Disturbance of State, than in any other Meetings whatsoever. But let us examine particularly the Heads of these Accusations.

You'll say, That *Assemblies and Meetings endanger the Publick Peace, and threaten the Commonwealth.* I answer: If this be so, Why are there daily such numerous Meetings in Markets, and Courts of Judicature?[142] Why are Crowds upon the Exchange,[143] and a Concourse of People in Cities suffered? You'll reply; These are Civil Assemblies; but Those that we object against are Ecclesiastical. I answer: 'Tis a likely thing indeed, that such Assemblies as are altogether remote from Civil Affairs, should be most apt to embroyl them. O, but Civil Assemblies are composed of men that differ from one another in matters of Religion; but these Ecclesiastical Meetings are of Persons that are all of one Opinion. As if an Agreement in matters of Religion, were in effect a Conspiracy against the Commonwealth; or as if men would not be so much the more warmly unanimous in Religion, the less liberty they had of Assembling. But it will be urged still, That Civil Assemblies are open, and free for any one to enter into; whereas Religious Conventicles are more private, and thereby give opportunity to Clandestine Machinations.[144] I answer, That this is not strictly true: For many Civil Assemblies are not open to every one.[145] And if some Religious Meetings be private, Who are they (I beseech you) that are to be blamed for it? those that desire, or those that forbid their being publick? Again; You'll say, That Religious Communion does exceedingly unite mens Minds and Affections to one another, and is therefore the more dangerous. But if this be so, Why is not the Magistrate afraid of his own Church; and why does he not forbid their Assemblies, as things dan-

142. The principal English law courts sat in Westminster Hall, which was constantly thronged with people.

143. *Exchange:* the Royal Exchange in London, or any other public marketplace. Locke has "corporations" or "guilds" (*collegiis*).

144. The Toleration Act required all places of worship to be unlocked during religious services.

145. Popple omits: "for corporations and the like are not."

gerous to his Government? You'll say, Because he himself is a Part, and even the Head of them. As if he were not also a Part of the Common-wealth, and the Head of the whole People.

Let us therefore deal plainly. The Magistrate is afraid of other Churches, but not of his own; because he is kind and favourable to the one, but severe and cruel to the other. These he treats like Children, and indulges them even to Wantonness: Those he uses as Slaves; and how blamelesly soever they demean themselves, recompenses them no other-wise than by Gallies,[146] Prisons, Confiscations, and Death. These he cher-ishes and defends: Those he continually scourges and oppresses. Let him turn the Tables: Or let those Dissenters enjoy but the same Priv-iledges in Civils as his other Subjects, and he will quickly find that these Religious Meetings will be no longer dangerous. For if men enter into Seditious Conspiracies, 'tis not Religion that inspires them to it in their Meetings; but their Sufferings and Oppressions that make them willing to ease themselves.[147] Just and Moderate Governments are every where quiet, every where safe. But Oppression raises Ferments, and makes Men struggle to cast off an uneasie and tyrannical Yoke.[148] I know that Sedi-tions are very frequently raised, upon pretence of Religion. But 'tis as true that, for Religion, Subjects are frequently ill treated, and live miserably. Believe me, the Stirs that are made proceed not from any peculiar Temper of this or that Church or Religious Society; but from the common Dis-position of all Mankind, who when they groan under any heavy Burthen, endeavour naturally to shake off the Yoke that galls their Necks. Suppose this Business of Religion were let alone, and that there were some other Distinction made between men and men, upon account of their different Complexions, Shapes, and Features; so that those who have black Hair (for example) or gray Eyes, should not enjoy the same Privileges as other

---

146. "Gallies": alternatively "slave prisons" (*ergastulum*). Another allusion to the French persecution of the Huguenots, thousands of whom were sent to the galleys.

147. "that make ... themselves": added by Popple.

148. "But Oppression ... Yoke": alternatively, "but when men are oppressed by injustice and tyranny they are always recalcitrant" (*semper reluctabuntur*). Popple's "struggle to cast off" seems stronger.

Citizens; that they should not be permitted either to buy or sell, or live by their Callings; that Parents should not have the Government and Education of their own Children;[149] that they should either be excluded from the Benefit of the Laws, or meet with partial Judges; can it be doubted but these Persons, thus distinguished from others by the Colour of their Hair and Eyes, and united together by one common Persecution, would be as dangerous to the Magistrate, as any others that had associated themselves meerly upon the account of Religion. Some enter into Company for Trade and Profit: Others, for want of Business, have their Clubs for Clarret:[150] Neighbourhood joyns some, and Religion others. But there is one only thing which gathers People into Seditious Commotions, and that is Oppression.

You'll say; What, will you have People to meet at Divine Service *against the Magistrates Will?* I answer; Why, I pray, against his Will? Is it not both lawful and necessary that they should meet? Against his Will, do you say? That's what I complain of. That is the very Root of all the Mischief.[151] Why are Assemblies less sufferable in a Church than in a Theater or Market?[152] Those that meet there are not either more vicious, or more turbulent, than those that meet elsewhere. The Business in that is, that they are ill used, and therefore they are not to be suffered. Take away the Partiality that is used towards them in matters of common Right; change the Laws; take away the Penalties unto which they are subjected; and all

149. Locke has in mind French edicts against Huguenots.

150. "Others, for want of Business, have their Clubs for Clarret": Popple's most striking extrapolation of Locke's text, which has "others, who are at leisure, for amusement" (*alios ad hilaritatem otium*). Popple had been a trader in claret. He had perhaps read Edward Whitaker's *Argument for Toleration* (1681), which remarks that "I see no cause of fearing any greater inconvenience in them [sects], to the church, or to the state, than is in so many several clubs of friendship, or companies of trade" (p. 15). Richard Baxter objected to definitions of a church that equated it with "a ship, a company of Christian merchants, or corporation" (*Answer to Stillingfleet*, 1681, p. 36). After "Clarret," Popple omits: "some meet for social intercourse because they live in the same city."

151. Popple omits: "and the disaster that has fallen on our estate." Livy, *History*, xxxix.15.

152. "Market": alternatively, "racecourse" (*circo*).

things will immediately become safe and peaceable. Nay, those that are averse to the Religion of the Magistrate, will think themselves so much the more bound to maintain the Peace of the Commonwealth, as their Condition is better in that place than elsewhere; And all the several separate Congregations, like so many Guardians of the Publick Peace, will watch one another,[153] that nothing may be innovated or changed in the Form of the Government: Because they can hope for nothing better than what they already enjoy; that is, an equal Condition with their Fellow-Subjects, under a just and moderate Government. Now if that Church, which agrees in Religion with the Prince, be esteemed the chief Support of any Civil Government, and that for no other Reason (as has already been shewn) than because the Prince is kind, and the Laws are favourable to it; how much greater will be the Security of a Government, where all good Subjects, of whatsoever Church they be, without any Distinction upon account of Religion, enjoying the same Favour of the Prince, and the same Benefit of the Laws, shall become the common Support and Guard of it; and where none will have any occasion to fear the Severity of the Laws, but those that do Injuries to their Neighbours, and offend against the Civil Peace?

That we may draw towards a Conclusion. The *Sum of all* we drive at is, *That every Man may enjoy the same Rights that are granted to others.* Is it permitted to worship God in the *Roman* manner? Let it be permitted to do it in the *Geneva* Form also. Is it permitted to speak *Latin* in the Market-place? Let those that have a mind to it, be permitted to do it also in the Church. Is it lawful for any man in his own House, to kneel, stand, sit, or use any other Posture; and to cloath himself in White or Black, in short or in long Garments? Let it not be made unlawful to eat Bread, drink Wine, or wash with Water, in the Church. In a Word: Whatsoever things are left free by Law in the common occasions of Life, let them remain free unto every Church in Divine Worship. Let no Mans Life, or Body, or House, or Estate, suffer any manner of Prejudice upon these Accounts. Can you allow of the *Presbyterian* Discipline? Why should not

153. A "reason of state" argument that a number of protoleration writers used: a plurality of denominations will tend to act as mutual checks and balances.

the *Episcopal* also have what they like?[154] Ecclesiastical Authority, whether it be administred by the Hands of a single Person, or many, is every where the same; and neither has any Jurisdiction in things Civil, nor any manner of Power of Compulsion, nor any thing at all to do with Riches and Revenues.

Ecclesiastical Assemblies, and Sermons, are justified by daily experience, and publick Allowance. These are allowed to People of some one Perswasion: Why not to all? If any thing pass in a Religious Meeting seditiously, and contrary to the Publick Peace, it is to be punished in the same manner, and no otherwise, than as if it had happened in a Fair or Market.[155] These Meetings ought not to be Sanctuaries for Factious and Flagitious[156] Fellows; Nor ought it to be less lawful for Men to meet in Churches than in Halls; Nor are one part of the Subjects to be esteemed more blameable, for their meeting together, than others. Every one is to be accountable for his own Actions; and no man is to be laid under a Suspicion, or Odium, for the Fault of another. Those that are Seditious, Murderers, Thieves, Robbers, Adulterers, Slanderers, &c. of whatsoever Church, whether National, or not, ought to be punished and suppressed. But those whose Doctrine is peaceable, and whose Manners are pure and blameless, ought to be upon equal Terms with their Fellow Subjects. Thus if Solemn Assemblies, Observations of Festivals, Publick Worship, be permitted to any one sort of Professors; all these things ought to be permitted to the *Presbyterians, Independents, Anabaptists, Arminians, Quakers,*[157] and others, with the same liberty. Nay if we may openly speak the Truth and as becomes one Man to another; neither *Pagan,* nor *Mahumetan,*

154. During the Civil Wars of the 1640s, episcopacy was destroyed and Presbyterianism established in England. A new form of Presbyterian dominion was again established in 1689, this time in Scotland. Whereas the English Toleration Act allowed freedom of worship to non-Anglicans, the Scottish parliament in 1689 established a Presbyterian national church that denied toleration to Episcopalians. In Holland, Lutherans, who had a form of episcopacy, were scarcely tolerated. Locke again shows his hostility to Calvinism.

155. Popple omits: "If a sermon in church contains anything seditious, it should be punished in the same way as if it had been preached in the market-place."

156. *Flagitious:* vicious.

157. This list is Popple's anglicization of Locke's different list: "Remonstrants,

nor *Jew*, ought to be excluded from the Civil Rights of the Common-wealth, because of his Religion.[158] The Gospel commands no such thing. The Church, which *judges not those that are without,* 1 Corinthians 5:12–13, wants it not. And the Commonwealth, which embraces indifferently all men that are honest, peaceable, and industrious, requires it not. Shall we suffer a *Pagan* to deal and trade with us, and shall we not suffer him to pray unto, and worship God? If we allow the *Jews* to have private Houses and Dwellings amongst us, Why should we not allow them to have Syna-gogues? Is their Doctrine more false, their Worship more abominable, or is the Civil Peace more endangered, by their meeting in publick, than in their private Houses? But if these things may be granted to *Jews* and *Pagans,* surely the condition of any Christians ought not to be worse than theirs in a Christian Commonwealth.

You'll say, perhaps, Yes, it ought to be: Because they are more inclin-able to Factions, Tumults, and Civil Wars. I answer: Is this the fault of the Christian Religion? If it be so, truly the Christian Religion is the worst of all Religions, and ought neither to be embraced by any particular Per-son, nor tolerated by any Commonwealth. For if this be the Genius, this the Nature of the Christian Religion, to be turbulent, and destructive to the Civil Peace; that Church it self which the Magistrate indulges[159] will not always be innocent. But far be it from us to say any such thing of that Religion, which carries the greatest opposition to Covetousness, Ambi-tion, Discord, Contention, and all manner of inordinate Desires; and is the most modest and peaceable Religion that ever was. We must there-fore seek another Cause of those Evils that are charged upon Religion. And if we consider right, we shall find it to consist wholly in the Subject

---

Anti-Remonstrants, Lutherans, Anabaptists, or Socinians." *Anabaptists* (often syn-onymous with "Baptists"): those who rejected infant baptism. Popple's deletion of Socinians suggests that his chief objection to the Toleration Act was its maintain-ing civil disabilities on dissenters rather than its theological stricture against anti-Trinitarianism. The French edition of 1710 restored Locke's original list.

158. Locke's toleration of Jews, Muslims, and others is categorical, though in the *Second Letter* he states that he hopes for their conversion. Much contemporary Christian philosemitism was grounded in apocalyptic aspiration for conversion.

159. "indulges": alternatively, "favours." The meaning here is a church established or actively supported by the state.

that I am treating of. It is not the Diversity of Opinions, (which cannot be avoided) but the Refusal of Toleration to those that are of different Opinions, (which might have been granted) that has produced all the Bustles and Wars that have been in the Christian World, upon account of Religion. The Heads and Leaders of the Church, moved by Avarice and insatiable desire of Dominion, making use of the immoderate Ambition of Magistrates, and the credulous Superstition of the giddy Multitude,[160] have incensed and animated them against those that dissent from themselves; by preaching unto them, contrary to the Laws of the Gospel, and to the Precepts of Charity, That Schismaticks and Hereticks are to be outed of their Possessions, and destroyed. And thus have they mixed together, and confounded two things that are in themselves most different, the Church and the Commonwealth. Now as it is very difficult for men patiently to suffer themselves to be stript of the Goods, which they have got by their honest Industry; and contrary to all the Laws of Equity, both Humane and Divine, to be delivered up for a Prey to other mens Violence and Rapine;[161] especially when they are otherwise altogether blameless, and that the Occasion for which they are thus treated, does not at all belong to the Jurisdiction of the Magistrate, but entirely to the Conscience of every particular man, for the Conduct of which he is acountable to God only; What else can be expected, but that these men, growing weary of the Evils under which they labour, should in the end think it lawful for them to resist Force with Force, and to defend their natural Rights (which are not forfeitable upon account of Religion) with Arms as well as they can?[162] That this has been hitherto the ordinary course of things, is abundantly evident in History: and that it will continue to be so hereafter, is but too apparent in Reason. It cannot indeed be otherwise, so long as the Principle of Persecution for Religion shall

160. "the credulous Superstition of the giddy Multitude:" alternatively, "the empty-headed people are always superstitious" (*populum superstitione semper vanum*).

161. Locke may have in mind the gangs of informers who, under the Conventicle Act, pocketed fines from dissenters whom they handed over to the authorities. See *Two Treatises of Government*, II, §§16, 137, 228.

162. Locke's most forceful assertion of a right of armed resistance against religious oppression. Popple has "natural Rights"; Locke has "rights which God and nature have granted him" (*jura sibi a Deo et natura concessa*).

prevail, as it has done hitherto, with Magistrate and People; and so long as those that ought to be the Preachers of Peace and Concord, shall continue, with all their Art and Strength, to excite men to Arms, and sound the Trumpet of War. But that Magistrates should thus suffer these Incendiaries, and Disturbers of the Publick Peace, might justly be wondred at; if it did not appear that they have been invited by them unto a Participation of the Spoil, and have therefore thought fit to make use of their Covetousness and Pride, as Means whereby to increase their own Power. For who does not see that *these Good Men* are indeed more Ministers of the Government, than Ministers of the Gospel; and that by flattering the Ambition, and favouring the Dominion of Princes and Men in Authority, they endeavour with all their might to promote that Tyranny in the Commonwealth, which otherwise they should not be able to establish in the Church?[163] This is the unhappy Agreement that we see between the Church and State. Whereas if each of them would contain it self within its own Bounds, the one attending to the worldly welfare of the Commonwealth, the other to the Salvation of Souls, it is impossible that any Discord should ever have happened between them. *Sed, pudet haec opprobria, &c.*[164] God Almighty grant, I beseech him, that the Gospel of Peace may at length be Preached, and that Civil Magistrates growing more careful to conform their own Consciences to the Law of God, and less solicitous about the binding of other mens Consciences by Humane Laws, may, like Fathers of their Countrey, direct all their Counsels and Endeavours to promote universally the Civil Welfare of all their Children; except only of such as are arrogant, ungovernable, and injurious to their Brethren; and that all Ecclesiastical men, who boast themselves to be the Successors of

---

163. It was a common anticlerical claim that church and state, clergy and prince, mutually conspired to support each other's aggrandizement. The *Letter to a Person of Quality* (1675), which Locke probably had a hand in composing, denounced a regime in which "priest and prince may, like Castor and Pollux, be worshipped together as divine in the same temple by us poor lay subjects." The phrase "Flattering the ambition, and favouring the dominion of princes" is an allusion to the doctrine of the divine right of kings, preached by the church as a quid pro quo for receiving coercive power over religious dissenters. See *Two Treatises of Government*, I, §3.

164. "Pudet haec opprobria nobis / Et dici potuisse et non potuisse refelli" (I am ashamed to say something so scandalous and yet which could not be answered). Ovid, *Metamorphoses*, i.758–59.

the Apostles, walking peaceably and modestly in the Apostles steps, without intermedling with State-Affairs, may apply themselves wholly to promote the Salvation of Souls.

Farewel.

POSTSCRIPT[165]

Perhaps it may not be amiss to add a few things concerning *Heresie* and *Schism*.[166] A Turk[167] is not, nor can be, either Heretick, or Schismatick to a *Christian:* and if any man fall off from the *Christian Faith* to *Mahumetism,* he does not thereby become a Heretick or Schismatick, but an Apostate, and an Infidel. This no body doubts of. And by this it appears that men of different Religions cannot be Hereticks or Schismaticks to one another.

We are to enquire therefore, what men are of the same Religion. Concerning which, it is manifest that those who have one and the same Rule of Faith and Worship, are of the same Religion; and those who have not the same Rule of Faith and Worship, are of different Religions. For since all things that belong unto that Religion, are contained in that Rule, it

165. The heading does not occur in the first edition. The postscript was perhaps written at a later time than the main body of the work. It was probably intended to have special pertinence to the Dutch Arminians, under pressure from Calvinists.

166. There was an ancient distinction between heresy and schism, the former being a deviation in theological doctrine and the latter in ecclesiastical discipline. In Locke's time, some dissenters, though schismatics in Anglican eyes, denounced Anglicans for heresy because they abandoned the Calvinist doctrine of predestination. Conversely, some conforming Anglicans were heretical in their unitarian views, yet were uninterested in the ceremonial and jurisdictional issues which drove dissenters into schismatic separation. Again, however, Locke's postscript probably has in mind divisions in the Dutch church.

167. *Turk:* Muslim.

follows necessarily, that those who agree in one Rule, are of one and the same Religion: and *vice versâ.* Thus *Turks* and *Christians* are of different Religions; because these take the *Holy Scriptures* to be the Rule of their Religion, and those the *Alcoran.* And for the same reason, there may be different Religions also even amongst *Christians.* The *Papists* and the *Lutherans,* though both of them profess Faith in Christ, and are therefore called *Christians,* yet are not both of the same Religion; because These acknowledge nothing but the *Holy Scriptures* to be the Rule and Foundation of their Religion; Those take in also Traditions[168] and the Decrees of Popes, and of all these together make the Rule of their Religion. And thus the Christians of St. *John*[169] (as they are called) and the Christians of *Geneva,* are of different Religions; because These also take only the Scriptures; and Those, I know not what Traditions, for the Rule of their Religion.

This being setled, it follows; *First,* that Heresie is a Separation made in Ecclesiastical Communion between men of the same Religion, for some Opinions no way contained in the Rule it self. And *Secondly,* That amongst those who acknowledge nothing but the Holy Scriptures to be their Rule of Faith, Heresie is a Separation made in their Christian Communion, for Opinions not contained in the express words of Scripture. Now this Separation may be made in a twofold manner.

1. When the greater part, or (by the Magistrate's Patronage) the stronger part, of the Church separates it self from others, by excluding them out of her Communion, because they will not profess their Belief of certain Opinions which are not to be found in the express words of Scripture. For it is not the paucity of those that are separated, nor the Authority of the Magistrate, that can make any man guilty of Heresie. But he

168. The "rule" of religion, and "traditions": Theologians debated the "Rule of Faith": Protestants held that Scripture alone was the Rule of Faith, and charged Catholics with corruptly augmenting Scripture with "tradition," embodied in theological writings and the decrees of popes and councils. Catholics retorted that Protestants were hermeneutically naive, since no text can be free of the need for interpretation, and such interpretation either has a coherent tradition or is an anarchy of private, unscholarly judgment.

169. *the Christians of St. John:* the Catholic order of the Knights of St. John of Malta.

only is an Heretick who divides the Church into parts, introduces Names and Marks of Distinction, and voluntarily makes a Separation because of such Opinions.

2. When any one separates himself from the Communion of a Church, because that Church does not publickly profess some certain Opinions which the Holy Scriptures do not expressly teach.

Both these are *Hereticks: because they err in Fundamentals, and they err obstinately against Knowledge.* For when they have determined the Holy Scriptures to be the only Foundation of Faith; they nevertheless lay down certain Propositions as fundamental, which are not in the Scripture; and because others will not acknowledge these additional Opinions of theirs, nor build upon them as if they were necessary and fundamental, they therefore make a Separation in the Church; either by withdrawing them-selves from the others, or expelling the others from them. Nor does it sig-nifie any thing for them to say that their Confessions and Symboles are agreeable to Scripture, and to the Analogy of Faith.[170] For if they be con-ceived in the express words of Scripture, there can be no question about them; because those are acknowledged by all Christians to be of Divine Inspiration, and therefore fundamental. But if they say that the Articles which they require to be profess'd, are Consequences deduced from the Scripture; it is undoubtedly well done of them to believe and profess such things as seem unto them so agreeable to the Rule of Faith; But it would be very ill done to obtrude those things upon others, unto whom they do not seem to be the indubitable Doctrines of the Scripture. And to make a Separation for such things as these, which neither are nor can be fun-damental, is to become Hereticks. For I do not think there is any man arrived to that degree of madness, as that he dare give out his Conse-quences and Interpretations of Scripture as Divine Inspirations, and com-pare the Articles of Faith that he has framed according to his own Fancy

---

170. *the Analogy of Faith* (Romans 12:6): the notion that an obscure passage in Scripture should be interpreted by analogy with a clear passage elsewhere. Locke here returns to the distinction between "things necessary" and "things indifferent" (fundamentals and nonfundamentals). Consistent with his 1667 *Essay*, he argues that the distinction, though valid (for he believes there are many inessentials), is unhelpful, since there is no brooking a person who, or a sect which, insists that an inessential is in fact essential.

with the Authority of the Scripture. I know there are some Propositions so evidently agreeable to Scripture, that no body can deny them to be drawn from thence; but about those therefore there can be no difference. This only I say, that however clearly we may think this or the other Doctrine to be deduced from Scripture, we ought not therefore to impose it upon others, as a necessary Article of Faith, because we believe it to be agreeable to the Rule of Faith; unless we would be content also that other Doctrines should be imposed upon us in the same manner; and that we should be compell'd to receive and profess all the different and contradictory Opinions of *Lutherans, Calvinists, Remonstrants, Anabaptists,* and other Sects, which the Contrivers of Symbols, Systems and Confessions, are accustomed to deliver unto their Followers as genuine and necessary Deductions from the Holy Scripture. I cannot but wonder at the extravagant arrogance of those Men who think that they themselves can explain things necessary to Salvation more clearly than the Holy Ghost, the Eternal and Infinite Wisdom of God.

Thus much concerning *Heresie;* which word in common use is applied only to the Doctrinal part of Religion. Let us now consider *Schism,* which is a Crime near akin to it. For both those words seem unto me to signifie an *ill-grounded Separation in Ecclesiastical Communion, made about things not necessary.* But since Use, which is the Supreme Law in matter of Language,[171] has determined that Heresie relates to Errors in Faith, and Schism to those in Worship or Discipline, we must consider them under that Distinction.

Schism then, for the same reasons that have already been alledged, is nothing else but a Separation made in the Communion of the Church, upon account of something in Divine Worship, or Ecclesiastical Discipline, that is not any necessary part of it. Now nothing in Worship or Discipline can be necessary to Christian Communion, but what Christ our Legislator, or the Apostles, by Inspiration of the Holy Spirit, have commanded in express words.

In a word: He that denies not any thing that the Holy Scriptures teach

171. "But . . . Language": alternatively, "use, which is the law that decides what is correct in speech." Horace, *Art of Poetry,* 71–72.

in express words, nor makes a Separation upon occasion of any thing that is not manifestly contained in the Sacred Text; however he may be nick-named by any Sect of Christians, and declared by some, or all of them to be utterly void of true Christianity, yet indeed and in truth this Man cannot be either a Heretick or a Schismatick.

These things might have been explained more largely, and more advantageously: but it is enough to have hinted at them, thus briefly, to a Person of your parts.

FINIS.

Excerpts from
A Third Letter for
Toleration

The Ends of Civil Society[1]

You[2] tell us farther, that *Commonwealths are instituted for the attaining of all the Benefits which Political Government can yield: and therefore if the spiritual and eternal Interests of Men may any way be procured or advanced by Political Government, the procuring and advancing those Interests must in all reason be received amongst the Ends of Civil Society, and so consequently fall within the compass of the Magistrate's Jurisdiction.* Concerning the extent of

1. *Third Letter,* chap. 2, pp. 60–72, citing *Second Letter,* pp. 51–52 (*Works,* pp. 211–25; 117–19).

2. Locke is responding to Jonas Proast, *The Argument of The Letter Concerning Toleration Briefly Consider'd and Answer'd* (Oxford, 1690) and *A Third Letter Concerning Toleration* (Oxford, 1691); his quotations occur at p. 18 of the former and pp. 56–62 of the latter. Proast (ca. 1642–1710) was chaplain of All Souls College, Oxford, 1677–98, and archdeacon of Berkshire, 1698–1710.

the Magistrate's Jurisdiction, and the Ends of Civil Society, whether the Author[3] or you have begg'd the Question, which is the chief business of your 56*th* and two or three following Pages, I shall leave it to the Readers to judg, and bring the matter, if you please, to a shorter Issue. The Question is, Whether the Magistrate has any power to interpose Force in Matters of Religion, or for the Salvation of Souls? The Argument against it is, That Civil Societies are not constituted for that End, and the Magistrate cannot use Force for Ends for which the Commonwealth was not constituted.

The End of a Commonwealth constituted can be supposed no other, than what Men in the Constitution of, and entring into it propos'd; and that could be nothing but Protection from such Injuries from other Men, which they desiring to avoid, nothing but Force could prevent or remedy: all things but this being as well attainable by Men living in Neighbourhood without the Bonds of a Commonwealth, they could propose to themselves no other thing but this in quitting their Natural Liberty, and putting themselves under the Umpirage of a *Civil Soveraign,* who therefore had the Force of all the Members of the Commonwealth put into his Hands, to make his Decrees to this end be obeyed.[4] Now since no Man, or Society of Men can by their Opinions in Religion, or Ways of Worship, do any Man who differed from them any Injury, which he could not avoid or redress, if he desired it, without the help of Force; the punishing any Opinion in Religion, or Ways of Worship by the Force given the Magistrate, could not be intended by those who constituted, or entred into the Commonwealth, and so could be no End of it, but quite the contrary. For Force from a stronger Hand to bring a Man to a Religion, which another thinks the true, being an Injury which in the State of Nature every one would avoid, Protection from any such injury is one of the Ends of a Commonwealth, and so every Man has a right to Toleration.

If you will say, that Commonwealths are not voluntary Societies constituted by Men, and by Men freely entered into, I shall desire you to prove it.

3. "the Author": that is, Locke. In the *Second Letter* and *Third Letter* Locke adopts the fiction that he is a third party defending the first *Letter.*
4. See *Two Treatises of Government,* II, especially §§87–89, 143, 155, 212, 227.

In the mean time allowing it you for good, that Commonwealths are constituted by God for Ends which he has appointed, without the consent and contrivance of Men:[5] If you say, that one of those Ends is the Propagation of the true Religion, and the Salvation of Mens Souls; I shall desire you to shew me any such End expresly appointed by God in Revelation; which since, as you confess, you cannot do, you have recourse to the general Law of Nature, and what is that? The Law of Reason, whereby every one is commissioned to do Good. And the propagating the true Religion for the Salvation of Mens Souls, being doing good, you say, the *Civil Soveraigns* are commissioned and required by that Law to use their Force for those Ends. But since by this Law all *Civil Soveraigns* are commissioned and obliged alike to use their *coactive*[6] *Power* for the propagating the true Religion, and the Salvation of Souls, and it is not possible for them to execute such a Commission, or obey that Law, but by using Force to bring Men to that Religion which they judg the true; by which use of Force much more Harm than Good would be done towards the propagating the true Religion in the World, as I have shewed elsewhere: therefore no such Commission, whose Execution would do more Harm than Good, more hinder than promote the End for which it is supposed given, can be a Commission from God by the Law of Nature. And this I suppose may satisfy you about the End of Civil Societies or Commonwealths, and answer what you say concerning the Ends attainable by them.[7] [. . .]

In the voluntary Institution and bestowing of Power, there is no Absurdity or Inconvenience at all, that Power, sufficient for several Ends, should be limited by those that give the Power only to one or some part of them. The Power which a General, commanding a potent Army, has, may be enough to take more Towns than one from the Enemy; or to suppress a domestick Sedition, and yet the Power of attaining those Benefits, which is in his Hand, will not authorize him to imploy the Force of the Army

---

5. See note 13, p. 74.

6. *coactive:* coercive.

7. Locke's claim, in this dense paragraph, is that, if the state is authorized to coerce in religion by the law of nature rather than by a Gospel commission, then all states, Christian or not, are licensed to coerce, and hence true believers will be persecuted.

therein, if he be commission'd only to besiege and take one certain Place. So it is in a Commonwealth. The Power that is in the Civil Soveraign is the Force of all the Subjects of the Commonwealth, which supposing it sufficient for other Ends, than the preserving the Members of the Commonwealth in Peace from Injury and Violence: yet if those who gave him that Power, limited the Application of it to that sole End, no Opinion of any other Benefits attainable by it can authorize him to use it otherwise. [...]

[Y]our Words are, *Doubtless Commonwealths are instituted for the attaining all the Benefits which Political Government can yield; and therefore if the spiritual and eternal Interests of Men may any way be procured or advanced by Political Government, the procuring and advancing those Interests, must in all Reason be reckon'd amongst the Ends of Civil Societies.*

To which I answer'd, "That if this be so, Then this Position must be true, *viz. That all Societies whatsoever are instituted for the attaining all the Benefits that they may any way yield;* there being nothing peculiar to Civil Society in the case, why that Society should be *instituted for the attaining all the Benefits it can any way yield,* and other Societies not. By which Argument it will follow, that all Societies are instituted for one and the same End, *i.e.,* for the *attaining all the Benefits that they can any way yield.* By which Account there will be no Difference between Church and State, a Commonwealth and an Army, or between a Family and the *East-India-*Company; all which have hitherto been thought distinct sorts of Societies, instituted for different Ends. If your Hypothesis hold good, one of the Ends of the Family must be to preach the Gospel, and administer the Sacraments; and one Business of an Army to teach Languages, and propagate Religion; because these are Benefits some way or other *attainable* by those Societies, unless you take want of Commission and Authority to be a sufficient Impediment: And that will be so too in other Cases." [...]

The natural Force of all the Members of any Society, or of those who by the Society can be procured to assist it, is in one Sense called the Power of that Society. This Power or Force is generally put into some one or few Persons Hands with Direction and Authority how to use it, and this in another Sense is called also the Power of the Society: And this is the Power you here speak of, and in these following Words, *viz. Several Socie-*

ties as they are instituted for different Ends; so likewise are they furnished with different Powers proportionate to their respective Ends. The Power therefore of any Society in this Sense, is nothing but the Authority and Direction given to those that have the Management of the Force or natural Power of the Society, how and to what Ends to use it, by which Commission the Ends of Societies are known and distinguished. [. . .]

[8]"'Tis a Benefit to have true Knowledg and Philosophy imbraced and assented to, in any Civil Society or Government. But will you say therefore, that it is a Benefit to the Society, or one of the Ends of Government, that all who are not Peripateticks[9] should be punished, to make Men find out the Truth, and profess it? This indeed might be thought a fit way to make some Men imbrace the Peripatetick Philosophy, but not a proper way to find the Truth. For, perhaps the Peripatetick Philosophy may not be true; perhaps a great many have not time, nor Parts[10] to study it; perhaps a great many who have studied it, cannot be convinced of the Truth of it: And therefore it cannot be a Benefit to the Commonwealth, nor one of the Ends of it, that these Members of the Society should be disturb'd, and diseas'd to no purpose, when they are guilty of no Fault. For just the same Reason, it cannot be a Benefit to Civil Society, that Men should be punished in *Denmark,* for not being *Lutherans,* in *Geneva* for not being *Calvinists,* and in *Vienna* for not being *Papists*; as a means to make them find out the True religion. For so, upon your Grounds, Men must be treated in those Places, as well as in *England* for not being of the Church of *England.* And then, I beseech you, consider the great Benefit will accrue to Men in Society by this Method; and I suppose it will be a hard thing for you to prove, That ever Civil Governments were instituted to punish Men for not being of this or that Sect in Religion; however by Accident, *indirectly, and at a distance,*[11] it may be an occasion to one perhaps of a thousand, or an hundred, to study that Controversy, which is all

---

8. This paragraph is verbatim from the *Second Letter,* p. 51 (*Works,* pp. 118–19).

9. *Peripateticks:* Aristotelians.

10. *Parts:* abilities.

11. "indirectly . . . distance": Locke snidely echoes Proast's persistent claim that coercion can induce true belief, albeit not directly, but "indirectly," by compelling people to listen to true teaching.

you expect from it. If it be a *Benefit,* pray tell me what *Benefit* it is. A Civil *Benefit* it cannot be. For Mens Civil Interests are disturb'd, injur'd, and impair'd by it. And what *Spiritual Benefit* that can be to any Multitude of Men, to be punished for Dissenting from a false or erroneous Profession, I would have you find out: unless it be a Spiritual Benefit to be in danger to be driven into a wrong way. For if in all differing Sects, one is in the wrong, 'tis a hundred to one but that from which any one Dissents, and is punished for Dissenting from, is the wrong."

You tell us, *the true religion is undoubtedly true.* If you had told us too, who is undoubtedly Judg of it, you had put all past doubt: but till you will be pleased to determine that, it will be undoubtedly true, that the King of *Denmark* is as Undoubtedly judg of it at *Copenhagen,* and the Emperor at *Vienna,* as the king of *England* in this Island: I do not say they judge as right, but they are by as much Right Judges, and therefore have as much Right to punish those who dissent from Lutheranism and Popery in those Countries, as any other Civil Magistrate has to punish any Dissenters from the National Religion[12] any where else. [...]

I say in the next Paragraph, *viz.* "That Commonwealths, or Civil Societies and Governments, if you will believe the Judicious Mr. *Hooker,* are, as St. *Peter* calls them, 1 Pet. ii. 13, Ἀνθρωπίνη κτίσις, *the Contrivance and Institution of Man.*"[13] To which you smartly reply, for your Choler[14] was up, *'Tis well for St.* Peter *that he had the judicious Mr. Hooker on his side.* And it would have been well for you too to have seen that Mr. *Hooker's* Authority was made use of not to confirm the Authority of St. *Peter,* but to confirm that sense I gave of St. *Peter's* words, which is not so clear in our Translation, but that there are those who, as I doubt not but you know, do not allow of it. But this being said when Passion it seems rather

---

12. *National Religion:* state religion. The term "Established Church" was not yet in use.

13. The Authorized Version of the Bible (called "our Translation" a few lines below) renders the Greek as "ordinance of man," but here Locke prefers a translation that better tallies with his own political philosophy. He makes the same point in *Two Treatises of Government,* I, §6, and regularly cites Richard Hooker's *Laws of Ecclesiastical Polity* (1594–97) in the *Two Treatises:* for example, II, §74.

14. *Choler:* anger. See note 15, following, for the reason for Proast's irritation.

imployed your Wit than your Judgment, though nothing to the purpose, may yet perhaps *indirectly and at a distance* do some service.

And now, Sir, if you can but imagine that Men in the corrupt State of Nature might be authorized and required by Reason, the Law of Nature, to avoid the Inconveniences of that State, and to that purpose to put the Power of governing them into some one or more Mens Hands, in such Forms, and under such Agreements as they should think fit: which Governors so set over them for a good End by their own choice, though they received all their Power from those, who by the Law of Nature had a Power to confer it on them, may very fitly be called *Powers ordained of God*,[15] being chosen and appointed by those who had Authority from God so to do. For he that receives Commission (limited according to the Discretion of him that gives it) from another who had Authority from his prince oo to do, may truly be said, so far as his Commission reaches, to be appointed or ordained by the Prince himself. Which may serve as an Answer to your next two Paragraphs, and to shew that there is no Opposition or Difficulty in all that St. *Peter,* St. *Paul,* or the Judicious Mr. *Hooker,* says; nor any thing, in what either of them says, to your purpose. And tho it be true, those Powers that are, *are ordained of God;* yet it may nevertheless be true, that the Power any one has, and the Ends for which he has it, may be by the Contrivance and Appointment of Men.

To my saying, "The Ends of Commonwealths appointed by the Institutors of them, could not be their spiritual and eternal Interest, because they could not stipulate about those one with another, nor submit this Interest to the Power of the Society, or any Soveraign they should set over them." You reply, *Very true, Sir; but they can submit to be punished in their Temporal Interest, if they despise or neglect those greater Interests.* How they

---

15. Locke echoes Romans 13:1 ("Let every soul be subject unto the higher powers. For there is no power but of God: the powers that be are ordained of God"), a standard text used by absolutists to defend the divine right of kings and the duty of nonresistance. He adopts a riposte familiar in the tradition of Calvinist resistance theory, that St. Paul's injunction may be construed as applying equally to rulers appointed by the people, and that there may be said to be a "divine right" of the people to erect governments. Hence Locke brings Romans 13 into line with 1 Peter 2:13.

can submit to be punished by any Men in their Temporal Interest, for that which they cannot submit to be judg'd by any Man, when you can shew, I shall admire your Politicks. Besides, if the Compact about Matters of Religion be, that those should *be punished in their Temporal, who neglect or despise* their Eternal *Interest*, who I beseech you is by this Agreement rather to be punished, a sober Dissenter, who appears concerned for Religion and his Salvation, or an irreligious profane or debauched Conformist? By such as *despise or neglect those greater Interests*, you here mean only Dissenters from the National Religion: for those only you punish, though you represent them under such a Description as belongs not peculiarly to them; but that matters not, so long as it best sutes your Occasion.

In your next Paragraph you wonder at my *News from the West-Indies*;[16] I suppose because you found it not in your Books of *Europe* or *Asia*. But whatever you may think, I assure you all the World is not *Mile-End*.[17] But that you may be no more surprized with News, let me ask you, Whether it be not possible that Men, to whom the Rivers and Woods afforded the spontaneous Provisions of Life, and so with no private Possessions of Land, had no inlarged Desires after Riches or Power; should live together in Society, make one People of one Language under one Chieftain, who shall have no other Power but to command them in time of War against their common Enemies, without any municipal Laws, Judges, or any Person with Superiority establish'd amongst them, but ended all their private Differences, if any arose, by the extemporary Determination of their Neighbours, or of Arbitrators chosen by the Parties. I ask you whether in such a Commonwealth, the Chieftain who was the only Man of Authority amongst them, had any Power to use the Force of the Commonwealth to any other End but the Defence of it against an Enemy, though other *Benefits* were *attainable* by it?[18]

---

16. *West-Indies:* Locke means America in general. The following passage illuminates remarks about Native Americans in *Two Treatises of Government*, II, chaps. 5 and 8, especially §§102, 108.

17. "Mile-End" is a district of London: Locke wittily puts down Proast's parochialism.

18. In the *Second Letter*, pp. 54–55 (*Works*, pp. 121–22), Locke wrote: "There are Nations in the *West-Indies* which have no other End of their Society, but their

The Civil Rights of Jews and Muslims[19]

To justify the largeness of the Author's Toleration, who would not have Jews, Mahometans and Pagans excluded from the Civil Rights of the Commonwealth, because of their Religion; I said, "I feared it will hardly be believed, that we pray in earnest for their Conversion, if we exclude them from the ordinary and profitable Means of it, either by driving them from us, or persecuting them when they are among us." You reply; *Now I confess I thought Men might live quietly enough among us, and enjoy the Protection of the Government against all Violence and Injuries, without being* endenizon'd,[20] *or made Members of the* Commonwealth; *which alone can entitle them to the* Civil Rights *and Privileges of it. But as to* Jews, Mahometans, *and* Pagans, *if any of them do not care to live among us, unless they may be admitted to the* Rights *and Privileges of the* Commonwealth; *the refusing them that Favour is not, I suppose, to be looked upon as* driving them from us, *or* excluding them from the ordinary and probable Means of Conversion; *but as a just and necessary Caution in a Christian Commonwealth, in respect to the Members of it: Who, if such as profess* Judaism, *or* Mahometanism, *or* Paganism, *were permitted to enjoy the same Rights with them, would be much the more in danger of being seduced by them; seeing they would lose no worldly Advantage by such a Change of their Religion: Whereas if they could not turn to any of those Religions, without forfeiting the* Civil Rights of the Commonwealth *by doing it, 'tis likely they would consider well before they did it, what ground there was to expect that they should get any thing by the Exchange, which would countervail the Loss they should sustain by it.* [. . .] Live amongst you then *Jews, Mahometans,* and *Pagans* may; but *endenizon'd* they must not be. But why? Are there not those who are *Members* of your *Commonwealth,* who do not *imbrace the Truth that must*

---

mutual defence against their common enemies. In these, their Captain, or Prince, is Sovereign Commander in time of War; but in time of Peace, neither he nor any body else has any Authority over any of the Society. You cannot deny but other, even temporal ends, are attainable by these Commonwealths, if they had been otherwise instituted and appointed to those ends."

19. *Third Letter,* chap. 3, pp. 75–78, citing *Second Letter,* p. 2 (*Works,* pp. 228–32; 62), and Proast, *Third Letter,* pp. 2–3.

20. *endenizon'd:* made a naturalized citizen.

save them, any more than they? What think you of Socinians, Papists, Anabaptists, Quakers, Presbyterians?[21] [. . .]

[I]f *the forfeiting the Civil Rights of the Commonwealth,* be the proper Remedy to keep Men in the Communion of the Church, why is it used to keep Men from *Judaism* or *Paganism,* and not from Phanaticism?[22] Upon this Account why might not Jews, Pagans, and Mahometans be admitted to the Rights of the Commonwealth, as far as Papists, Independents,[23] and Quakers? But you distribute to every one according to your good Pleasure; and doubtless are fully justified by these following Words: *And whether this be not a reasonable and necessary Caution, any Man may judg, who does but consider within how few Ages after the Flood Superstition and Idolatry prevailed over the World, and how apt even God's own peculiar People were to receive that mortal Infection notwithstanding all that he did to keep them from it.*

What the State of Religion was in the first Ages after the Flood, is so imperfectly known now, that as I have shewed you in another Place,[24] you can make little Advantage to your Cause from thence. And since it was the same Corruption then, which as you own,[25] withdraws Men now from the true Religion, and hinders it from prevailing by its own Light, without the Assistance of Force; and it is the same Corruption that keeps *Dissenters,* as well as *Jews, Mahometans* and *Pagans,* from imbracing of the Truth: why different Degrees of Punishments should be used to them, till there be found in them different Degrees of Obstinacy, would need some better Reason. Why this common *Pravity of humane Nature* should make Judaism, Mahometism or Paganism more catching than any sort of Nonconformity, which hinders Men from imbracing the true Religion; so that Jews, Mahometans and Pagans must, for fear of infecting others, be shut out from the Commonwealth, when others are not, I would fain[26] know?

21. For Socinians and Anabaptists, see p. 30, note 66, and p. 58, note 157.
22. *Phanaticism:* Locke defers to the standard hostile term for Protestant dissenters.
23. *Independents:* Congregationalists.
24. See p. 98.
25. *own:* admit.
26. *fain:* gladly.

Whatever it was that so disposed the Jews to Idolatry before the Captivity, sure it is, they firmly resisted it, and refused to change, not only where they might have done it on equal terms, but have had great Advantage to boot; and therefore 'tis possible that there is something in this matter, which neither you nor I do fully comprehend, and may with a becoming Humility sit down and confess, that in this, as well as other Parts of his Providence, God's Ways are past finding out. But this we may be certain from this Instance of the Jews, that it is not reasonable to conclude, that because they were once inclin'd to Idolatry, that therefore they, or any other People are in *Danger* to turn Pagans, whenever they *shall lose no worldly Advantage by such a Change.* But if we may oppose nearer and known Instances to more remote and uncertain, look into the World, and tell me, since Jesus Christ brought Life and Immortality to light through the Gospel, where the Christian Religion meeting Judaism, Mahometism or Paganism upon equal terms, lost so plainly by it, that you have Reason to suspect the Members of a Christian Commonwealth would *be in Danger to be seduced* to either of *them,* if *they should lose no worldly Advantage by such a Change of their Religion,* rather than likely to increase among them? Till you can find then some better Reason for excluding Jews, *&c.* from *the Rights of the Commonwealth,* you must give us leave to look on this as a bare Pretence. Besides, I think you are under a Mistake, which shews your Pretence against admitting Jews, Mahometans and Pagans, to the Civil Rights of the Commonwealth, is ill grounded; for what Law I pray is there in *England,* that they *who turn to any of those Religions, forfeit the Civil Rights of the Commonwealth by doing it?* Such a Law I desire you to shew me; and if you cannot, all this Pretence is out of doors,[27] and Men of your Church, since on that Account *they would lose no worldly Advantage by the Change, are in as much Danger to be seduced,* whether Jews, Mahometans and Pagans, are indenizon'd or no.

---

27. *out of doors:* irrelevant.

The Sectarianism of Creed-Makers[28]

I easily grant that our *Saviour pray'd that all might be one in that holy Religion which he taught them,* and in that very Prayer teaches what that Religion is, *This is Life eternal, that they might know thee the only true God, and Jesus Christ whom thou hast sent* (John 17:3). But must it be expected, that therefore they should all be of one Mind in things not necessary to Salvation? For whatever Unity it was our Saviour pray'd for here, 'tis certain the Apostles themselves did not all of them agree in every thing: but even the chief of them have had Differences amongst them in Matters of Religion, as appears, Galatians 2:11.

An Agreement in Truths necessary to Salvation, and the maintaining of Charity and brotherly Kindness with the Diversity of Opinions in other things, is that which will very well consist with Christian Unity, and is all possibly to be had in this world, in such an incurable Weakness and Difference of Mens Understandings. This probably would contribute more to the Conversion of *Jews, Mahometans* and *Pagans,* if there were proposed to them and others, for their Admittance into the Church, only the plain simple Truths of the Gospel necessary to Salvation, than all the fruitless Pudder[29] and Talk about uniting Christians in Matters of less Moment, according to the Draught and Prescription of a certain set of Men any where.

What Blame will lie on the Authors and Promoters of Sects and Divisions, and (let me add) Animosities amongst Christians, *when Christ comes to make Inquisition why no more Jews, Mahometans and Pagans were converted,* they who are concerned *ought certainly well to consider.* And to abate in great measure this Mischief for the future, they who talk so much of *Sects and Divisions,* would do well to consider too, whether those are not most Authors and Promoters of Sects and Divisions, who impose Creeds, Ceremonies and Articles of Mens making; and make things not necessary to Salvation, the necessary terms of Communion, excluding and driving from them such as out of Conscience and Perswasion cannot assent and submit to them, and treating them as if they were utter Aliens from the

---

28. *Third Letter,* chap. 3, pp. 82–85 (*Works,* pp. 237–40), citing Proast, *Third Letter,* p. 4.

29. *Pudder:* fuss.

Church of God, and such as were deservedly shut out as unfit to be Members of it: who narrow Christianity within Bounds of their own making, and which the Gospel knows nothing of; and often for things by themselves confessed indifferent, thrust Men out of their Communion, and then punish them for not being of it.

Who sees not, but the Bond of Unity might be preserved, in the different Perswasions of Men concerning things not necessary to Salvation, if they were not made necessary to Church-Communion? What two thinking Men of the Church of *England* are there, who differ not one from the other in several material Points of Religion? who nevertheless are Members of the same Church, and in Unity one with another. Make but one of those Points the *Shibboleth* of a Party, and erect it into an Article of the National Church, and they are presently divided; and he of the two, whose Judgment happens not to agree with National Orthodoxy, is immediately cut off from Communion. Who I beseech you is it in this Case that makes the Sect? Is it not those who contract the Church of Christ within Limits of their own Contrivance? who by Articles and Ceremonies of their own forming, separate from their Communion all that have not Perswasions which just jump with their Model?

'Tis frivolous here to pretend Authority. No Man has or can have Authority to shut any one out of the Church of Christ, for that for which Christ himself will not shut him out of Heaven. Whosoever does so, is truly the Author and Promoter of Schism and Division, sets up a Sect, and tears in Pieces the Church of Christ, of which every one who believes, and practises what is necessary to Salvation, is a Part and Member; and cannot, without the Guilt of Schism, be separated from, or kept out of its external Communion. In this *lording it over the Heritage of God* (1 Peter 5:2–3), and thus *overseeing* by Imposition on the unwilling, and not consenting, which seems to be the meaning of St. *Peter,* most of the lasting Sects which so mangle Christianity, had their Original, and continue to have their Support: and were it not for these establish'd Sects under the specious Names of National Churches,[30] which by their contracted and

---

30. One of the clearest indications that Locke objected in principle to established churches.

arbitrary Limits of Communion, justify against themselves the Separation and like Narrowness of others, the Difference of Opinions which do not so much begin to be, as to appear and be owned[31] under Toleration, would either make no Sect nor Division; or else if they were so extravagant as to be opposite to what is necessary to Salvation, and so necessitate a Separation, the clear Light of the Gospel, joined with a strict Discipline of Manners,[32] would quickly chase them out of the World. But whilst needless Impositions, and moot Points in Divinity are established by the Penal Laws of Kingdoms, and the specious Pretences of Authority, what Hopes is there that there should be such an Union amongst Christians any where, as might invite a rational Turk[33] or Infidel to imbrace a Religion, whereof he is told they have a Revelation from God, which yet in some Places he is not suffered to read, and in no Place shall he be permitted to understand for himself,[34] or to follow according to the best of his Understanding, when it shall at all thwart (though in things confessed not necessary to Salvation) any of those select Points of Doctrine, Discipline, or outward Worship, whereof the National Church has been pleased to make up its Articles, Polity, and Ceremonies? And I ask, what a sober sensible Heathen must think of the Divisions amongst Christians not owing to Toleration, if he should find in an Island, where Christianity seems to be in its greatest Purity, the South and North Parts establishing Churches upon the Differences of only whether fewer or more, thus and thus chosen, should govern;[35] tho the Revelation they both pretend be their Rule, say nothing directly one way or t'other:[36] each contending with so much Eagerness, that they deny each other to be Churches of

31. *owned:* acknowledged.

32. *Manners:* morals.

33. *Turk:* Muslim.

34. "some Places ... for himself": Locke evenhandedly indicts Catholics and Protestants.

35. Locke alludes to the fact that in 1689 episcopacy was overthrown in Scotland and Presbyterianism established, so that the two kingdoms of Britain now had distinct official churches. With the Act of Union in 1707 this pluralism became more anomalous because it now existed within a single state. Throughout Locke's writings on toleration, he is silent about the fact that Ireland was overwhelmingly Catholic.

36. Locke makes clear his belief that neither episcopacy nor presbytery are prescribed in Scripture.

Christ, that is, in effect, to be true Christians? To which if one should add Transubstantiation, Consubstantiation, Real Presence,[37] Articles and Distinctions set up by Men without Authority from Scripture, and other less Differences, (which good Christians may dissent about without endangering their Salvations) *established by Law* in the several Parts of Christendom: I ask, Whether the Magistrates interposing in Matters of Religion, and establishing National Churches by the Force and Penalties of Civil Laws, with their distinct (and at home reputed necessary) Confessions and Ceremonies, do not by Law and Power authorize and perpetuate Sects among Christians, to the great Prejudice of Christianity, and Scandal to Infidels, more than any thing that can arise from a mutual Toleration, with Charity and a good Life?

Those who have so much in their Mouths, the *Authors of Sects and Divisions,* with so little advantage to their Cause, I shall desire to consider, whether National Churches established as now they are, are not as much Sects and Divisions in Christianity, as smaller Collections, under the name of distinct Churches, are in respect of the National? only with this difference, that these Subdivisions and discountenanced Sects, wanting Power to enforce their peculiar Doctrines and Discipline, usually live more friendly like Christians, and seem only to demand Christian Liberty; whereby there is less appearance of Unchristian Division among them: Whereas those National Sects, being back'd by the Civil Power, which they never fail to make use of, at least as a pretence of Authority over their Brethren, usually breathe out nothing but Force and Persecution, to the great Reproach, Shame, and Dishonour of the Christian Religion.

The Reformation of Manners[38]

I said, "That if the Magistrates would severely and impartially set themselves against Vice in whomsoever it is found, and leave Men to their own Consciences in their Articles of Faith, and Ways of Worship, true Religion would spread wider, and be more fruitful in the Lives of its Professors, than ever hitherto it has done by the imposing of Creeds and

37. Three divergent doctrines concerning the nature of the Eucharist.
38. *Third Letter,* pp. 85–86, citing *Second Letter,* p. 5 (*Works,* pp. 241–42; 65–66), and Proast, *Third Letter,* p. 13. The "reformation of manners" was a common phrase

Ceremonies." Here I call only Immorality of Manners, *Vice;* you on the contrary, in your Answer, give the Name of *Vice* to Errors in Opinion, and Difference in Ways of Worship from the National Church: for this is the Matter in question between us, express it as you please. This being a Contest only about the signification of a short Syllable in the English Tongue, we must leave to the Masters of that Language to judg which of these two is the proper use of it. But yet from my using the word *Vice,* you conclude presently, (taking it in your Sense, not mine) that the Magistrate has a Power in *England* (for *England* we are speaking of) to punish Dissenters from the National Religion, because it is a *Vice.* I will, if you please, in what I said, change the word *Vice* into that I meant by it, and say thus, "If the Magistrates will severely and impartially set themselves against the Dishonesty and Debauchery of Mens Lives, and such Immoralities as I contra-distinguish from Error in speculative Opinions of Religion, and Ways of Worship": and then pray see how your Answer will look, for thus it runs, *It seems then with you the rejecting the true Religion, and refusing to worship God in decent Ways prescribed by those to whom God has left the ordering of those Matters, are not comprehended in the name* Vice. But you tell me, *If I except these things, and will not allow them to be called by the name of* Vice, *perhaps other Men may think it as reasonable to except some other things,* (i.e., from being called Vices) *which they have a kindness for: For instance, some may perhaps except arbitrary Divorce, Polygamy, Concubinage, simple Fornication, or Marrying within Degrees thought forbidden.* Let them except these, and if you will, Drunkenness, Theft, and Murder too, from the name of *Vice;* nay, call them Vertues: Will they by their calling them so, be exempt from the Magistrate's Power of punishing them? Or can they claim an Impunity by what I have said? Will these Immoralities by the Names any one shall give, or forbear to give to them, become *Articles of Faith, or Ways of Worship?* Which is all, as I expresly say in the Words you here cite of mine, that I would have the Magistrates leave Men to their own Consciences in.

---

in the 1690s, reformers calling for a "moral revolution" to match the political revolution of 1688.

England's Penal Laws[39]

[Y]ou bemoan the decaying State of Religion amongst us at present, by reason of taking off the Penalties from Protestant Dissenters: And I beseech you what Penalties were they? Such whereby many have been ruined in their Fortunes; such whereby many have lost their Liberties, and some their Lives in Prisons; such as have sent some into Banishment, stripp'd of all they had. These were the *Penal Laws* by which the National Religion was establish'd in *England;* and these you call *moderate:*[40] for you say, *Where-ever true Religion or sound Christianity has been Nationally received and established by moderate Penal Laws;* and I hope you do not here exclude *England* from having its Religion so *established by Law,* which we so often hear of; or if to serve the present occasion, you should, would you also deny, that in the following Words you speak of the present Relaxation in *England?*[41] where after your *Appeal* to all observing People for the dismal Consequences, which you suppose to have every-where followed from such Relaxations, you add these pathetical Words, *Not to speak of what at this time our Eyes cannot but see, for fear of giving offence:* so heavy does the present *Relaxation* sit on your Mind; which since it is of *Penal Laws* you call *moderate,* I shall shew you what they are.

In the first Year of Q. *Elizabeth,* there was a Penalty of 1*s.*[42] a Sunday and Holiday[43] laid upon every one, who came not to the Common Prayer then established. This Penalty of 1*s.* a time not prevailing, as was desired,

39. *Third Letter,* chap. 4, pp. 125–26 (*Works,* pp. 286–88), citing Proast, *Third Letter,* p. 34.

40. "moderate": Proast insists that the penalties he advocates are moderate, seeking thereby to distance Protestantism from the cruelties of Catholic persecution.

41. Formally, the Toleration Act merely suspended the penalties for nonconformity, rather than repealing the laws for conformity *per se;* high churchmen could therefore construe it as a temporary relaxation. The act nowhere used the word *toleration.* Its formal title was "An Act for Exempting Their Majesties' Protestant Subjects, Dissenting from the Church of England, from the Penalties of Certain Laws."

42. *s:* shilling; *l:* pound; *d:* pence. There were twenty shillings to the pound and twelve pence to the shilling. The statutes cited in this paragraph are the Uniformity Act (1559) and two Acts to Retain the Queen's Subjects in Obedience (1581, 1593).

43. *Holiday:* holy day.

in the twenty third Year of her Reign was increased to 20*l.* a Month, and Imprisonment for Non-payment within three Months after Judgment given. In the twenty ninth Year of *Eliz.* To draw this yet closer, and make it more forcible, 'twas enacted, That whoever upon one Conviction did not continue to pay on the 20*l. per* Month, without any other Conviction or Proceeding against him till he submitted and conformed, should forfeit all his Goods, and two Thirds of his Land for his Life. But this being not yet thought sufficient, it was in the *35th* Year of that Queen completed, and the *moderate Penal Laws* upon which our *National Religion* was *established,* and whose *Relaxation* you cannot bear, but from thence date the *Decay of the very Spirit and Life of Christianity,* were brought to perfection: For then going to Conventicles, or a Month's Absence from Church, was to be punished with Imprisonment, till the Offender conformed: and if he conformed not within three Months, then he was to abjure the Realm, and forfeit all his Goods and Chattels for ever, and his Lands and Tenements during his Life: And if he would not abjure, or abjuring, did not depart the Realm within a time prefix'd, or returned again, he was to suffer Death as a Felon. And thus your *moderate Penal Laws* stood for the *established Religion,* till their Penalties were in respect of Protestant Dissenters, lately taken off.[44] And now let the Reader judg whether your pretence to moderate Punishments, or my Suspicion of what a Man of your Principles might have in store for Dissenters, have more of *Modesty* or *Conscience* in it; since you openly declare your regret for the taking away such an Establishment, as by the gradual increase of Penalties reached Mens Estates, Liberties and Lives; and which you must be presumed to allow and approve of, till you tell us plainly, where, according to your Measures,

44. The Elizabethan statutes were called laws against *recusancy* (refusal to attend church) and affected all such absentees, though initially the targets were Catholics. During the Restoration there was doubt about whether these laws applied to Protestant dissenters, but the judges insisted they did. The Whigs tried to pass a bill reversing this construal. Locke's recognition that the recusancy laws had been in force against Protestant dissenters, and hence that dissent was a capital offense, confirms (as he remarks a few lines later) that English persecution extended to "life" as well as "liberty and estate." Accordingly, religious coercion was among the sharpest forms of tyranny: see *Two Treatises of Government,* II, §§209, 221–22. Locke does not recite here the further (non-capital) penal laws enacted against Protestant dissenters in the 1660s.

those Penalties should; or, according to your Principles, they could have stopp'd.

Prejudice and Sincere Seeking [45]

You speak more than once of Mens being brought to lay aside their *Prejudices* to make them consider as they ought, and judg right of Matters in Religion; and I grant without doing so they cannot: But it is impossible for Force to make them do it, unless it could show them, which are Prejudices in their Minds, and distinguish them from the Truths there. Who is there almost that has not *Prejudices,* that he does not know to be so; and what can Force do in that Case? It can no more remove them, to make way for Truth, than it can remove one Truth to make way for another; or rather remove an establish'd Truth, or that which is look'd on as an unquestionable Principle (for so are often Mens Prejudices) to make way for a Truth not yet known, nor appearing to be one. 'Tis not every one knows, or can bring himself to *Des Cartes's* way of doubting, and strip his Thoughts of all Opinions, till he brings them to self-evident Principles, and then upon them builds all his future Tenents.[46]

Do not think all the World, who are not of your Church, abandon themselves to an utter Carelessness of their future State. You cannot but allow there are many Turks who sincerely seek Truth, to whom yet you could never bring *Evidence sufficient* to convince them of the Truth of the Christian Religion, whilst they looked on it as a Principle not to be question'd, that the Alcoran was of Divine Revelation. This possibly you will tell me is a *Prejudice,* and so it is; but yet if this Man shall tell you 'tis no more a *Prejudice* in him, than it is a *Prejudice* in any one amongst Christians, who having not examin'd it, lays it down as an unquestionable Principle of his Religion, that the Scripture is the Word of God; what

---

45. *Third Letter,* chap. 5, pp. 135–36 (*Works,* pp. 297–99), citing Proast, *Third Letter,* p. 42. Proast argues that people should be punished for obstinate dissent, "as long as [they] reject the true religion tendered them with sufficient evidence of the truth of it . . . because it is impossible for any man innocently to reject the true religion so tendered to him."

46. René Descartes, *Discourse on Method* (1637). *Tenents:* tenets.

will you answer to him? And yet it would shake a great many Christians in their Religion, if they should lay by that Prejudice, and suspend their Judgment of it, until they had made it out to themselves with *Evidence sufficient* to convince one who is not prejudiced in Favour of it; and it would require more Time, Books, Languages, Learning and Skill, than falls to most Mens share to establish them therein, if you will not allow them, in this so distinguishing and fundamental a Point, to rely on the Learning, Knowledg and Judgment of some *Persons* whom they have in *Reverence* or *Admiration*. This though you blame it as an ill way, yet you can allow in one of your own Religion, even to that Degree, that he may be ignorant of *the Grounds* of his Religion. And why then may you not allow it to a Turk, not as a good way, or as having led him to the Truth; but as a way, as fit for him, as for one of your Church to acquiesce in; and as fit to exempt him from your Force, as to exempt any one of your Church from it?

On the Test Act[47]

You go on, *And therefore if such Persons profane the Sacrament to keep their Places, or to obtain Licenses to sell Ale, this is an horrible Wickedness.*[48] I excuse them not. *But it is their own, and they alone must answer for it.* Yes, and those who threatned poor ignorant and *irreligious* Ale-sellers, whose Livelihood it was, to take away their Licences, if they did not conform and receive the Sacrament; may be thought perhaps to have something to answer for. You add, *But it is very unjust to impute it to those who make such Laws, and use such Force, or to say that they prostitute holy things, and drive Men to profane them.* Nor is it just to insinuate in your Answer, as if that

47. *Third Letter,* chap. 8, pp. 173–74 (*Works,* pp. 342–43), citing Proast, *Third Letter,* pp. 22–23.

48. The allusion to *places,* i.e., public offices, is to the Corporation and Test Acts (1661, 1673), by which officeholders were obliged to affirm their orthodoxy by annually receiving the Eucharist in the Church of England. Proast broaches what, in Queen Anne's reign, would become the Occasional Conformity Controversy, when Tories tried to legislate to end the practice by which dissenters took the sacrament merely to obtain office. As for ale-sellers, during the purges in the 1680s, all kinds of tradesmen were forced to take the sacrament in order to keep their businesses. In the *Second Letter* Locke referred to men "driven to take the Sacrament to keep their Places, or to obtain Licences to sell Ale" (p. 11; *Works,* p. 73).

had been said which was not. But if it be true that a poor ignorant loose irreligious Wretch should be threatned to be turn'd out of his Calling and Livelihood, if he would not take the Sacrament: May it not be said these holy things have been so low prostituted? And if this be not profaning them, pray tell me what is?

Penal Laws Do Not Make People Reconsider Their Religion[49]

To shew the Usefulness of Force, your way apply'd, I said, "Where the Law punish'd Dissenters without telling them it is to make them consider, they may through Ignorance and Oversight neglect to do It." Your Answer is, *But where the Law provides sufficient means of Instruction for all, as well as Punishment for Dissenters, it is so plain to all concern'd, that the Punishment is intended to make them consider, that* you *see no danger of Mens neglecting to do it, through Ignorance and Oversight.* I hope you mean by *consider,* so to *consider* as not only to imbrace in an outward Profession (for then all you say is but a poor Fallacy, for such a Considering amounts to no more but bare outward Conformity); but so to *consider, study* and *examine* Matters of Religion, as really to imbrace, what one is convinced to be the true, with Faith and Obedience. If it be so plain and easy to understand, that a Law, that speaks nothing of it, should yet be intended to make Men *consider,* search and *study,* to find out the *Truth that must save them;* I wish you had shew'd us this Plainness. For I confess many of all degrees,[50] that I have purposely asked about it, did not ever see, or so much as dream, that the Act of Uniformity, or against Conventicles,[51] or the Penalties in either of them, were ever intended to make Men seriously study Religion, and make it their business to find the *Truth which must save them;* but barely to make Men conform. But perhaps you have met

49. *Third Letter,* chap. 9, pp. 226–29, citing *Second Letter,* p. 15 (*Works,* pp. 403–6; 78), and Proast, *Third Letter,* p. 28.

50. *degrees:* statuses, classes.

51. The Uniformity Act (1662) and Conventicle Act (1670) were among the principal penal laws for conformity passed during the Restoration.

with Handicrafts-Men, and Country-Farmers, Maid-Servants, and Day-Labourers, who have quicker Understandings, and reason better about the Intention of the Law, for these as well as others are *concern'd*. If you have not, 'tis to be fear'd, your saying *it is so plain, that you see no danger of Mens neglecting to do it, through Ignorance or Oversight*, is more for its serving your purpose, than from any Experience you have, that it is so.

When you will enquire into this Matter, you will, I guess, find the People so ignorant amidst that great *Plainness* you speak of, that not one of twenty of any degree, amongst Conformists or Nonconformists, ever understood the Penalty of 12*d.* a Sunday, or any other of our Penal Laws against Nonconformity, to be intended to set Men upon studying the True Religion, and impartially examining what is necessary to Salvation. And if you would come to *Hudibras's* [52] Decision, I believe he would have a good Wager of it, who should give you a Guinea for each one who had thought so, and receive but a Shilling for every one who had not. Indeed you do not say, it is plain everywhere, but only *where the Law provides sufficient means of Instruction for all, as well as Punishment for Dissenters.* From whence, I think it will follow, that that contributes nothing to make it plain, or else that the Law has not provided sufficient means of Instruction in *England*, where so very few find this to be so plain. If by this *sufficient Provision of means of Instruction for all*; you mean, Persons maintain'd at the Publick Charge to preach, and officiate in the publick Exercise of the National Religion; I suppose you needed not this Restriction, there being few Places which have an establish'd National Religion, where there is not such *means of Instruction provided:* if you intend any other *means of Instruction*, I know none *the Law* has provided in *England* but the 39 Articles, [53] the Liturgy, and the Scripture, and how either of them by it self, or these altogether, with a National Clergy, make it plain, that the Penalties laid on Nonconformity, are intended to make Men *consider, study, and impartially examine Matters of Religion*, you would do well to shew. For Magistrates usually know (and therefore make their Laws accordingly) that the People seldom carry either their Interpretation or Practice

---

52. Samuel Butler's *Hudibras* (1663) was one of the Restoration's most popular burlesque poems.

53. The Thirty-Nine Articles constitute the creed of the Church of England.

beyond what the express Letter of the Law requires of them. You would do well also to shew, that a sufficient provision of means of Instruction, cannot but be understood to require an effectual Use of them, which the Law that makes that provision says nothing of. But on the contrary, contents it self with something very short of it: For Conformity or Coming to Church, is at least as far from *considering, studying* and *impartially examining* Matters of Religion, so as to *imbrace the Truth upon Conviction and with an obedient Heart,* as being present at a Discourse concerning Mathematicks, and studying Mathematicks, so as to become a knowing Mathematician, are different one from the other.

People generally think they have done their Duties abundantly, if they have been at Church, whether they mind[54] any thing done there or no: this they call serving of God, as if it were their whole Duty; so backward are they to understand more, though it be plain the Law of God expresly requires more. But that they have fully satisfied the Law of the Land, no body doubts; nor is it easy to answer what was replied to me on this occasion, *viz.* If the Magistrate *intended* any thing more in those Laws but Conformity, would he not have said it? To which let me add, if the Magistrate *intended Conformity as the fruit of Conviction,* would he not have taken some care to have them instructed before they conformed, and examin'd when they did? but 'tis *presumable* their Ignorance, Corruption and Lusts, all drop off in the Church-porch, and that they become perfectly good Christians as soon as they have taken their Seats in the Church.

The Charge of Scepticism and Epicureanism[55]

Epicurism and Atheism, say you, are found *constantly to spread themselves upon the Relaxation of moderate Penal Laws.* We will suppose your History to be full of Instances of such *Relaxations,* which you will in good time communicate to the World, that wants this Assistance from your

54. *mind:* notice.

55. *Third Letter,* chap. 9, pp. 236–38 (*Works,* pp. 414–16), citing Proast, *Third Letter,* pp. 34–35, 47. *Epicureanism:* libertinism (from the Greek philosopher Epicurus, who advocated a hedonistic ethics).

Observation. But were this to be justified out of History, yet would it not be any Argument against Toleration; unless your History can furnish you with a new sort of Religion founded in Atheism. However, you do well to charge the spreading of Atheism upon Toleration in Matters of Religion, as an Argument against those who deny *Atheism* (which takes away all Religion) to have any Right to Toleration at all. But perhaps (as is usual for those who think all the World should see with their Eyes, and receive their Systems for unquestionable Verities) Zeal for your own way makes you call all *Atheism,* that agrees not with it. That which makes me doubt of this, are these following words; *Not to speak of what at this time our Eyes cannot but see for fear of giving Offence: Though I hope it will be none to any that have a just Concern for Truth and Piety, to take notice of the Books and Pamphlets which now fly so thick about this Kingdom, manifestly tending to the multiplying of Sects and Divisions, and even to the promoting of* Scepticism *in Religion among us. In which number,* you say, you *shall not much need* my *pardon, if* you *reckon the First and Second Letter concerning Toleration.* Wherein, by a broad Insinuation, you impute the spreading of *Atheism* among us, to the late *Relaxation* made in favour of Protestant Dissenters: and yet all that you take notice of as a proof of this, is, *the Books and Pamphlets which now fly so thick about this Kingdom, manifestly tending to the multiplying of Sects and Divisions, and even to the promoting of Scepticism in Religion amongst us;* and for instance, you name *the First and Second Letter concerning Toleration.* If one may guess at the others by these, The *Atheism and Scepticism* you accuse them of will have but little more in it, than an Opposition to your Hypothesis; on which, the whole business of Religion must so turn, that whatever agrees not with your System, must presently, by Interpretation, be concluded to *tend* to the promoting of *Atheism* or *Scepticism* in Religion. For I challenge you to shew in either of those two Letters you mention, one word tending to *Epicurism, Atheism* or *Scepticism* in Religion.

But, Sir, against the next time you are to give an account of *Books and Pamphlets tending to the promoting Scepticism in Religion amongst us,* I shall mind you of the *third Letter concerning Toleration,* to be added to the Catalogue, which asserting and building upon this, that *True Religion may be known by those who profess it, to be the only True Religion,* does not a little towards betraying the Christian Religion to Scepticks. For what greater advantage can be given them, than to teach, that one may know the True Religion? thereby putting into their hands a Right to demand it to be demonstrated to them, that the Christian Religion is true, and bringing on the Professors of it a necessity of doing it. I have heard it complain'd of as one great Artifice of Scepticks, to require Demonstrations where they neither could be had, nor were necessary. But if the True Religion may be known to Men to be so, a Sceptick may require, and you cannot blame him if he does not receive your Religion, upon the strongest probable Arguments, without Demonstration.

And if one should demand of you Demonstration of the Truths of your Religion, which I beseech you, would you do, either renounce your Assertion, that it may be known to be true, or else undertake to demonstrate it to him?

And as for *the decay of the very Life and Spirit of Christianity,* and the *spreading of Epicurism* amongst us: I ask, what can more tend to the promoting of them than this Doctrine, which is to be found in the same Letter, *viz.* That it is *presumable* that those who *conform, do it upon Reason and Conviction?* When you can instance in any thing so much tending to the promoting of *Scepticism in Religion* and *Epicurism,* in *the first or second Letter concerning Toleration,* we shall have reason to think you have some ground for what you say.

As to *Epicurism,* the spreading whereof you likewise impute to the *Relaxation* of your moderate Penal Laws; That so far as it is distinct from *Atheism,* I think regards Mens Lives more than their Religions, *i.e.,* speculative Opinions in Religion and Ways of Worship, which is that we mean by Religion, as concern'd in Toleration. And for the Toleration of corrupt Manners, and the Debaucheries of Life, neither our Author, nor I do plead for it; but say it is properly the Magistrate's Business, by Punishments, to restrain and suppress them. I do not therefore blame your Zeal against *Atheism* and *Epicurism;* but you discover a great Zeal against something else, in charging them on Toleration, when it is in the Magistrate's power to restrain and suppress them by more effectual Laws than those for Church-Conformity. For there are those who will tell you that an outward Profession of the National Religion, even where it is the True Religion, is no more opposite to, or inconsistent with *Atheism* or *Epicurism,* than the owning of another Religion, especially any Christian Profession, that differs from it. And therefore you, in vain, impute *Atheism* or *Epicurism* to the Relaxation of Penal Laws, that require no more than an outward Conformity to the National Church.

The Pastoral Care of Corrupt Conformists[56]

The Backwardness and Lusts that hinder an *impartial Examination,* as you describe it, is general. The Corruption of Nature which hinders a *real imbracing* the true Religion, that also you tell us here, is universal. I ask a Remedy for these in your way. You say *the Law* for Conformity *is general, excepts none.* Very likely, *none* that do not conform; but punishes *none* who conforming, do neither *impartially examine* nor *really imbrace* the true Religion. From whence I conclude, there is no corruption of Nature in those, who are brought up or join in outward Communion with the Church of *England.* But *as to Ignorance, Negligence, and Prejudice,* you say you *desire* me, *or any Man else, to tell what better course can be taken to cure them, than that which* you *have mentioned.* If your Church can find no better way to cure Ignorance and Prejudice, and the Negligence, that is in Men, to examine Matters of Religion and heartily Imbrace the true, than what is impracticable upon Conformists, then of all others, Conformists are in the most deplorable Estate. But, as I remember, you have been told of a better way, which is, the discoursing with Men seriously and friendly about Matters in Religion, by those whose Profession is the Care of Souls; examining what they do not understand, and where, either through Laziness, Prejudice or Difficulty, they do stick; and applying to

56. *Third Letter,* chap. 9, pp. 252–53 (*Works,* pp. 432–34), citing Proast, *Argument,* pp. 6–12, and *Third Letter,* pp. 6–8. Locke continues to stress that conformists are as much in need as nonconformists of engaging in proper consideration of their beliefs, yet the penal laws did not touch them. He advocates a vigorous regime of pastoral catechesis, beyond mere pulpit hectoring and coercive laws.

their several Diseases proper Cures, which it is as impossible to do by a general Harangue, once or twice a Week out of the Pulpit, as to fit all Mens Feet with one Shoe, or cure all Mens Ails with one, though very wholsome, Diet-drink. To be thus *instant in season, and out of season,*[57] some Men have thought a better way of Cure, than a Desire, only to have Men driven by the Whip, either in your, or the Magistrate's hands, into the Sheepfold: where when they are once, whether they understand or no, their Ministers Sermons; whether they are, or can be better for them or no; whether they are ignorant and hypocritical Conformists, and in that way like[58] to remain so, rather than to become knowing and sincere Converts, some Bishops have thought it not sufficiently enquired;[59] but this no body is to mention, for whoever does so, *makes himself an occasion to shew his good Will to the Clergy.*

This had not been said by me here, now I see how apt you are to be put out of temper with any thing of this kind (though it be in every serious Man's Mouth) had not you desired me to shew you a better way than Force, your way apply'd. And to use your way of Arguing, since bare Preaching, as now us'd, 'tis plain, will not do, there is no other means left but this to deal with the corrupt Nature of Conformists; for Miracles are now ceased, and Penalties they are free from; therefore, by your way of concluding, *no other being left,* this of Visiting at home, conferring and instructing, and admonishing Men there, and the like Means, proposed by the Reverend Author of the *Pastoral Care,*[60] is necessary; and Men, whose business is the Care of Souls, are *obliged* to use it.

---

57. 2 Timothy 4:2.

58. *like:* likely.

59. Locke pulls rank: now, after the Revolution, there were latitudinarian bishops who accepted the Toleration Act and developed new pastoral strategies for the Anglican Church.

60. Gilbert Burnet, *A Discourse of the Pastoral Care* (1692). Burnet was bishop of Salisbury. Locke several times recommends his treatise as a pastoral handbook for postpenal times. He accuses Proast of advocating coercion by the state as a substitute for remedying pastoral failure in the clergy.

The Reformation of Manners Once More[61]

You give us in this and the foregoing Pages, the Grounds of your *Fear*, It is the *Corruption of humane Nature* which opposes the True Religion. You express it thus, *Idolatry prevailing against it* (the True Religion) *not by its own Light and Strength, for it could have nothing of either, but merely by the Advantage it had in the Corruption and Pravity of humane Nature, finding out to it self more agreeable Religions than the true. For,* say you, *whatever Hardships some False Religions may impose, it will however, always be easier to carnal and worldly-minded Men, to give even their First-born for their Transgressions, than to mortify their Lusts from which they spring, which no Religion but the True, requires of them.* I wonder, saying this, how you could any longer mistake the Magistrate's Duty, in reference to Religion, and not see wherein *Force* truly can and ought to be serviceable to it. What you have said, plainly shews you, that the Assistance the Magistrate's Authority can give to the True Religion, is in the subduing of Lusts, and its being directed against Pride, Injustice, Rapine, Luxury and Debauchery, and those Immoralities which come properly under his Cognisance, and may be corrected by Punishments; and not by the imposing of *Creeds and Ceremonies,* as you tell us. *Sound* and *Decent,* you might have left out, whereof their Fancies, and not the Law of God, will always be Judg and consequently the Rule.

The Case between the true and false Religions, as you have stated it, in short, stands thus, *True Religion has always Light and Strength of its own sufficient to prevail with all that seriously consider it, and without prejudice. Idolatry* or False Religions *have nothing of Light or Strength to prevail with.* Why then does not the true Religion prevail against the false, having so much the advantage in Light and Strength? The Counter-ballance of *Prejudice* hinders. And wherein does that consist? The Drunkard must part with his Cups and Companions, and the Voluptuous Man with his Pleasures. The Proud and Vain must lay by all Excess in Apparel, Furniture and Attendance; and Money, the support of all these, must be got

---

61. *Third Letter,* chap. 10, pp. 282–83 (*Works,* pp. 468–69), citing Proast, *Third Letter,* pp. 7, 13.

only by the ways of Justice, Honesty, and fair Industry. And every one must live peaceably, uprightly, and friendly with his Neighbour. Here then the Magistrate's assistance is wanting: Here they may and ought to interpose their Power, and by Severities, against Drunkenness, Lasciviousness, and all sorts of Debauchery; by a steady and unrelaxed Punishment of all the ways of Fraud and Injustice; and by their Administration, Countenance, and Example, reduce the Irregularities of Mens Manners into order, and bring Sobriety, Peaceableness, Industry and Honesty into Fashion. This is their proper Business every-where; and for this they have a Commission from God, both by the Light of Nature and Revelation; and by this, removing the great Counterpoise, which lies in strictness of Life, and is so strong a Bias, with the greatest part, against the true Religion, they would cast the Ballance on that side. For if Men were forced by the Magistrate to live sober, honest and strict Lives, whatever their Religion were, would not the advantage be on the side of Truth, when the gratifying of their Lusts were not to be obtained by forsaking her?

The History of Idolatry[62]

[Y]ou may meet with Men (whose reading yet I will not compare with yours) who think they have found in History, that Princes and those in Power, first corrupted the True Religion, by setting up the Images and Symbols of their Predecessors in their Temples; which, by their Influence, and the ready Obedience of the Priests they appointed, were in succession of Time, propos'd to the People as Objects of their Worship. Thus they think they *find in History that* Isis, Queen of *Egypt,* with her Counsellor *Thoth,* instituted the Funeral-Rites of King *Osiris,* by the Honour done to the sacred Ox. They think they *find* also *in History,* that the same *Thoth,* who was also King of *Egypt* in his turn, invented the Figures of the first *Egyptian* Gods, *Saturn, Dagon, Jupiter Hammon,* and the rest: that is, the Figures of their Statues or Idols; and that he instituted the Worship and Sacrifices of these Gods: And his Institutions were so well assisted

62. *Third Letter,* chap. 10, pp. 288–92 (*Works,* pp. 475–80), citing Proast, *Third Letter,* p. 6.

by those in Authority, and observed by the Priests they set up, that the Worship of those Gods soon became the Religion of that, and a Pattern to other Nations. And here we may perhaps, with good reason, place the rise and original of Idolatry after the Flood, there being nothing of this kind more ancient. So ready was the Ambition, Vanity, or Superstition of Princes, to introduce their Predecessors into the Divine Worship of the People, to secure to themselves the greater Veneration from their Subjects, as descended from the Gods; or to erect such a Worship, and such a Priesthood, as might awe the blinded and seduced People into that Obedience they desired. Thus *Ham*, by the Authority of his Successors, the Rulers of *Egypt*, is first brought for the Honour of his Name and Memory into their Temples, and never left, till he is erected into a God, and made *Jupiter Hammon*, &c. which Fashion took afterwards with the Princes of other Countries.

Was not the great God of the Eastern Nations, *Baal*, or *Jupiter Belus*, one of the first Kings of *Assyria?* And which, I pray, is the more likely, that Courts, by their Instruments the Priests, should thus advance the Honour of Kings amongst the People for the ends of Ambition and Power; or the People find out these refined Ways of doing it, and introduce them into Courts for the enslaving themselves? What Idolatry does your History tell you of among the Greeks, before *Phoroneus* and *Danaus*, Kings of the *Argives*, and *Cecrops* and *Theseus* Kings of *Attica*, and *Cadmus* King of *Thebes*, introduced it? An Art of Rule 'tis probable they borrowed from the *Egyptians*. So that if you had not vouch'd the Silence of History, without consulting it, you would possibly have found, that in the first Ages, Princes, by their Influence and Aid, by the Help and Artifice of the Priests they imploy'd, their Fables of their Gods, their Mysteries and Oracles, and all the Assistance they could give it by their Authority, did so much against the Truth, before direct Force was grown into fashion, and appear'd openly, that there would be little reason of putting the Guard and Propagation of the True Religion, into their hands now, and arming them with Force to promote it.

That this was the Original of Idolatry in the World, and that it was borrowed by other Magistrates from the *Egyptians*, is farther evident in that this Worship was setled in *Egypt*, and grown the National Religion there, before the Gods of *Greece,* and several other Idolatrous Countries, were born. For though they took their Pattern of Deifying their deceased Princes, from the *Egyptians,* and kept, as near as they could, to the Number and Genealogies of the *Egyptian* Gods; yet they took the Names still of some great Men of their own, which they accommodated to the Mythology of the *Egyptians.* Thus, by the assistance of the *Powers in being,* Idolatry entred into the World after the Flood. Whereof, if there were not so clear Footsteps in History, why yet should you not imagine Princes and Magistrates, ingaged in False Religions, as ready to imploy their Power for the maintaining and promoting their False Religions in those days, as we find them now? And therefore, what you say in the next Words, of the entrance of Idolatry *into the World, and the Entertainment* it found *in it,* will not pass for so very evident without Proof, though you tell us never so confidently, that you *suppose, besides the Corruption of humane Nature, there can no other Cause be assigned of it, or none more probable than this, That the Powers then in being, did not what they might and ought to have done* (*i.e.* if you mean it to your purpose, use Force your way, to make Men *consider,* or to *impose Creeds and Ways of Worship*) *towards the preventing or checking that horrible Apostacy.*

I grant that the entrance and growth of Idolatry, might be owing to the Negligence of the *Powers in being,* in that they *did not do what they might and ought to have done,* in using their Authority to suppress the Enormities of Mens Manners, and correct the Irregularity of their Lives. But this was not all the Assistance they gave to that *horrible Apostacy:* They were, as far as History gives us any light, the Promoters of it, and Leaders in it, and did what they ought not to have done, by setting up False Religions, and using their Authority to establish them, to serve their corrupt and ambitious Designs.

National Religions, establish'd by Authority, and inforced by the Powers in being, we hear of every where, as far back as we have any account of the rise and growth of the Religions of the World. Shew me any place, within those few Generations, wherein you say the Apostacy prevail'd after the Flood, where the Magistrates, being of the True Religion, the Subjects by the Liberty of a Toleration, were led into False Religions, and then you will produce something against Liberty of Conscience. But to talk of that great Apostacy, as wholly owing to Toleration, when you cannot produce one Instance of Toleration then in the World, is to say what you please.

That the majority of Mankind were then, and always have been, by the *Corruption and Pravity of humane Nature,* led away, and kept from imbracing the True Religion, is past doubt. But whether this be owing to Toleration, in Matters of Religion, is the Question. *David* describes an horrible Corruption and Apostacy in his time, so as to say, *There is none that doth good, no not one;*[63] and yet I do not think you will say, a Toleration, then in that Kingdom, was the cause of it. If the greatest part cannot be ill without a Toleration, I am afraid you must be fain to find out a Toleration in every Country, and in all Ages of the World. For I think it is true, of all Times and Places, that the *Broad way* that leadeth to Destruction, has had most Travellers. I would be glad to know where it was that Force, your way apply'd, *i.e.,* with Punishments only upon Nonconformists, ever prevail'd to bring the greater number into the *Narrow-way, that leads unto Life;* which our Saviour tells us, there are *few* that *find.*[64]

The *Corruption of Humane Nature,* you say, opposes the True Religion. I grant it you. There was also, say you, an *horrible Apostacy* after the Flood; let this also be granted you: and yet from hence it will not follow, that the True Religion cannot subsist and prevail in the World without the assistance of Force, your way apply'd, till you have shewn, that the False Religions, which were the Inventions of Men, grew up under Toleration, and not by the Encouragement and Assistance of the Powers in being.

How near soever therefore, the *True Religion* was to be *extinguish'd within a few Generations* after the Flood, (which whether more in danger then, than in most Ages since, is more than you can shew). This will be still the Question, Whether the Liberty of Toleration, or the Authority of the Powers in being, contributed most to it? And whether *there can be no other, no more probable Cause* assigned, than the want of Force, your way apply'd, I shall leave the Reader to judg. This I am sure, whatever Causes any one else shall *assign,* are as well proved as yours, if they offer them only as their Conjectures.

63. Psalm 14:3.
64. Matthew 7:13–14.

Not but that I think Men could run into false and foolish Ways of Worship, without the Instigation or Assistance of humane Authority; but the Powers of the World, as far as we have any History, having been always forward enough (*True Religion* as little serving Princes as private Mens *Lusts*) to take up Wrong Religions, and as forward to imploy their Authority to impose the Religion, good or bad, which they had once taken up, I can see no reason why the not using of Force, by the Princes of the World, should be assigned as the sole, or so much as the most *probable Cause* of propagating the False Religions of the World, or extirpating the True; or how you can so positively say, Idolatry *prevail'd without any assistance from the Powers in being.*

Since therefore History leads us to the Magistrates, as the Authors and Promoters of Idolatry in the World, to which we may suppose their not suppressing of Vice, joined as another Cause of the spreading of False Religions, you were best consider, whether you can still *suppose there can no other Cause be assigned,* of the prevailing of the Worship of False Gods, but the Magistrate's not interposing his Authority in matters of Religion. For that that cannot with any probability at all be assigned as any Cause, I shall give you this further Reason. You impute the prevailing of False Religions, to *the Corruption and Pravity of Humane Nature, left to it self, unbridled by Authority.* Now, if Force, your way applied, does not at all *bridle the Corruption and Pravity of Humane Nature,* the Magistrate's not so interposing his Authority, cannot be *assigned* as any *Cause* at all of that Apostacy. So that let that Apostacy have what rise, and spread as far as you please, it will not make one jot for Force, your way applied, or shew that that can receive any assistance your way from Authority. For your use of Authority and Force, being only to bring Men to an outward Conformity to the National Religion, it leaves the *Corruption and Pravity of Humane Nature,* as *unbridled* as before.

Writing for Party[65]

The *Party* you *write* for is *God,* you say. But if all you have said, aims or amounts to nothing more than that the Church of *England,* as now establish'd by Law, in its Doctrines, Ceremonies and Discipline, should be supported by the Power of the Magistrate, and Men by Force be driven into it; I fear the World will think you have very narrow Thoughts of *God;* or that that is not the *Party* you write for. 'Tis true, you all along speak of bringing Men *to the True Religion.* But to evidence to you, that by *the only True Religion,* you mean only that of the Church of *England;* I tell you, that upon your Principles, you cannot name any other Church now in the World, (and I again demand of you to do it) for the promoting whereof, or punishing Dissenters from it, the Magistrate has the same Right to use Force, as you pretend he has here in *England.* Till you therefore name some such other True Church and True Religion, besides that of *England,* your saying that *God* is the *Party* you *write for,* will rather shew that you make bold with his Name, than that you do not write for another *Party.*

You say too, you write not *for any Party, but the Souls of Men.* You write indeed, and contend earnestly, that Men should be brought into an outward Conformity to the Church of *England.* But that they imbrace that Profession upon Reason and Conviction, you are content to have it *presumable,* without any farther Enquiry or Examination. And those who are once in the outward Communion of the National Church, however ignorant or irreligious they are, you leave there unassisted by your only *competent Means, Force;* without which, you tell us, the *True Religion, by its own Light and Strength, is not able to prevail* against Mens Lusts and the Corruption of Nature, so as to be consider'd as it ought, and heartily imbraced. And this drop'd not from your Pen by chance: But you professedly make Excuses for those of the National Religion who are ignorant of the *Grounds* of it; And give us Reasons why Force cannot be used to those who outwardly conform, to make them consider so as sincerely to imbrace, believe and obey, the Truth that must save them. But the Rev-

---

65. *Third Letter,* chap. 10, pp. 347–49 (*Works,* pp. 542–45), citing Proast, *Third Letter,* p. 79.

erend Author of the *Pastoral Care*[66] tells you, *PARTY is the true Name of making Converts, except they become at the same time good Men.*

If the use of Force be necessary for the Salvation of Souls; and Mens Souls be the *Party* you write for; you will be suspected to have betrayed your *Party,* if your Method and necessary Means of Salvation reach no farther than to bring Men to outward Conformity, though to the True Church; and after that abandons them to their *Lusts* and *depraved Natures,* destitute of the help of Force, your *necessary* and *competent Means* of Salvation.

This way of managing the Matter, whatever you intend, seems rather, in the Fitness of it, to be for another *Party.* But since you assure us you write for nothing but *God and Mens Souls,* it can only be said you had a good Intention, but ill Luck; since your Scheme, put into the Language of the Country, will fit any National Church and Clergy in the World, that can but suppose it self the True; and that I presume none of them will fail to do.

You were more than ordinary reserv'd and gracious when you tell me, That *what Party I write for,* you *will not undertake to say.* But having told me, that my Letter tends *to the promoting of Scepticism in Religion;* you thought ('tis like) that was sufficient to show the *Party* I write for; and so you might safely end your Letter with words that looked like civil. But that you may another time be a little better informed what *Party* I write for, I will tell you. They are those who in every Nation *fear God, work Righteousness, and are accepted with him;*[67] and not those who in every nation are zealous for Humane Constitutions, cry up nothing so much as outward Conformity to the National Religion; and are accepted by those who are the Promoters of it. Those that I write for are those, who, according to the Light of their own Consciences, are every-where in earnest in Matters of their own Salvation, without any desire to impose on others; A *Party* so seldom favour'd by any of the Powers or Sects of the World; A *Party* that has so few Preferments to bestow; so few Benefices

66. Burnet, *Pastoral Care,* p. 201.
67. Acts 10:35.

to reward the Endeavours of any one who appears for it, that I conclude I shall easily be believ'd when I say, that neither Hopes of Preferment, nor a Design to recommend my self to those I live amongst, has biassed my Understanding, or misled me in my Undertaking. So much Truth as serves the turn of any particular Church, and can be accommodated to the narrow Interest of some Human Constitution, is indeed often received with applause, and the Publisher[68] finds his account in it. But I think I may say, Truth (in its full Latitude, of those generous Principles of the Gospel, which so much recommend and inculcate universal Charity, and a Freedom from the Inventions and Impositions of Men in the things of God), has so seldom had a fair and favourable Hearing any where, that he must be very ignorant of the History and Nature of Man, however digni-fied and distinguish'd, who proposes to himself any secular Advantage by writing for her.

68. *Publisher:* disseminator.

An Essay
Concerning
Toleration

In the question of liberty of conscience, which has for some years been so much bandied among us, one thing that hath chiefly perplexed the question, kept up the dispute, and increased the animosity, hath been (I conceive) this, that both parties have with equal zeal and mistake too much enlarged their pretensions, whilst one side preach up absolute obedience, and the other claim universal liberty in matters of conscience, without assigning what those things are which have a title to liberty or showing the boundaries of imposition and obedience.

To clear the way to this I shall lay down this for a foundation, which I think will not be questioned or denied. I shall assert:

That the whole trust,[1] power and authority of the magistrate is vested

---

1. Locke's later theme of government as fiduciary, a trust, is already visible in this *Essay,* composed in 1667. See *Two Treatises of Government,* II, §§149, 156.

in him for no other purpose, but to be made use of for the good, preservation, and peace of men in that society over which he is set, and therefore that this alone is and ought to be the standard and measure according to which he ought to square and proportion his laws, model and frame his government. For if men could live peaceably and quietly together without uniting under certain laws and growing[2] into a commonwealth, there would be no need at all of magistrates or polities, which were only made to preserve men in this world from the fraud and violence of one another, so that what was the end of erecting of government, ought alone to be the measure of its proceeding.

There are some that tell us that monarchy is *jure divino.*[3] I will not now dispute this opinion but only mind[4] the assertors of it, that if they mean by this (as certainly they must), that the sole supreme arbitrary power and disposal of all things is and ought to be by divine right in a single person, 'tis to be suspected they have forgot what country they were born in, under what laws they live and certainly cannot but be obliged to declare Magna Charta to be downright heresy. If they mean by monarchy *jure divino,* not an absolute but limited monarchy (which I think is an absurdity, if not a contradiction) they ought to show us his charter from heaven, and let us see where God hath given the magistrate a power to do anything but barely in order to the preservation of his subjects in this life, or else leave us at liberty to believe it as we please, since nobody is bound, or can allow anyone's pretensions to a power (which he himself confesses limited), farther than he shows his title.

There are others who affirm that all the power and authority the magistrate hath is derived from the grant and consent of the people, and to those I say it cannot be supposed the people should give any one or more of their fellow men an authority over them for any other purpose than their own preservation, or extend the limits of their jurisdiction beyond the limits of this life.

This being premised that the magistrate ought to do or meddle with nothing but barely in order to securing the civil peace and proprieties[5] of

---

2. *growing:* in MS Locke c. 28, Locke amends this to "entering."
3. *jure divino:* by divine right.
4. *mind:* remind.
5. *proprieties:* properties. This usage occurs several times below.

his subjects, let us next consider the opinions and actions of men, which in reference to toleration divide themselves into three sorts.

First, are all such opinions and actions as in themselves concern not government or society at all, and such are all purely speculative opinions, and divine worship.

Second, are such as in their own nature are neither good nor bad but yet concern society and men's conversations one with another, and these are all practical opinions and actions in matters of indifference.[6]

Third,[7] are such too as concern society, but are also good or bad in their own nature and these are moral virtues and vices.

I. I say that the first sort only, *viz.*, speculative opinions and divine worship are those things alone which have an absolute and universal right to toleration. First, purely speculative opinions as the belief of the trinity, purgatory, transubstantiation, antipodes,[8] Christ's personal reign on earth, etc., and that in these every man has his unlimited freedom, appears. Because bare speculations give no bias to my conversation with men, nor having any influence on my actions as I am a member of any society, but being such as would be still the same with all the consequences of them though there were no other person besides myself in the world, cannot by any means either disturb the state or inconvenience my neighbour and so come not within the magistrate's cognizance. Besides, no man can give another man power (and it would be to no purpose if God should) over that over which he has no power himself. Now, that a man cannot command his own understanding, or positively determine today what opinion he will be of tomorrow, is evident from experience, and the nature of the understanding, which can no more apprehend things otherwise than they appear to it, than the eye see other colours than it doth in the rainbow whether those colours be really there or no.[9]

The other thing that has just claim to an unlimited toleration is the

6. *matters of indifference* or *things indifferent:* see note 75, p. 33.

7. The sections I, II, and III below address each of these three points in turn.

8. "antipodes": Locke may have in mind Copernican cosmology, for which Galileo was condemned by the Inquisition; but he may be thinking of the medieval heresy that the sphericity of the earth implied the existence of peoples whose origins were independent of Adam.

9. At this point, MS Locke c. 28 contains Addition A: see below.

place, time and manner of worshiping my God. Because this is a thing wholly between God and me, and of an eternal concernment above the reach and extent of polities and government, which are but for my well-being in this world. For the magistrate is but an umpire between man and man.[10] He can right me against my neighbour but cannot defend me against my God. Whatever evil I suffer by obeying him in other things he can make me amends in this world, but if he force me to a wrong religion, he can make me no reparation in the other world. To which let me add that even in things of this world over which the magistrate has an authority, he never does, and it would be unjustice if he should, any farther than it concerns the good of the public, enjoin men the care of their private civil concernments, or force them to a prosecution of their own private interests, but only protects them from being invaded and injured in them by others, (which is a perfect toleration). And therefore we may well suppose he hath nothing at all to do with my private interest in another world, and that he ought not to prescribe me the way or require my diligence in the prosecution of that good which is of a far higher concernment to me than anything within his power, having no more certain or more infallible knowledge of the way to attain it than I myself, where we are both equally inquirers, both equally subjects, and wherein he can give me no security, that I shall not, nor make me any recompense if I do, miscarry. Can it be reasonable that he that cannot compel me to buy a house should force me his way to venture the purchase of heaven, that he that cannot in justice prescribe me rules of preserving my health, should enjoin me methods of saving my soul, he that cannot choose a wife for me should choose a religion. But if God (which is the point in question) would have men forced to heaven, it must not be by the outward violence of the magistrate on men's bodies, but the inward constraints of his own spirit on their minds, which are not to be wrought on by any human compulsion, the way to salvation not being any forced exterior performance, but the voluntary and secret choice of the mind; and it cannot be supposed that God would make use of any means, which could not reach, but would rather cross, the attainment of the end. Nor can it be

10. Compare *Two Treatises of Government*, II, §87.

thought that men should give the magistrate a power to choose for them their way to salvation which is too great to give away, if not impossible to part with, since whatever the magistrate enjoined in the worship of God, men must in this necessarily follow what they themselves thought best, since no consideration could be sufficient to force a man from or to that, which he was fully persuaded, was the way to infinite happiness or infinite misery.[11] Religious worship being that homage which I pay to that God I adore in a way I judge acceptable to him, and so being an action or commerce passing only between God and myself, hath in its own nature no reference at all to my governor or to my neighbour, and so necessarily produces no action which disturbs the community. For kneeling or sitting at the sacrament[12] can in itself tend no more to the disturbance of the government, or injury of my neighbour, than sitting or standing at my own table; wearing a cope or surplice[13] in the church, can no more alarm or threaten the peace of the state, than wearing a cloak or coat in the market; being rebaptised no more make a tempest in the commonwealth than it doth in the river, nor than barely washing myself would do in either. If I observe the Friday with the Mahometan, or the Saturday with the Jew, or the Sunday with the Christian, whether I pray with or without a form, whether I worship God in the various and pompous ceremonies of the papists, or in the plainer way of the Calvinists, I see nothing in any of these, if they be done sincerely and out of conscience, that can of itself make me either the worse subject to my prince, or worse neighbour to my fellow subject. Unless it be, that I will out of pride, or overweeningness of my own opinion, and a secret conceit of my own infallibility, taking to myself something of a godlike power, force and compel others to be of my mind, or censure and malign them if they be not. This indeed often

11. A second version in the Huntington MS adds a sentence here: "Nor do I find that the doctrine of Christianity does invest the magistrate with any new power or give him any more jurisdictions in matters of religion, than he had before from the nature of government in general, or the constitution of that society he is entrusted with."

12. Puritan dissenters objected to the church's requirement that worshippers kneel to receive the Eucharist, as they thought it showed a quasi-popish veneration.

13. Puritans disliked the church's white surplice as being popish and preferred the black "Geneva gown."

happens, but 'tis not the fault of the worship, but the men. And is not the consequence of this or that form of devotion, but the product of depraved ambitious human nature, which successively makes use of all sorts of religion, as Ahab did of keeping a fast: which was not the cause, but means and artifice to take away Naboth's vineyard.[14] Which miscarriages of some professors[15] do no more discredit any religion (for the same happens in all) than Ahab's rapine does fasting.

From what is premised I think will follow:[16]

That in speculations and religious worship every man hath a perfect uncontrolled liberty, which he may freely use without or contrary to the magistrate's command, without any guilt or sin at all: provided always that it be all done sincerely and out of conscience to God according to the best of his knowledge and persuasion. But if there be any ambition, pride, revenge, faction, or any such alloy that mixes itself with what he calls conscience, so much there is of guilt, and so much he shall answer for at the day of judgement.[17]

II. I say all practical principles or opinions by which men think themselves obliged to regulate their actions with one another. As that men may breed their children or dispose of their estates as they please, that men may work or rest when they think fit, that polygamy and divorce are lawful or unlawful, etc.[18] These opinions and the actions flowing from them,

14. 1 Kings 21:1–16. Although Ahab piously fasted, he and his wife Jezebel evilly conspired to have Naboth killed so that they could seize his vineyard.

15. *professors:* those who proclaim or follow a religion.

16. At this point, MS Locke c. 28 contains Addition B: see below. However, the addition might more plausibly precede this sentence.

17. A second version in the Huntington MS adds a sentence here: "Query. Whether it will not hence also follow, that any man or party keeping within the former rules may not lawfully by force [...] defend themselves against the magistrate that would by force impose anything on them in opinion or worship, where neither of them directly tend to the disturbance of his government since in this he would then invade them in that over which he has no power, nor do they owe him any more subjection than they do, a foreign prince, whose subjects they are not." See note 21, p. 133.

18. It is striking that Locke considers polygamy and divorce to be "things indifferent." He takes the same view elsewhere: e.g., *Two Treatises of Government*, II, §65, 81–82.

with all other things indifferent, have a title also to toleration; but yet only so far as they do not tend to the disturbance of the state, or do not cause greater inconveniences than advantages to the community. For all these opinions, except such of them, as are apparently destructive to human society, being things either of indifference or doubt, and neither the magistrate or subject being on either side infallible, he ought no farther to consider them, than as the making laws and interposing his authority in such opinions may conduce to the welfare and safety of his people. But yet no such opinion has any right to toleration, on this ground, that it is a matter of conscience, and some men are persuaded that it is either a sin or a duty. Because the conscience, or persuasion of the subject, cannot possibly be a measure by which the magistrate can, or ought to frame his laws, which ought to be suited to the good of all his subjects, not the persuasions of a part: which often happening to be contrary one to another must produce contrary laws. And there being nothing so indifferent which the consciences of some or other, do not check at,[19] a toleration of men in all that which they pretend out of conscience they cannot submit to, will wholly take away all the civil laws and all the magistrate's power, and so there will be no law, nor government, if you deny the magistrate's authority in indifferent things, over which it is acknowledged on all hands that he has jurisdiction. And therefore the errors, or scruples of anyone's conscience, which lead him to, or deter him from the doing of anything, do not destroy the magistrate's power nor alter the nature of the thing which is still indifferent. For I will not doubt here to call all these practical opinions in respect of the lawmaker indifferent, though perhaps they are not so in themselves. For however the magistrate be persuaded in himself of the reasonableness or absurdity, necessity or unlawfulness of any of them, and is possibly in the right, yet whilst he acknowledges himself not infallible, he ought to regard them in making of his laws, no otherwise, than as things indifferent, except only as that being enjoined, tolerated, or forbidden, they carry with them the civil good and welfare of the people. Though at the same time he be obliged strictly to suit his personal actions to the dictates of his own conscience and persuasion in these very opin-

---

19. *check at:* balk at.

ions. For not being made infallible in reference to others, by being made a governor over them, he shall hereafter be accountable to God for his actions as a man, according as they are suited to his own conscience and persuasion; but shall be accountable for his laws and administration as a magistrate, according as they are intended to the good, preservation, and quiet of all his subjects in this world as much as is possible, which is a rule so certain and so clear, that he can scarce err in it unless he do it wilfully.

But before I proceed to show the limits of restraint and liberty in reference to these things, it will be necessary to set down the several degrees of imposition, that are, or may be used in matters of opinion.

1. The prohibiting to publish or vent[20] any opinion.

2. Forcing to renounce or abjure any opinion.

3. Compelling to declare an assent to the contrary opinion.

There are answerable to these the same degrees of toleration.

From all which I conclude:

A. That the magistrate may prohibit the publishing of any of these opinions when they tend to the disturbance of the government because they are then under his cognizance and jurisdiction.

B. That no man ought to be forced to renounce his opinion, or assent to the contrary, because such a compulsion cannot produce any real effect to that purpose for which it is designed. It cannot alter men's minds, it can only force them to be hypocrites, and by this way the magistrate is so far from bringing men to embrace the truth of his opinion, that he only constrains them to lie for their own. Nor does this injunction at all conduce to the peace or security of the government but quite the contrary. Because hereby the magistrate does not make anyone to be one jot the more of his mind, but to be very much more his enemy.

C. That any actions flowing from any of these opinions, as also in all other indifferent things, the magistrate has a power to command or forbid so far as they tend to the peace, safety or security of his people, whereof though he be judge, yet he ought still to have a great care, that no such laws be made, no such restraints established, for any other reason, but because the necessity of the state, and the welfare of the people called

---

20. *vent:* express.

for them. And perhaps it will not be sufficient, that he barely thinks such impositions, and such rigour necessary, or convenient, unless he hath seriously and impartially considered, and debated whether they be so or no: and his opinion (if he mistake) will no more justify him in the making of such laws, than the conscience or opinion of the subject will excuse him, if he disobey them; if consideration and enquiry could have better informed either of them. And I think it will easily be granted, that the making of laws to any other end, but only for the security of the government and protection of the people in their lives, estates, and liberties, i.e., the preservation of the whole, will meet with the severest doom at the great tribunal, not only because the abuse of that power and trust which is in the lawmaker's hands, produces greater and more unavoidable mischief than anything else to mankind, for whose good only governments were instituted, but also, because he is not accountable to any tribunal here. Nor can there be a greater provocation to the supreme preserver of mankind, than that the magistrate should make use of that power, which was given him only for the preservation of all his subjects, and every particular person amongst them, as far as it is practicable, should misuse it to the service of his pleasure, vanity, or passion, and employ it to the disquieting or oppression of his fellow men, between whom and himself in respect of the king of kings there is but a small and accidental difference.

D. That if the magistrate in these opinions or actions by laws and impositions endeavour to restrain, or compel men, contrary to the sincere persuasions of their own consciences; they ought to do what their consciences require of them, as far as without violence they can; but withal are bound at the same time quietly to submit to the penalties the law inflicts on such disobedience.[21] For by this means they secure to themselves their grand concernment in another world, and disturb not the peace of this; offend not against their allegiance either to God or the king but give both their due, the interest of the magistrate and their own being both safe. And certainly he is a hypocrite, and only pretends conscience and aims

---

21. Locke, in 1667, appears to be far from advocating a right of resistance, for in this paragraph he adopts the conventional view that, if we disobey the magistrate for conscience's sake, we must passively suffer the consequences (but see note 17, p. 110).

at something else in this world, who will not, by obeying his conscience and submitting also to the law, purchase heaven for himself and peace for his country though at the rate[22] of his estate, liberty, or life itself. But here also the private person, as well as the magistrate in the former case, must take great care that his conscience or opinion do not mislead him, in the obstinate pursuit or flight[23] of anything as necessary or unlawful, which in truth is not so, lest by such an error, or wilfulness, he come to be punished for the same disobedience in this world and the other too. For liberty of conscience being the great privilege of the subject, as the right of imposing is the great prerogative of the magistrate, they ought the more narrowly to be watched, that they do not mislead either magistrate or subject, because of the fair pretences they have. Those wrongs being the most dangerous, most carefully to be avoided, and such as God will most severely punish, which are done under the specious semblances and appearances of right.

III. I say there are, besides the two former, a third sort of actions, which are thought good or bad in themselves, *viz.*, the duties of the second table[24] or trespasses against it or the moral virtues of the philosophers.[25] These, though they are the vigorous active part of religion, and that wherein men's consciences are very much concerned, yet I find, that they make but a little part of the disputes of liberty of conscience. I know not whether it be, that if men were more zealous for these, they would be less contentious about the other.[26] But this is certain, that the countenancing virtue is so necessary a prop to a state, and the allowance of some vices brings so certain a disturbance and ruin to society, that it was never found that any magistrate did; nor can be suspected, that he ever will, establish vice by a law, or prohibit the practice of virtue. Which does by its own authority,

22. *rate:* cost.

23. *flight:* a soaring or sally of the imagination or intellect.

24. *second table:* the latter half of the Ten Commandments, concerning morality (Exodus 20:12–17).

25. Locke has in mind the pagan moralists such as Aristotle and Cicero.

26. It was a common sentiment of tolerationists that Restoration society mistakenly expended its efforts upon disciplining worship rather than morality. Those who were tolerant as to worship could be vigorous as to "reformation of manners."

and the advantages it brings to all governments sufficiently establish itself everywhere. Yet give me leave to say, however strange it may seem, that the lawmaker hath nothing to do with moral virtues and vices, nor ought to enjoin the duties of the second table any otherwise, than barely as they are subservient to the good and preservation of mankind under government.[27] For could public societies well subsist, or men enjoy peace or safety, without the enforcing of those duties, by the injunctions and penalties of laws, it is certain the lawmaker ought not to prescribe any rules about them, but leave the practice of them entirely to the discretion and consciences of his people. For could even these moral virtues and vices be separated from the relation they have to the weal[28] of the public, and cease to be a means to settle or disturb men's peace and proprieties, they would then become only the private and super-political concernment between God and a man's soul, wherein the magistrate's authority is not to interpose. God hath appointed the magistrate his vicegerent[29] in this world, with power to command; but 'tis but like other deputies, to command only in the affairs of that place where he is vicegerent. Whoever meddle in the concernments of the other world, have no other power, but to entreat and persuade. The magistrate hath nothing to do with the good of men's souls or their concernments in another life but is ordained and entrusted with his power only for the quiet and comfortable living of men in society one with another, as has been already sufficiently proved.

And it is yet farther evident, that the magistrate commands not the practice of virtues, because they are virtues, and oblige the conscience, or are the duties of man to God and the way to his mercy and favour, but because they are the advantages of man with man, and most of them the strong ties and bonds of society; which cannot be loosened, without shattering the whole frame. For some of them, which have not that influence on the state, and yet are vices and acknowledged to be so as much as any, as covetousness, disobedience to parents, ingratitude, malice, revenge, and several others, the magistrate never draws his sword against. Nor can it

27. Locke appears here to take a more liberal view of the state's role in relation to morality than he later would in the *Letter Concerning Toleration*.

28. *weal:* well-being.

29. *vicegerent:* delegate, deputy.

be said, that these are neglected, because they cannot be known, when the secretest of them, revenge and malice, put the distinction in judicature between manslaughter and murder. Yea even charity itself, which is certainly the great duty both of a man and a Christian, hath not yet, in its full latitude, a universal right to toleration: since there are some parts, and instances of it, which the magistrate hath absolutely forbidden, and that, for ought I could ever hear, without any offence to the tenderest consciences. For who doubts that to relieve with an alms the poor, though beggars (if one see them in want), is, if considered absolutely, a virtue and every particular man's duty, yet this is amongst us prohibited by a law[30] and the rigour of a penalty, and yet nobody in this case complains of the violation of his conscience, or the loss of his liberty, which certainly, if it were an unlawful restraint upon the conscience could not be overlooked by so many tender and scrupulous men. God does sometimes (so much does he take care of the preservation of governments) make his law in some degrees submit, and comply with man's; his law forbids the vice, but the law of man often makes the measures of it. There have been commonwealths that have made theft lawful for such as were not caught in the fact, and perhaps 'twas as guiltless a thing to steal a horse at Sparta, as to win a horse race in England. For the magistrate having a power to appoint ways of transferring proprieties, from one man to another, may establish any, so they be universal, equal and without violence, and suited to the interest and welfare of that society, as this was at Sparta, who being a warlike people found this no ill way, to teach their citizens, vigilance, boldness and activity.[31] This I only note by the by, to show how much the good of the commonwealth is the standard of all human laws, when it

30. Locke has in mind the Statute of Labourers (1349): "Because that many [able-bodied] beggars, as long as they may live of begging, do refuse to labour, giving themselves to idleness and vice, and sometimes to theft and other abominations; none upon the said pain of imprisonment shall, under the colour of pity or alms, give anything to such, which may labour, or presume to favour them, so that thereby they may be compelled to labour for their necessary living."

31. For the right of theft and the quasi-communism of Sparta, see Plutarch, *Life of Lycurgus*, 17, and Aristotle, *Politics*, 1263a35–38. Locke had used this example in his *Essays on the Law of Nature*. Note that Locke appears to allow the legitimacy of state regulation of property. Compare *Two Treatises of Government*, II, §120.

seems to limit and alter the obligation even of some of the laws of God, and change the nature of vice and virtue.[32] Hence it is that the magistrate who could make theft innocent could not yet make perjury or breach of faith lawful, because destructive to human society.

From this power therefore that the magistrate hath over good and bad actions I think it will follow:

1. That he is not bound to punish all, i.e., he may tolerate some vices, for I would fain know what government in the world doth not;

2. That he ought not to command the practice of any vice, because such an injunction cannot be subservient to the good of the people, or preservation of the government;

3. That if it can be supposed that he should command the practice of any vice, the conscientious and scandalized subject is bound to disobey his injunction, but submit to his penalty. As in the former case.

These I suppose are the limits of imposition and liberty, and these three several sorts of things wherein men's consciences are concerned have right to such a latitude of toleration as I have set down and no more, if they are considered separately and abstractly in themselves.

But yet there are two cases or circumstances which may still upon the same grounds vary the magistrate's usage of the men that claim this right to toleration.

1. Since men usually take up their religion in gross, and assume to themselves the opinions of their party all at once in a bundle, it often happens, that they mix with their religious worship, and speculative opinions, other doctrines absolutely destructive to the society wherein they live, as is evident in the Roman Catholics that are subjects of any prince but the pope. These therefore blending such opinions with their religion, reverencing them as fundamental truths, and submitting to them as articles of their faith, ought not to be tolerated by the magistrate in the exercise of their religion unless he can be secured, that he can allow one part, without the spreading of the other, and that the propagation of these dangerous

---

32. Locke here sails close to the Hobbesian view that good and evil are "but names," subject to human conventions.

opinions may be separated from their religious worship, which I suppose is very hard to be done.[33]

2. [34]Since experience vouches the practice, and men are not all saints that pretend conscience, I think I shall not injure any party, if I say, that most men, at least factions of men, when they have power sufficient, make use of it, right or wrong, for their own advantage, and the establishment of themselves in authority, few men forbearing to grasp at dominion that have power to seize and hold it.[35] When therefore men herd themselves into companies with distinctions from the public, and a stricter confederacy with those of their own denomination and party, than other their fellow subjects; whether the distinction be religious or ridiculous it matters not, otherwise than as the ties of religion are stronger, and the pretences of conscience fairer, and apter to draw partisans, and therefore the more to be suspected and the more heedfully to be watched; when, I say, any such distinct party is grown, or growing so numerous as to appear dangerous to the magistrate, and seem visibly to threaten the peace of the state, the magistrate may and ought to use all ways either of policy or power that shall be convenient, to lessen, break and suppress the party and so prevent the mischief. For though their separation were really in nothing but religious worship, and he should use as the last remedy force and severity against them, who did nothing but worship God in their own way, yet did he not really persecute their religion or punish them for that more than, in a battle, the conqueror kills men for wearing white rib-

33. Locke is emphatic that Catholics cannot be tolerated, though this is not because of their theology or worship, but because they are dangerous to civil society. He expands below on the dangers of Catholicism. There were a number of attempts by Catholics, especially in the 1660s, to formulate an oath acceptable to themselves and the English state by which they would distinguish their theology from doctrines held to be uncivil. In Locke's preliminary draft in the Huntington MS he states more explicitly "that papists and all other men have a right to toleration of their religious worship and speculative opinions"; it is only their opinions "destructive to any government but the pope's" which "have no title to toleration."

34. In MS Locke c. 28 this section (to "here dispute" near the start of the next but one paragraph) is deleted, and replaced by a new passage: Addition C.

35. It was a common accusation against Protestant dissenters who pleaded for toleration that they had themselves been coercive when in power during the Civil Wars. The present paragraph reflects the government's concern in the late 1660s to find some reliable way of distinguishing between safe and dangerous dissenters.

bons in their hats, or any other badge about them, but because this was a mark that they were enemies and dangerous. Religion, i.e., this or that form of worship, being the cause of their union and correspondence;[36] not of their factiousness and turbulency. For the praying to God in this or that place or posture, does no more make men factious, or at enmity one with another, nor ought otherwise to be treated, than the wearing of hats or turbans, which yet either of them may do by being a note of distinction, and giving men an opportunity to number their forces, know their strength, be confident of one another, and readily unite upon any occasion. So that they are not restrained because of this or that opinion or worship, but because such a number of any opinion whatsoever, who dissented, would be dangerous. The same thing would happen if any fashion of clothes distinct from that of the magistrate, and those that adhere to him, should spread itself, and become the badge of a very considerable part of the people, who thereupon grew into a very strict correspondence and friendship one with another. Might not this well give the magistrate cause of jealousy, and make him with penalties forbid the fashion; not because unlawful, but because of the danger it might occasion? Thus a lay cloak may have the same effect with an ecclesiastical cowl or any other religious habit.

And perhaps the Quakers, were they numerous enough to become dangerous to the state, would deserve the magistrate's care and watchfulness to break and suppress them, were they no other way distinguished from the rest of his subjects, but by the bare keeping on their hats,[37] as much as if they had a set form of religion separate from the state. In which case nobody would think, that the not standing bare were a thing the magistrate levelled his severity against, any otherwise, than as it united a great number of men who, though they dissented from him in a very indifferent and trivial circumstance, yet might thereby endanger the government. And in such case he may endeavor to suppress and weaken or dissolve any party of men, which religion or any other thing hath united to

36. *correspondence:* connection or communication.

37. The Quakers were notorious for refusing "hat honour" to their social superiors: they held that, since we are all equally the children of God, we ought not to defer to human hierarchies.

the manifest danger of his government by all those means, that shall be most convenient for that purpose, whereof he is to be judge, nor shall he be accountable in the other world, for what he does directly in order to the preservation and peace of his people according to the best of his knowledge.

Whether force and compulsion be the right way to this end I will not here dispute, but this I dare affirm, that it is the worst, the last to be used, and with the greatest caution. For these reasons:

A. Because it brings that upon a man, which that he might be fenced[38] from is the only reason why he is a member of the commonwealth, *viz.*, violence. For were there no fear of violence, there would be no government in the world, nor any need of it.

B. Because the magistrate in using of force, does in part cross what he pretends to, which is to promote the safety of all. For the preservation as much as is possible of the propriety, quiet and life of every individual being his duty; he is obliged not to disturb, or destroy some, for the quiet, or safety of the rest, till it has been tried, whether there be not ways to save all. For so far as he undoes or destroys any of his subjects, for the security of the rest, so far he opposes his own design, which is professed and ought to be only for preservation, to which even the meanest have a title. 'Twould be but an uncharitable as well as unskillful way of cure, and such as nobody would use or consent to, to cut off so much as an ulcered toe, though tending to a gangrene, till all other gentler remedies had proved unsuccessful; though it be a part as low as the earth, and far distant from the head.

I can see but one objection that can be made to this, and that is, that by the application of gentler remedies, such slow methods may make you lose the opportunity of those remedies that if timely would be effectual. Whereas in your faint way of proceeding the malady increases, the faction grows strong, gathers head, and becomes your masters.

To this I answer. That parties and factions grow slowly and by degrees, have their times of infancy and weakness, as well as full growth and strength, and become not formidable in an instant: but give sufficient time for experimenting other kind of cures, without any danger by the

38. *fenced:* protected.

delay. But if the magistrate chance to find the dissenters so numerous, as to be in a condition to cope with him, I see not what he can gain by force and severity, when he thereby gives them the fairer pretence to embody,[39] and arm, and makes them all unite the firmer against him. But this bordering something upon that part of the question, which concerns more the interest of the magistrate than his duty, I shall refer to a fitter place.[40]

Hitherto I have only traced out the bounds that God hath set to the power of the magistrate and the obedience of the subject, both which are subjects and equally owe obedience to the great king of kings who expects from them the performance of those duties which are incumbent on them in their several stations and conditions, the sum whereof is that:

1. There are some opinions and actions that are wholly separate from the concernment of the state, and have no direct influence upon men's lives in society, and those are, all speculative opinions and religious worship, and these have a clear title to universal toleration, which the magistrate ought not to intrench on.

2. There are some opinions and actions, which are in their natural tendency absolutely destructive to human society, as that faith may be broken with heretics,[41] that if the magistrate doth not reform religion the subjects may,[42] that one is bound to broach and propagate any opinion he believes himself and such like; and in actions all manner of fraud and injustice, etc. And these the magistrate ought not to tolerate at all.

3. There is a third sort of opinions and actions which in themselves do not inconvenience or advantage human society, but only as the temper of the state and posture of affairs may vary their influence to good or bad, as that polygamy is lawful or unlawful, that flesh or fish is to be eaten or abstained from at certain seasons. And such other practical opinions and all actions conversant about matters of indifference. And these have a right to toleration so far only as they do not interfere with the advantages of the public or serve any way to disturb the government.

And thus far of toleration as it concerns the magistrate's duty. Having

---

39. *embody:* organize.
40. In fact, within half a page Locke turns to prudential arguments for toleration.
41. A doctrine alleged of Catholics: see note 127, p. 50.
42. A doctrine alleged of Calvinists and radical Puritans.

showed what he is bound in conscience to do, it will not be amiss to consider a little what he ought to do in prudence.[43]

But because the duties of men are contained in general established rules, but their prudence is regulated by circumstances relating to themselves in particular, it will be necessary in showing how much toleration is the magistrate's interest, to come to particulars.

To consider therefore the state of England at present. There is but this one question in the whole matter and that is whether toleration or imposition be the readiest way to secure the safety and peace and promote the welfare of this kingdom.

As to securing your safety and peace, there is but one way which is that your friends at home be many and vigorous,[44] and your enemies few and contemptible. Or at least that the inequality of their number make it very dangerous and difficult for malcontents to molest you.

As to promoting the welfare of the kingdom which consists in riches and power, to this most immediately conduces the number and industry of your subjects.[45]

What influence toleration hath on all these cannot be well seen without considering the different parties now among us. Which may well be comprehended under these two, papist and fanatic.[46]

I. 1. As to the papists, 'tis certain that several of their dangerous opinions which are absolutely destructive to all governments but the pope's ought not to be tolerated in propagating those opinions, and whosoever shall spread or publish any of them the magistrate is bound to suppress so far as may be sufficient to restrain it. And this rule reaches not only

43. About the time Locke was writing, economic and demographic "reason of state" arguments in favor of toleration became fashionable.

44. Here and below there are indications of Locke's preoccupation, shared by contemporaries, with encouraging demographic growth. A common "reason of state" argument was that toleration encouraged immigration and enhanced population and commerce.

45. "your subjects": some commentators have suggested that the *Essay* was written as material that Lord Ashley could present to the king; note also "your safety," "your friends," and "your enemies" in the preceding paragraph; "number and industry": compare *Two Treatises of Government*, II, §42.

46. *fanatic:* the common contemporary term for Protestant dissenters.

the papists but any other sort of men amongst us. For such restraint will something hinder the spreading of those doctrines, which will always be of ill consequence and like serpents can never be prevailed on by kind usage to lay by their venom.

2. Papists are not to enjoy the benefit of toleration because where they have power they think themselves bound to deny it to others. For it is unreasonable that any should have a free liberty of their religion, who do not acknowledge it as a principle of theirs that nobody ought to persecute or molest another because he dissents from him in religion. For toleration being settled by the magistrate as a foundation whereon to establish the peace and quiet of his people, by tolerating any who enjoy the benefit of this indulgence, which at the same time they condemn as unlawful, he only cherishes those who profess themselves obliged to disturb his government as soon as they shall be able.

3. It being impossible either by indulgence[47] or severity to make papists, whilst papists, friends to your government, being enemies to it both in their principles and interest, and therefore considering them as irreconcilable enemies of whose fidelity you can never be secured, whilst they owe a blind obedience to an infallible pope, who has the keys of their consciences tied to his girdle, and can upon occasion dispense with all their oaths, promises and the obligations they have to their prince, especially being a heretic, and arm them to the disturbance of the government, I think they ought not to enjoy the benefit of toleration.[48]

Because toleration can never, but restraint may, lessen their number or at least not increase it, as it does usually all other opinions which grow and spread by persecution, and recommend themselves to bystanders by the hardships they undergo, men being forward to have compassion for sufferers and esteem for that religion as pure, and the professors of it as sincere which can stand the test of persecution. But I think it is far otherwise with Catholics who are less apt to be pitied than others because they receive no other usage than what the cruelty of their own principles and practices are known to deserve. Most men judging those severities they

47. "indulgence": the other manuscripts of the *Essay* have *toleration*. Locke, like his contemporaries, uses the two words more or less interchangeably.
48. On the intolerable principles of Catholics, see note 33, p. 118.

complain of, as just punishments due to them as enemies to the state rather than persecutions of conscientious men for their religion, which indeed it is not. Nor can they be thought to be punished merely for their consciences who own themselves at the same time subjects of a foreign and enemy prince.[49] Besides the principles and doctrines of that religion are less apt to take inquisitive heads and unstable minds, men commonly in their voluntary changes do pursue liberty and enthusiasm,[50] wherein they are still free and at their own disposal rather than give themselves up to the authority and impositions of others. This is certain that toleration cannot make them divide amongst themselves, nor a severe hand over them (as in other dissenting parties) make them cement with the fanatics (whose principles and worship and tempers are so utterly inconsistent), and by that means increasing the number of the united malcontents make the danger greater.[51] Add to this that popery having been brought in upon the ignorant and zealous world by the art and industry of their clergy, and kept up by the same artifice backed by power and force, it is the most likely of any religion to decay where the secular power handles them severely, or at least takes from them those encouragements and supports they received by their own clergy.

But if restraint of the papists do not lessen the number of our enemies in bringing any of them over to us, yet it increases the number, it strengthens the hands of our friends, and knits all the Protestant parties firmer to our assistance and defence. For the interest of the king of England as head of the Protestants will be much improved by the discountenancing of popery amongst us. The different parties will sooner unite in a common friendship with us, when they find we really separate from and

49. Locke takes for granted that the papacy is a secular power, which claims sovereignty over the whole world. Compare *Two Treatises of Government*, II, §§217, 220.

50. *enthusiasm:* a recent coinage, denoting excessive religious exaltation, or wild claims to private inspiration. The "sober" religion of orthodox Protestantism was thought a middle way between (Catholic) "superstition" and (sectarian) "enthusiasm." In 1698 Locke added a chapter, "Of Enthusiasm," to the fourth edition of his *Essay Concerning Human Understanding*.

51. King James II, during his short reign (1685–88), would attempt precisely such an improbable alliance of Catholics and dissenters, as common seekers after toleration in the face of an intolerant Church of England.

set ourselves against the common enemy both to our church and all Protestant professions. This will be a hostage of our friendship to them, and a security that they shall not be deceived in the confidence they have of us, and the sincerity of the accord we make with them.

II. All the rest of dissenters come under the opprobrious name of fanatics,[52] which I think, by the way, might with more prudence be laid aside and forgotten than made use of. For what understanding man in a disordered state would find out and fix notes of distinction, a thing to be coveted only by those that are factious, or, by giving one common name to different parties, teach those to unite whom he is concerned to divide and keep at a distance one among another.

But to come to what is more material, I think it is agreed on all hands, that it is necessary the fanatics should be made useful and assisting and as much as possible firm to the government as it now stands. Both as to secure it from disturbance at home and defend it against invasions from abroad which nothing can possibly bring to pass but what is able to alter their minds and bring them over to your profession. Or else if they do not part with their opinions, yet may persuade them to lay by their animosity, and become friends to the state though they are not sons of the church.

What efficacy force and severity hath to alter the opinions of mankind, though all history be full of examples, and there is scarce an instance to be found of any opinion driven out of the world by persecution but where the violence of it at once swept away all the professors too. I desire nobody to go farther than his own bosom for an experiment[53] whether ever violence gained anything upon his opinion, whether even arguments managed with heat do not lose something of their efficacy, and have not made him the more obstinate in his opinion, so chary is human nature to preserve the liberty of that part wherein lies the dignity of a man, which,

52. There were several disparate varieties of Protestant dissenters, the chief groups being the Presbyterians, Congregationalists (Independents), Baptists, and Quakers. As Locke points out below, their theological differences were profound, although hostile labeling by their enemies, and the shared experience of persecution, tended to drive them together.

53. *an experiment:* practical acquaintance with, experience of.

could it be imposed on, would make him but little different from a beast. I ask those who in the late times[54] so firmly stood the ineffectual persecution[55] themselves and found how little it obtained on their opinions, and yet are now so forward to try it upon others, whether all the severity in the world could have drawn them one step nearer to a hearty and sincere embracing the opinions that were then uppermost, let them not say it was because they knew they were in the right, for every man in what he believes, has so far this persuasion that he is in the right. But how little this obstinacy or constancy depends upon knowledge, may appear in those galley slaves who return from Turkey,[56] who though they have endured all manner of miseries rather than part with their religion, yet one would guess by the lives and principles of most of them, that they had no knowledge of the doctrine and practise of Christianity at all. Who thinks not that those poor captives who (for renouncing a religion they were not over instructed in nor during the enjoyment of their freedom at home over zealous for) might have regained their liberty, for changing their opinion would not (had their chains given them leave) have cut the throats of those cruel patrons who used them so severely to whom they would yet have done no violence had they been treated civilly like fair prisoners of war. Whereby we may see 'twill be a hazardous attempt for those who design it,[57] if they are not much the greater number, to compel dissenters by force and ill usage to be true to that government and serviceable to that interest, which instead of an equal protection affords them no other treatment but disgrace, punishment and persecution: unless those who would thus enforce a uniformity will make chains for all those to whom

54. *late times:* the Civil Wars and Interregnum (1642–60). Locke appeals to intolerant Anglicans to recall how their own convictions were not broken by their proscription during the period of the Puritan hegemony.

55. "ineffectual persecution": MS Locke c. 28 has "ineffectual force of persecution."

56. Enslavement of European Christians occurred frequently. *Turkey* probably here means Muslim North Africa and the Near East generally.

57. In place of the next several lines ("if they ... upon them"), MS Locke c. 28 has: "to bring this island to a condition of a galley where the greater part shall be reduced to the condition of slaves, be forced with blows to row the vessel, but share in none of the lading, nor have any privilege or protection unless they will make chains for all those who are to be used like Turks, and persuade them to stand still whilst they put them on."

they will allow no liberty and persuade them also to stand still whilst they put them upon them. For let divines preach duty as long as they will, 'twas never known that men lay down quietly under the oppression and submitted their backs to the blows of others when they thought they had strength enough to defend themselves. I say not this to justify such proceedings, which in the former part of this discourse I think I have sufficiently condemned. But to show what the nature and practice of mankind is and what has usually been the consequence of persecution.

Besides the forcible introducing of opinions keeps people off from closing with them by giving men unavoidable jealousies, that it is not truth that is thus carried on, but interest and dominion that is sought in making proselytes by compulsion. For who takes this course to convince anyone of the certain truths of mathematics? 'Tis likely 'twill be said that those are truths on which depends not my happiness. I grant it, and am much indebted to the man that takes care I should be happy, but 'tis hard to think that that comes from charity to my soul which brings such ill usage to my body, or that he is much concerned I should be happy in another world who is pleased to see me miserable in this. I wonder that those who have such a zealous regard to the good of others, do not a little more look after the relief of the poor or think themselves concerned to guard the estates of the rich, which certainly are good things too and make a part of one's happiness, if we may believe the lives of those who tell us the joys of heaven but endeavor as much as others for large possessions on earth.

But, after all this, could persecution not only now and then conquer a tender faint-hearted fanatic, which yet it rarely does and that usually by the loss of two or three orthodox, could it I say at once drive in all dissenters within the pale of the church, it would not thereby secure but much more threaten the government and make the danger as much greater as it is to have a false, secret but exasperated enemy rather than a fair open adversary. For punishment and fear may make men dissemble, but not convincing anybody's reason, cannot possibly make them assent to the opinion, but will certainly make them hate the person of their persecutor and give them the greater aversion to both; such compliers only prefer impunity to the declaring of their own opinion, but do not thereby approve of yours. Fear of your power, not love of your government, is that which restrains them, and, if that be the chain that ties them to you, it would certainly hold them surer were they open dissenters, than being secret malcontents, because it would not only be something easier to be worn but harder to be knocked off. At least this is certain that compelling men to your opinion any other way than by convincing them of the truth of it, makes them no more your friends, than forcing the poor Indians by droves into the rivers to be baptised made them Christians.[58]

Though force cannot master the opinions men have, nor plant new ones in their breasts, yet courtesy, friendship and soft usage may, for several (I think I may say most) men whose business or laziness keep them from examining take many of their opinions upon trust, even in things of religion, but never take them from any man of whose knowledge, friendship and sincerity they have not very good thoughts. Which it is impossible they should have of one that persecutes them.

But inquisitive men, though they are not of another's mind because of his kindness, yet they are the more willing to be convinced and will be apt to search after reasons that may persuade them to be so whom they are obliged to love.

Since force is a wrong way to bring dissenters off from their persuasions, and by drawing them to your opinion you cement them fast to the state, it will certainly prevail much less with those to be your friends who steadfastly retain their persuasion. He that differs in an opinion is only so far at a distance from you, but if you use him ill for that which he believes to be the right he is then at perfect enmity, the one is barely a separation, the other a quarrel. Nor is that all the mischief which severity will do among us as the state of things is at present, for force and harsh usage will not only increase the animosity but number of enemies. For the fanatics taken all together being numerous,[59] and possibly more than the

---

58. It was a Protestant commonplace to deplore the forced conversion of native Americans by the Spaniards. Compare *The Constitutions of Carolina*, p. 146.

59. Nobody knew what proportion of the population were dissenters, though it was widely believed they were more numerous than is likely to have been the case. Modern estimates suggest ten percent (perhaps twenty in large towns), but dissent was in any case an inexact status, since many people were "partial" or "occasional" conformists. In 1660–62 about one fifth of the clergy broke away, or were driven, from the reestablished church. The number of Catholics was likewise exaggerated, and probably was no more than two percent.

hearty friends to the state religion, are yet crumbled into different parties amongst themselves, and are at as much distance one from another as from you, if you drive them not farther off by the treatment they receive from you, for their bare opinions are as inconsistent one with another as with the Church of England. People therefore that are so shattered into different factions are best secured by toleration since being in as good a condition under you, as they can hope for under any, 'tis not like[ly] they should join, to set up any other, whom they cannot be certain will use them so well. But if you persecute them you make them all of one party and interest against you, tempt them to shake off your yoke and venture for a new government wherein everyone has hopes to get the dominion themselves or better usage under others, who cannot but see that the same severity of the government which helped them to power and partisans to get up, will give others the same desire and same strength to pull them down, and therefore it may be expected they will be cautious how they exercise it. But if you think the different parties are already grown to a consistency and formed into one body and interest against you, whether it were the hardships they suffered under you made them unite or no, when they are so many as to equal or exceed you in number as perhaps they do in England, force will be but an ill and hazardous way to bring them to submission.

If uniformity in England be so necessary as many pretend, and compulsion be the way to it, I demand of those who are so zealous for it, whether they really intend by force to have it or no. If they do not, it is not only imprudent but malicious under that pretence, by ineffectual punishments to disquiet and torment their brethren. For to show how little persecution, if not in the extremest degree, has been able to establish uniformity, I shall ask but this one plain question, was there ever a free toleration in this kingdom. If there were not I desire to know of any of the clergy who were once sequestered,[60] how they came to be turned out of their livings and whether impositions and severity were able to preserve the Church of England and hinder the growth of puritans even before the war.[61] If therefore violence be to settle uniformity 'tis in vain to mince the

60. *sequestered:* sequestrated. See note 54, p. 126.
61. The regime of Archbishop William Laud before the outbreak of the Civil Wars in 1642 was notorious for its rigorous prosecution of Puritan nonconformists.

matter. That severity which must produce it cannot stop short of the total destruction and extirpation of all dissenters at once, and how well this will agree with the doctrine of Christianity, the principles of our church and reformation from popery, I leave them to judge who can think the massacre of France[62] worthy their imitation; and desire them to consider if death, for nothing less can make uniformity, were the penalty of not coming to common prayer, and joining in all our church worship, how much such a law would settle the quiet and secure the government of the kingdom.

The Romish religion that had been but a little while planted and taken but small root in Japan[63] (for the poor converts had but little of the efficacious truths and light of Christianity conveyed to them by those teachers who make ignorance the mother of devotion,[64] and knew very little beyond an *ave Maria*, or *paternoster*)[65] could not be extirpated but by the death of many thousands, which too prevailed not at all to lessen their numbers till they extended the severity beyond the delinquents and made it death not only to the family that entertained a priest but also to all of both the families that were next neighbours on either hand though they were strangers or enemies to the new religion. And invented exquisite lingering torments worse than a thousand deaths which though some had strength enough to endure fourteen days together yet many renounced their religion, whose names were all registered with a design that when the professors of Christianity were all destroyed, these too should be butchered all on a day, never thinking the opinion rooted out beyond possibility of spreading again, as long as there were any alive who were the least acquainted with it or had almost heard anything of Christianity more than the name. Nor are the Christians that trade there to this day suffered to discourse, fold their hands, or use any gesture that may show the differ-

62. The slaughter of Protestants in the St. Bartholomew's Day Massacre (1572).

63. Locke proceeds to give an account of the bloody suppression of Christianity in Japan that began in 1614. It is not clear from which of several possible sources Locke drew his knowledge of these events.

64. "ignorance [is] the mother of devotion": a principle proverbially attributed to Catholics. It was allegedly the saying of Pope Gregory the Great when he destroyed the Palatine Library in ca. 600.

65. The most common prayers in Catholicism: the Hail Mary and the Our Father (the Lord's Prayer).

ence of their religion. If anyone think uniformity in our church ought to be restored though by such a method as this, he will do well to consider how many subjects the king will have left by that time it is done. There is this one thing more observable in the case, which is, that it was not to set up uniformity in religion (for they tolerate seven or eight sects and some so different as is the belief of the mortality or immortality of the soul, nor is the magistrate at all curious or inquisitive what sect his subjects are of, or does in the least force them to his religion), nor any aversion to Christianity, which they suffered a good while quietly to grow up among them, till the doctrine of the popish priest gave them jealousies that religion was but their pretence but empire their design, and made them fear the subversion of their state, which suspicion their own priests improved all they could to the extirpation of this growing religion.

But to show the danger of establishing uniformity.

To give a full prospect of this subject there remain yet these following particulars to be handled:

1. To show what influence toleration is like to have upon the number and industry of your people on which depends the power and riches of the kingdom.

2. That if force must compel all to a uniformity in England, to consider what party alone, or what parties are likeliest to unite to make a force able to compel the rest.

3. To show that all that speak against toleration seem to suppose that severity and force are the only arts of government and way to suppress any faction, which is a mistake.

4. That for the most part the matters of controversy and distinction between sects, are no parts or very inconsiderable ones and appendixes of true religion.

5. To consider how it comes to pass that Christian religion hath made more factions, wars, and disturbances in civil societies than any other, and whether toleration and latitudinism[66] would prevent those evils.

---

66. *latitudinism:* more commonly, *latitudinarianism,* a recently coined term. It denoted a commitment, grounded in belief in the wide ambit of "things indifferent,"

6. That toleration conduces no otherwise to the settlement of a government than as it makes the majority of one mind and encourages virtue in all, which is done by making and executing strict laws concerning virtue and vice, but making the terms of church communion as large as may be, i.e., that your articles in speculative opinions be few and large, and ceremonies in worship few and easy. Which is latitudinism.

7. That the defining and undertaking to prove several doctrines which are confessed to be incomprehensible and to be no otherwise known but by revelation,[67] and requiring men to assent to them in the terms proposed by the doctors of your several churches, must needs make a great many atheists.

> But of these when I have more leisure:
> Sic Cogitavit Atticus[68] 1667[69]

Additions to the *Essay*

A. I must only remark before I leave this head of speculative opinions that the belief of a deity is not to be reckoned amongst purely speculative opinions, for it being the foundation of all morality, and that which influences the whole life and actions of men, without which a man is to be counted no other than one of the most dangerous sorts of wild beasts, and so incapable of all society.

B. 'Twill be said that if a toleration shall be allowed as due to all the parts of religious worship it will shut out the magistrate's power from

---

to securing a scheme of "comprehension," by which the terms and conditions of the Church of England would be liberalized so that moderate dissenters could rejoin the church. Locke insists that there must also be toleration for those who remain outside the pale. It is striking that, in the next paragraph, Locke commits to comprehension. While he held that toleration, in the sense of a plurality of denominations, must be conceded, it was not the most desirable outcome.

67. Probably the several doctrines entailed in that of the Trinity. Note that Locke (whose later theology is often said to have been anti-Trinitarian) here implies that the doctrine of the Trinity is demonstrable from Scripture.

68. Locke used the coterie name "Atticus" around this time. Atticus was a friend of Cicero.

69. In the notebook "Adversaria 1661" there follow two further additions, D and E.

making laws about those things over which it is acknowledged on all hands that he has a power, *viz.*, things indifferent, as many things made use of in religious worship are, *viz.*, wearing a white or a black garment, kneeling or not kneeling, etc. To which I answer, that in religious worship nothing is indifferent, for it being the using of those habits, gestures, etc., and no other, which I think acceptable to God in my worshipping of him, however they may be in their own nature perfectly indifferent, yet when I am worshipping my God in a way I think he has prescribed and will approve of, I cannot alter, omit, or add any circumstance in that which I think the true way of worship. And therefore if the magistrate permit me to be of a profession or church different from his, 'tis incongruous that he should prescribe any one circumstance of my worship, and 'tis strange to conceive upon what grounds of uniformity any different profession of Christians can be prohibited in a Christian country, where the Jewish religion (which is directly opposite to the principles of Christianity) is tolerated; and would it not be irrational, where the Jewish religion is permitted, that the Christian magistrate, upon pretence of his power in indifferent things, should enjoin or forbid anything, or any way interpose in their way or manner of worship?[70]

C. And that which may render them yet more incapable of toleration is when, [in addition] to these doctrines dangerous to government, they have the power of a neighbour prince of the same religion at hand to countenance and back them upon any occasion.[71]

The objection usually made against toleration, that the magistrate's great business being to preserve [the] peace and quiet of the government, he is obliged not to tolerate different religions in his country, since they bring distinctions wherein men unite and incorporate into bodies separate from the public, they may occasion disorder, conspiracies and seditions in the commonwealth and endanger the government.

I answer: if all things that may occasion disorder or conspiracy in a commonwealth must not be endured in it, all discontented and active men

70. On the readmission of the Jews to England, see note 78, p. 34.

71. The "neighbour prince" presumably means France. However, English fear of French ambitions did not crystallize until around 1672; previously the old fear of Spain lingered and figured prominently in Cromwell's foreign policy in the 1650s.

must be removed, and whispering must be less tolerated than preaching, as much likelier to carry on and foment a conspiracy. And if all numbers of men joined in a union and corporation distinct from the public be not to be suffered, all charters of towns, especially great ones, are presently to be taken away. Men united in religion have as little and perhaps less interest against the government than those united in the privileges of a corporation. This I am sure: they are less dangerous as being more scattered and not formed into that order. And the minds of men are so various in matters of religion, and so nice and scrupulous in things of an eternal concernment, that where men are indifferently tolerated, and persecution and force does not drive them together, they are apt to divide and subdivide into so many little bodies, and always with the greatest enmity to those they last parted from or stand nearest to, that they are a guard one upon another, and the public can have no apprehensions of them as long as they have their equal share of common justice and protection. And if the example of old Rome (where so many different opinions, gods, and ways of worship were promiscuously tolerated) be of any weight, we have reason to imagine that no religion can become suspected to the state of ill intention to it, till the government first by a partial usage of them, different from the rest of the subjects, declare its ill intentions to its professors, and so make a state business of it. And if any rational man can imagine that force and compulsion can at any time be the right way to get an opinion or religion out of the world, or to break a party of men that unite in the profession of it, this I dare affirm:

D. Methinks the clergy should, like ambassadors, endeavour to entreat, convince and persuade men to the truth rather than thus solicit the magistrate to force them into their fold. This was the way that gained admittance for Christianity and spread the religion they profess so far into the world: whereas whilst they once a week uncharitably preach against, and the rest of the week as impudently rail at their dissenting brethren, and do not endeavour by the meekness and tender methods of the Gospel, and by the soft cords of love, to draw men to them, but would have even those compelled under their jurisdiction whom they never take care to instruct in their opinions, for I think I may say that preaching a sermon once a week at rovers,[72] perhaps learned, perhaps otherwise, doth very little towards instructing men in the knowledge of faith, which after many years hearing one may be still ignorant of, and is seldom effectual to persuade them to good lives. This makes some men suspect that 'tis not the feeding of the sheep[73] but the benefit of the fleece that makes these men endeavour by such methods to enlarge their fold. This I am sure is quite contrary to the first way which nursed up Christianity.

E. Though the magistrate have a power of commanding or forbidding things indifferent which have a relation to religion, yet this can only be within that church whereof he himself is a member, who being a lawgiver in matters indifferent in the commonwealth under his jurisdiction, as it is purely a civil society, for their peace, is fittest also to be lawgiver in the religious society (which yet must be understood to be only a voluntary society and during every member's pleasure), in matters indifferent, for decency and order,[74] for the peace of that too. But I do not see how hereby he hath any power to order and direct even matters indifferent in the circumstances of a worship, or within a church whereof he is not professor or member. 'Tis true he may forbid such things as may tend to the disturbance of the peace of the commonwealth to be done by any of his people, whether they esteem them civil or religious. This is his proper business; but to command or direct any circumstances of a worship as part of that religious worship which he himself does not profess nor approve, is altogether without[75] his authority, and absurd to suppose. Can anyone think it reasonable, yea, or practicable, that a Christian prince should direct the form of Mahometan worship, the whole religion being thought by him false and profane, and vice versa?; and yet it is not impossible that a Christian prince should have Mahometan subjects who may deserve all civil freedom; and *de facto* the Turk hath Christian subjects. As absurd would it be that a magistrate, either Popish, Protestant, Lutheran, Presbyterian, Quaker, etc. should prescribe a form

72. *at rovers:* at random, haphazardly.
73. John 21:16.
74. 1 Corinthians 14:40.
75. *without:* outside, outwith.

to any or all of the differing churches in their way of worship. The reason whereof is because religious worship being that homage which every man pays to his God, he cannot do it in any other way, nor use any other rites, ceremonies, nor forms, even of indifferent things, than he himself is persuaded are acceptable and pleasing to that God he worships; which depending upon his opinion of his God, and what will best please him, it is impossible for one man to prescribe or direct any one circumstance of it to another: and this being a thing different and independent wholly from every man's concerns in the civil society, which hath nothing to do with a man's affairs in the other world, the magistrate hath here no more right to intermeddle than any private man, and has less right to direct the form of it, than he hath to prescribe to a subject of his in what manner he shall do his homage to another prince to whom he is feudatory, for something which he holds immediately from him, which, whether it be standing, kneeling, or prostrate, bareheaded or barefooted, whether in this or that habit, etc. concerns not his allegiance to him at all, nor his well government of his people. For though the things in themselves are perfectly indifferent, and it may be trivial, yet, to the worshipper, when he considers them as required by his God, or forbidden, pleasing or displeasing to the invisible power he addresses to, they are by no means so, and till you have altered his opinion (which persuasion can only do) you can by no means, nor without the greatest tyranny, prescribe him a way of worship; which was so unreasonable to do, that we find little bustle about it, and scarce any attempts towards it by the magistrates in the several societies of mankind till Christianity was well grown up in the world, and was become a national religion;[76] and since that [time] it hath been the cause of more disorders, tumults and bloodshed than all other causes put together.

But far be it from anyone to think Christ the author of those disorders, or that such fatal mischiefs are the consequence of his doctrine, though they have grown up with it. Antichrist hath sown these tares in the field[77] of the church; the rise whereof hath been only hence, that the clergy, by

76. *national religion:* state religion. Locke is referring to the fourth century, when the Roman Empire became Christian.
77. Matthew 13:25.

degrees, as Christianity spread, affecting dominion, laid claim to a priest-hood, derived by succession from Christ,[78] and so independent from the civil power, receiving (as they pretend) by the imposition of hands, and some other ceremonies agreed on (but variously) by the priesthoods of the several factions, an indelible character, particular sanctity, and a power immediately from heaven to do several things which are not lawful to be done by other men. The chief whereof are: (1) To teach opinions concerning God, a future state, and ways of worship. (2) To do and perform themselves certain rites exclusive of others. (3) To punish dissenters from their doctrines and rules. Whereas (1) it is evident from Scripture, that all priesthood terminated in the great high priest, Jesus Christ, who was the last priest.[79] (2) There are no footsteps in Scripture of any so set apart, with such powers as they pretend to, after the apostles' time, nor that had any indelible character. (3) That it is to be made out, that there is nothing which a priest can do, which another man without any such ordination, (if other circumstances of fitness, and an appointment to it, not disturbing peace and order, concur), may not lawfully perform and do, and the church and worship of God be preserved, as the peace of the state may be by justices of [the] peace, and other officers, who had no ordination or laying on of hands, to fit them to be justices, and by taking away their commissions may cease to be so. So ministers, as well as justices, are necessary, one for the administration of religious public worship, the other of civil justice; but an indelible character, peculiar sanctity of the function, or a power immediately derived from heaven, is not necessary, or as much as convenient, for either.

But the clergy (as they call themselves, of the Christian religion, in imitation of the Jewish priesthood) having, almost ever since the first ages of the church, laid claim to this power separate from civil government, as received from God himself, have, wherever the civil magistrate hath been Christian and of their opinion, and superior in power to the clergy, and they not able to cope with him, pretended this power only to be spiritual, and to extend no farther; but yet still pressed, as a duty on the magistrate,

78. See note 34, p. 17.
79. Hebrews 7:23–25, 10:11–12.

to punish and persecute those who they disliked and declared against. And so where they excommunicated, their under officer, the magistrate, was to execute; and to reward princes for thus doing their drudgery, they have (whenever princes have been serviceable to their ends) been careful to preach up monarchy *jure divino;* for commonwealths have hitherto been less favourable to their power. But notwithstanding the *jus divinum* of monarchy, when any prince hath dared to dissent from their doctrines or forms, or been less apt to execute the decrees of the hierarchy, they have been the first and forwardest in giving check to his authority and disturbance to his government. And princes, on the other side, being apt to hearken to such as seem to advance their authority, and bring in religion to the assistance of their absolute power, have been generally very ready to worry those sheep who have ever so little straggled out of those shepherds' folds, where they were kept in order to be shorn by them both, and to be howled on, both upon subjects and neighbours at their pleasure: and hence have come most of those calamities which have so long disturbed and wasted Christendom. Whilst the magistrate, being persuaded it is his duty to punish those the clergy please to call heretics, schismatics, or fanatics, or else taught to apprehend danger from dissenters in religion, thinks it his interest to suppress them; [and] persecutes all who observe not the same forms in religious worship which is set up in his country. The people, on the other side, finding the mischiefs that fall on them for worshipping God according to their own persuasions, enter into confederacies and combinations to secure themselves as well as they can; so that oppression and vexation on one side, self-defence and desire of religious liberty on the other, create dislikes, jealousies, apprehensions and factions, which seldom fail to break out into downright persecution, or open war.

But notwithstanding the liberality of the clergy to princes, when they have not strength enough to deal with them, be very large; yet when they are once in a condition to strive with him for mastery, then is it seen how far their spiritual power extends, and how, *in ordine ad spiritualia*,[80] absolute temporal power comes in. So that ordination, that begins in priesthood, if it be let alone, will certainly grow up to absolute empire; and

---

80. Into the spiritual order.

though Christ declares himself to have no kingdom of this world,[81] his successors have (whenever they can but grasp the power) a large commission to execute, and that rigorously, civil dominion. The popedom hath been a large and lasting instance of this. And what presbytery could do, even in its infancy when it had a little humbled the magistrate, let Scotland show.[82]

81. John 18:36.

82. Locke presumably refers to Scotland in the era of the domineering Andrew Melville in the 1570s. In his *Two Tracts,* he cited one of many accounts of Presbyterian tyranny in Scotland: John Maxwell, *The Burthen of Issachar* (1646), reprinted in 1663 as *Presbytery Displayd.*

Fragments on Toleration

Infallibility

While in any state and society of men the right of making laws is the highest and greatest power, certainly next and almost equal to this is the authority of interpreting these laws. For what is the point of drawing up dumb, silent statements of laws, if anybody may attach a new meaning to the words to suit his own taste, find some remote interpretation, and twist the words to fit the situation and his own opinion? Observing this, sharp-sighted priests have violated both these powers in their efforts to establish in every way that control over the conduct and consciences of men which they so strongly claim. On the one hand these persons force upon the church their own traditions which grow up continually as the occasion demands, and they contend that these possess the force of laws and oblige men's consciences. On the other hand the priests insist that the Roman pontiff is the sole and infallible interpreter of the Holy Bible. Nor does it matter very much what God himself dictated to his people on Mount Sinai, or what our lawgiver, Christ, declared on the Mount of Olives,[1] as long as, loftier than either, the seven hills of Rome dominate both. Blindness is certainly inevitable, where Heaven itself does not have enough light to guide our steps. Or does that same God, who made the tongue and organs of speech and who gave the use of language to mankind, address men in such a way that he cannot be understood without an interpreter? Who will explain the mind of God better than God himself? Or perhaps the words of God are obscure and ambiguous, while those of men are clear and certain? Is he who first made the souls of men unable to instruct them? Or does Christ so address the waves and storms that they do understand and speak to men alone so that they do not?[2] Or, indeed, will the eyes of the blind heed his words which open ears are unable to grasp? Does he instruct ignorant and wretched mankind in such a way that the diseases understand his commands better than the diseased? The prophets, the apostles, even his own Son clothed in human form and not unaware of our weakness and ignorance—all of these God sent so that he might teach men what he wanted to be done, that mankind might know what the worship and reverence of the deity should be and what unity and fellowship should exist among themselves. After so many emissaries there is by now no need for an interpreter. So it is agreed that it is not necessary that an infallible interpreter of Holy Scripture be granted in the church.

Firstly, because an infallible interpreter of this sort has not existed since the time of the apostles; for here the argument from fact to necessity is valid. It cannot be doubted that God, who promised to preserve his church continuously until the end of time,[3] will provide that nothing necessary to it should be lacking. That there has been no infallible interpreter is sufficiently shown by the disagreements of Christians among themselves about divine matters; and the dissension of opinions (and these notions are not only various but contradictory) troubled the diverse members of the church dispersed in various regions of the world and divided them into factions. All this, perhaps the priests will say, is only the quarrel

1. The Ten Commandments were delivered on Mount Sinai, and the Sermon on the Mount at the Mount of Olives.
2. Matthew 8:23–27.
3. Matthew 16:18–22.

and battle of the true church—that is to say their own—with the ignorant and heretical. Yet, it is obvious enough to anyone, however slightly
acquainted with ecclesiastical history, that even in the Church of Rome
and its infallible interpreter opinions about faith and morals and interpretations of Holy Scripture differ enormously.

Secondly, that which is not necessary would be utterly useless to both
the faith and peace of the church. Even granting that some infallible
interpreter of Holy Scripture be given, he will still not be able, however
[*word illegible*] he may be, to contribute anything to the solution of problems of faith or to the establishment of peace among Christians, unless he
can infallibly show that he is infallible. Since he cannot prove this about
himself, for nobody's testimony about himself is acceptable, and since the
Scripture is silent, I cannot easily discover how he can be recognised. So
we cannot expect any remedy from this quarter for so great a disagreement and so many errors; for there is no difference between everyone's
being subject to error and someone's being infallible but unknown and
uncertain. What help is it to be certain about something when you are
uncertain about the person? How anxiously you must anticipate a cure for
vice and ignorance from someone, when you do not know whether the
man to whose trust you commit yourself is a doctor or a charlatan.

As to the Scripture whose interpreter we seek—since it was written at
different times and not in the same style, embraces within itself various
arguments, and contains the history of past events, rules of conduct, and
the articles of faith, it can be considered in many ways.

1. Thus, there are many things contrived for arrogance and the display
of learning, which are frivolous and empty quibbles that have not arisen
from Holy Scripture, but are violently expressed by the hollow talents
of madmen. Of such a kind are the questions, "What was the forbidden
fruit of Paradise?", "Where was that lovely garden?", and others of that
sort, which neither need an interpreter nor deserve a reader. Problems of
this sort can perhaps exercise petty minds but scarcely detain a sober and
pious man. Although these are difficult matters to know, they can safely
be ignored. Moreover, they hardly seem to concern the Scripture, which is
the standard of faith and conduct.

2. The Holy Scripture also contains within it the profound myster-

ies of divine matters which utterly transcend the human intellect. These, although they are obscure, nevertheless cannot have an interpreter. For, since to interpret is nothing else than to bring out the meaning of obscure words and to express unfamiliar language clearly in words of everyday speech, here such interpretation is clearly impossible, because God has proclaimed in the clearest and most unambiguous terms what he wanted men to know and believe. Whoever attempts to explain the trinity of persons in the divine nature in words other than those in which God has revealed it brings not so much light to the Scripture as darkness. We can add to this the union of divine and human nature in the person of the mediator, the infinity and eternity of God, and several other matters, the truth of which is certain and is to be believed, but the way in which they are true cannot be expressed in discourse nor grasped by the mind. Whatever it is that impedes us in these matters, it is certainly not the obscurity of the words but the magnitude of the matters themselves and the weakness of our minds. Whoever wants to interpret these things ought to bring to them not an extensive vocabulary and a facility of expression but a power and an intellect new to human souls.

3. There are other things in Holy Writ, things most necessary to salvation, so clear and unambiguous that virtually nobody can doubt them, for to hear is to understand them. Such are the principal duties of a Christian man—justice, chastity, charity, and benevolence—which certainly have little need of an interpreter, since they are so clearly transmitted that if any interpretation were added, it would in turn inevitably require another interpretation.

4. There are some precepts and instructions in Holy Writ of a more general nature. For example, there is that passage to the Corinthians: "Doth not even nature itself (i.e., custom) teach you that, if a man has long hair, it is a shame to him?"[4] Scripture does not state what length of hair is too long, and so it is to be determined by the church. Similarly, it is stated in chapter 14: "Let all things be done decently and in order."[5] Since these precepts relate to matters which are in themselves and by their

4. 1 Corinthians 11:14.
5. 1 Corinthians 14:40.

nature indifferent[6] and can neither be applied to everyday life nor govern human behaviour without an interpreter, in these and other similar cases I agree that an infallible interpreter is given, possible, and needed. Such interpreters are the fathers and leaders of every church, who in these matters can be called infallible, but as I see it, their infallibility is directive not definitive. To be sure, the shepherds of the church can perhaps err while they are leading, but the sheep certainly cannot err while they are following. The path of obedience is safe and secure. For, since obedience is a certain and undeniable duty of Christian people, even if the interpretation of a text of Scripture is perhaps uncertain, the man who errs least is he who follows what is sure and applies himself to both obedience and the peace of the church. Interpreters of such divine laws can be called "infallible," since even if they can perhaps be deceived themselves, they cannot mislead others.

In the interpretation of Scripture, however, how much is to be granted to each individual and how much to the authority of the church, and then what is achieved by reason and what by the illumination of the Holy Spirit is not so easy and straightforward to state. Great caution must be exercised, however, lest by relying too heavily on our reason we disregard our faith, or by neglecting the mysteries of the gospel embrace philosophy instead of religion. On the other hand, enthusiasm[7] must be carefully avoided, lest, while we await the inspiration of the Holy Spirit, we honour and worship our own dreams. It is certainly true that much is contributed to the interpretation of the Holy Bible by learning, much by reason, and finally much by the Holy Spirit's enlightening the minds of men. However, the most certain interpreter of Scripture is Scripture itself, and it alone is infallible.

6. *indifferent:* see note 75, p. 33.
7. *enthusiasm:* see note 50, p. 124.

The Constitutions of Carolina

(95) No man shall be permitted to be a freeman of Carolina, or to have any estate or habitation within it, that doth not acknowledge a God, and that God is publicly and solemnly to be worshipped.

(97)[8] But since the natives of that place, who will be concerned in our plantation, are utterly strangers to Christianity, whose idolatry, ignorance, or mistake, gives us no right to expel, or use them ill; and those who remove from other parts to plant[9] there, will unavoidably be of different opinions concerning matters of religion, the liberty whereof they will expect to have allowed them, and it will not be reasonable for us, on this account, to keep them out; that civil peace may be maintained amidst the diversity of opinions, and our agreement and compact with all men may be duly and faithfully observed, the violation whereof, upon what pretence soever, cannot be without great offence to Almighty God, and great scandal to the true religion that we profess; and also, that Jews, heathens, and other dissenters from the purity of Christian religion may not be scared and kept at a distance from it, but, by having an opportunity of acquainting themselves with the truth and reasonableness of its doctrines, and the peaceableness and inoffensiveness of its professors,[10] may, by good usage and persuasion, and all those convincing methods of gentleness and meekness, suitable to the rules and design of the Gospel, be won over to embrace, and unfeignedly receive the truth: therefore, any seven or more persons agreeing in any religion shall constitute a church or profession, to which they shall give some name to distinguish it from others.

(98) The terms of admittance and communion with any church or pro-

8. A new article 96 was inserted in the published 1670 version which is absent in the manuscript: "As the country comes to be sufficiently planted and distributed into fit divisions, it shall belong to the parliament to take care for the building of churches, and the public maintenance of divines, to be employed in the exercise of religion, according to the Church of England, which, being the only true and orthodox, and the national religion of all the king's dominions, is so also of Carolina, and therefore it alone shall be allowed to receive public maintenance by grant of parliament." Pierre Des Maizeaux stated that Locke did not approve of this clause (*A Collection of Several Pieces of Mr. John Locke*, 1720, p. 42).

9. *plant:* settle.

10. *professor:* one who proclaims or follows a religion.

fession shall be written in a book and therein be subscribed by all the members of the said church or profession, which book shall be kept by the public register of the precinct where they reside.

(99) The time of everyone's subscription and admittance shall be dated in the said book or religious record.

(100) In the terms of communion of every church or profession, these following shall be three, without which no agreement or assembly of men, upon pretence of religion, shall be accounted a church or profession, within these rules: (i) That there is a God. (ii) That God is publicly to be worshipped. (iii) That it is lawful, and the duty of every man, being thereunto called by those that govern, to bear witness to truth; and that every church or profession shall, in their terms of communion, set down the external way whereby they witness a truth as in the presence of God, whether it be by laying hands on, or kissing the Bible, as in the Church of England,[11] or by holding up the hand, or any other sensible[12] way.[13]

(101) No person above seventeen years of age shall have any benefit or protection of the law, or be capable of any place of profit or honour, who is not a member of some church or profession, having his name recorded in some one, and but one religious record at once.

(102) No person of any other church or profession shall disturb or molest any religious assembly.

(103) No person whatsoever shall speak anything in their religious assembly irreverently or seditiously of the government or governors, or states matters.

(104) Any person subscribing the terms of communion in the record of the said church or profession before the precinct register, and any five members of the church or profession, shall be thereby made a member of the said church or profession.

(105) Any person striking out his own name out of any religious record,

---

11. "Church of England": the manuscript has "Protestant and Papist churches."

12. *sensible:* apprehensible to the senses.

13. This passage seeks to exclude "Nicodemism," the notion that it is legitimate to keep one's religious allegiance secret. Some Protestant sects were suspected of this, and Catholics were accused of permitting dissimulation in their relations with heretics. The term derives from John 3:1–2.

or his name being struck out by any officer thereunto authorised by each church of profession respectively, shall cease to be a member of that church or profession.

(106) No person shall use any reproachful, reviling, or abusive language against the religion of any church or profession, that being the certain way of disturbing the public peace, and of hindering the conversion of any to the truth, by engaging them in quarrels and animosities, to the hatred of the professors and that profession, which otherwise they might be brought to assent to.

(107) Since charity obliges us to wish well to the souls of all men, and religion ought to alter nothing in any man's civil estate or right, it shall be lawful for slaves as well as others, to enter themselves, and be of what church any of them shall think best, and thereof be as fully members as any freemen. But yet no slave shall hereby be exempted from that civil dominion his master hath over him, but be in all other things in the same state and condition he was in before.

(108) Assemblies, upon what pretence soever of religion, not observing and performing the abovesaid rules, shall not be esteemed as churches, but unlawful meetings, and be punished as other riots.[14]

(109) No person whatsoever shall disturb, molest, or persecute another for his speculative opinions in religion, or his way of worship.

(110) Every freeman of Carolina shall have absolute power and authority over his negro slaves, of what opinion or religion soever.

Against Samuel Parker

Society[15] is necessary to the preservation of human nature. Government necessary to the preservation of society, the end whereof is peace. One supreme necessary in every city for the preservation of the government. First, because there cannot be two supremes; second, because co-ordinate distinct powers may command the same person contrary obedience,

14. In law, a *riot* was not necessarily violent, merely an unlawful assembly.

15. The first two paragraphs are Locke's summary of Parker's argument in his *Discourse of Ecclesiastical Politie.* Samuel Parker (1640–88) was chaplain to Archbishop Sheldon, 1667–72, and bishop of Oxford, 1686–88.

which he cannot be obliged to. This supreme is the civil magistrate. The civil magistrate must have under his power all that may concern the end of government, i.e., peace. Religion and conscience are more apt to disturb the peace than even vice itself; first, because men are most apt to mistake [it], because backed with zeal, the glory of God, and the good of men's souls, martyrdom; [second,] they make men more resolute, confident, turbulent, etc.; whereas vice discovered is out of countenance. *Ergo*, it is necessary the magistrate should have power over men's consciences in matters of religion. This power is to be exercised with the most severity and strictness, because ordinary severity will not do.

Fathers have an absolute power over their children. This paternal power grew into several monarchies. These monarchs by this paternal right were also priests. Sovereignty and priesthood [were] jointly vested in the same person for [the] first 2500 years. Ecclesiastical supremacy [was] exercised by the Jewish kings, though the priesthood was vested in other persons. Christ, having no temporal power, exercised none, nor could give the magistrate none about his religion, which was to be propagated by patience and submission. But, instead of civil coercive power to keep up ecclesiastical discipline, there was given the church a miraculous power to punish as well as eject offenders by excommunication. This lasted in the church till the magistrate became Christian and then ceased as no longer necessary, because then the government of religion resolved in the magistrate and was restored, though the priests commissioned by our Saviour kept the ministerial function, and so the Christian magistrate hath again the power over religion.

[SP][16] *'Tis absolutely necessary to the peace and tranquillity of the commonwealth, which, though it be the prime and most important end of government, can never be sufficiently secured, unless religion be subject to the authority of the supreme power, in that it has the strongest influence upon human affairs.*

[JL] Whether [this] proves anything but that the magistrate's business being only to preserve peace, those wrong opinions are to be restrained

16. The extracts in italics are from Parker's *Discourse*, to which Locke responds. The initials of the interlocutors have been inserted at the beginning of each paragraph.

that have a tendency to disturb it? (and this is by every sober man to be allowed).[17]

[SP] *As true piety secures the public weal by taming and civilising the passions of men, and inuring them to a mild, gentle and governable spirit: so superstition and wrong notions of God and his worship are the most powerful engines to overturn its settlement. And therefore unless princes have power to bind their subjects to that religion that they apprehend most advantageous to public peace and tranquillity, and restrain those religious mistakes that tend to its subversion, they are no better than statues and images of authority, and want[18] that part of their power that is most necessary to a right discharge of their government.*

[JL] Whether assigning those ill effects that follow to "mistakes" [and] "wrong notions of God and his worship," he does not suppose the magistrate's power to proceed from his being in the right? Whether by "bind the subject to his religion," he means that, whether the magistrate's opinion be right or wrong, he has power to force the subject to renounce his own opinions, however quiet and peaceable, and declare assent and consent to those of the magistrate? And, if so, why Christ and the apostles directed not their discourses and addressed their miracles to the princes and magistrates of the world to persuade them, whereas by preaching to and converting the people they, according to this doctrine, [lay] under a necessity of being either seditious or martyrs.

[SP] *If conscience be ever able to break down the restraints of government, and all men have licence to follow their own persuasions, the mischief is infinite, and the folly endless; . . . there never yet was any commonwealth that gave a real liberty to men's imaginations, that was not suddenly overrun with numberless divisions and subdivisions of sects: as was notorious in the late confusions, when liberty of conscience was laid as the foundation of settlement.*

[JL] Whether subdivision of opinions into small sects be of such danger to the government?

[SP] *Because the Church of Rome, by her unreasonable impositions, has invaded the fundamental liberties of mankind, they presently conclude[19] all*

17. *allowed:* accepted, agreed with.
18. *want:* lack.
19. "they presently conclude": they [the dissenters] now include.

restraints upon licentious practices and persuasions about religion under the hated name of popery.

[JL] What fundamental liberties of mankind were invaded by the Church of Rome that will not be in the same condition under the civil magistrate, according to his doctrine?, since the power of the Church of Rome was allowed and their decrees enforced by the will of the civil magistrate?

[SP] *'Tis enough at present to have proved in general the absolute necessity that affairs of religion should be subject to government; . . . if the prince's jurisdiction be limited to civil affairs, and the concerns of religion be subject to another government, then may subjects be obliged to (what is impossible) contradictory commands. . . . But, seeing no man can be subject to contradictory obligations, 'tis by consequence utterly impossible he should be subject to two supreme powers.*

[JL] The end of government being public peace, 'tis no question the supreme power must have an uncontrollable right to judge and ordain all things that may conduce to it, but yet the question will be whether uniformity established by a law be (as is here supposed) a necessary means to it?, i.e., whether it be at all dangerous to the magistrate that, he believing free will, some of his subjects shall believe predestination, or whether it be more necessary for his government to make laws for wearing surplices than it is for wearing vests?

[SP] *The wisdom of providence . . . so ordered affairs, that no man could be born into the world without being subject to some superior: every father being by nature vested with a right to govern his children. And the first governments in the world were established purely upon the natural rights of paternal authority, which afterward grew up to a kingly power by the increase of posterity; . . . and hence it came to pass that in the first ages of the world, monarchy was its only government.*

[JL] Whether, allowing the paternal right of government (which is asserted not proved), that paternal monarchy descended upon [the] death of the father it descended wholly to the eldest son, or else all the brothers had an equal power over their respective issues. If the first, then monarchy is certainly *jure naturali*,[20] but then there can be but one rightful

---

20. *jure naturali:* by natural right.

monarch in the whole world, i.e., the right heir of Adam; if the second, all governments, whether monarchical or other, is only from the consent of the people.

[SP] *Nothing more concerns the interest of the civil magistrate than to take care what particular doctrines of religion are taught within his dominions, because some are peculiarly advantageous to the ends of government, and others as naturally tending to its disturbance. . . . It must needs above all things concern princes, to look to the doctrine and articles of men's belief.*

[JL] Whether hence it will follow that the magistrate ought to force men by severity of laws and penalties to be of the same mind with him in the speculative opinions in religion, or worship God with the same ceremonies? That the magistrate should restrain seditious doctrines who denies, but because he may, then has he power over all other doctrines to forbid or impose? If he has not, your argument is short, if he hath, how far is this short of Mr Hobbes's doctrine? [21]

[SP] *Fanaticism is both the greatest and the easiest vice that is incident to religion; 'tis a weed that thrives in all soils, and there is the same fanatic spirit that mixes itself with all the religions in the world.*

[JL] Whether this fanatic spirit be not the same passion, fired with religious zeal, whose fanatic heats he in that same paragraph accuses of having committed such dire outrages, massacres, and butchery, and done such mischiefs among men, and if it mixes itself with all religions? I desire him to examine, though he be of the Church of England, what spirit that is which sets him so zealously to stir up the magistrate to persecute all those who dissent from him in those opinions or ways of worship the public support whereof is to give him preferment?

Civil and Ecclesiastical Power

There is a twofold society, of which almost all men in the world are members, and that from the twofold concernment they have to attain a twofold happiness; *viz.* that of this world and that of the other: and hence there arises these two following societies, *viz.* religious and civil.

21. Hobbes, because of the arguments in bks. 3 and 4 of *Leviathan* (1651), was taken to be the extreme exponent of the submission of religion to the civil power.

State (1)[22] The end of civil society is civil peace and prosperity, or the preservation of the society and every member thereof in a free and peaceable enjoyment of all the good things of this life that belong to each of them; but beyond the concernments of this life, this society hath nothing to do at all.

Church (1) The end of religious society is the attaining happiness after this life in another world.

State (2) The terms of communion with, or being a part of this society, is promise of obedience to the laws of it.

Church (2) The terms of communion or condition of being members of this society, is promise of obedience to the laws of it.

State (3) The proper matter, *circa quam*,[23] of the laws of this society are all things tending to the end above-mentioned, i.e., civil happiness; and are in effect almost all moral and indifferent things, which yet are not the proper matter of the laws of this society, till the doing or omitting of any of them come to have a tendency to the end above-mentioned.

Church (3) The proper matter of the laws of this society are all things tending to the attainment of future bliss, which are of three sorts. (i) *Credenda,* or matters of faith and opinion, which terminate in the understanding. (ii) *Cultus religiosus,* which contains in it both the ways of expressing our honour and adoration of the deity, and of address to him for the obtaining any good from him. (iii) *Moralia,* or the right management of our actions in respect of ourselves and others.

State (4) The means to procure obedience to the laws of this society, and thereby preserve it, is force or punishment; i.e., the abridgement of anyone's share of the good things of the world, within the reach of this society, and sometimes a total deprivation, as in capital punishments.

Church (4) The means to preserve obedience to the laws of this society are the hopes and fears of happiness and misery in another world. But though the laws of this society be in order to happiness in another world, and so the penalties annexed to them are also of another world; yet the society being in this world and to be continued here, there is some means

22. The numeration and repetition of the headings "state" and "church" are not in the manuscript; instead, the paragraphs appear in parallel columns, headed "Civil Society or the State" and "Religious Society or the Church."

23. *circa quam:* about which.

necessary for the preservation of the society here, which is the expulsion of such members as obey not the laws of it, or disturb its order.

State. And this, I think, is the whole end, latitude, and extent of civil power and society.

Church. And this, I think, is the whole end, latitude, and extent of ecclesiastical power and religious society.

This being, as I suppose, the distinct bounds of church and state, let us a little compare them together.

The Parallel:

State (1) The end of civil society is present enjoyment of what this world affords.

Church (1) The end of church communion, future expectation of what is to be had in the other world.

State (2) Another end of civil society is the preservation of the society or government itself for its own sake.

Church (2) The preservation of the society in religious communion is only in order to the conveying and propagating those laws and truths which concern our well-being in another world.

State and Church (3) The terms of communion must be the same in all societies.

State (4) The laws of a commonwealth are mutable, being made within the society by an authority not distinct from it, nor exterior to it.

Church (4) The laws of religious society, bating[24] those which are only subservient to the order necessary to their execution, are immutable, not subject to any authority of the society, but only proposed by and within the society, but made by a lawgiver without[25] the society, and paramount to it.

State (5) The proper means to procure obedience to the law of the civil society, and thereby attain the end, civil happiness, is force or punishment. First, it is [the] effectual and adequate way for the preservation of

24. *bating:* excepting.
25. *without:* outside, outwith.

the society, and of civil happiness, [which] is the immediate and natural consequence of the execution of the law. Second, it is just, for the breach of laws being mostly the prejudice and diminution of another man's right, and always tending to the dissolution of the society, in the continuance whereof every man's particular right is comprehended, it is just that he who has impaired another man's good should suffer the diminution of his own. Third, 'tis within the power of the society, which can exert its own strength against offenders, the sword being put into the magistrate's hands to that purpose. But civil society hath nothing to do without its own limits, which is civil happiness.

Church (5) The proper enforcement of obedience to the laws of religion is the rewards and punishments of the other world. But civil punishment is not so. First, because it is ineffectual to that purpose; for punishment is never sufficient to keep men to the obedience of any law, where the evil it brings is not certainly greater than the good which is obtained or expected from the disobedience. And therefore no temporal worldly punishment can be sufficient to persuade a man to that, or from that, way which he believes leads to everlasting happiness or misery. Second, because it is unjust, in reference both to *credenda* and *cultus*, that I should be despoiled of my good things of this world, where I disturb not in the least the enjoyment of others; for my faith or religious worship hurts not another man in any concernment of his. And in moral transgressions, the third and real part of religion, the religious society cannot punish, because it then invades the civil society, and wrests the magistrate's sword out of his hand. In civil society one man's good is involved and complicated with another, but in religious societies every man's concerns are separate, and one man's transgression hurts not another any farther than he imitates him, and if he err, he errs at his own private cost. Therefore I think no external punishment, i.e., deprivation or diminution of the good of this life, belongs to the church. Only because for the propagation of the truth (which every society believes to be its own religion) it is equity[26] it should remove those two evils which will hinder its propagation: (i) disturbance within, which is contradiction or disobedience of any of its members to its doctrines and

26. "it is equity": it is equitable that.

discipline; (ii) infamy without, which is the scandalous lives or disallowed profession of any of its members. And the proper way to do this, which is in its power, is to exclude and disown such vicious members.

State and Church (6) Church membership is perfectly voluntary, and may end whenever anyone pleases without any prejudice to him, but in civil society it is not so.

But because religious societies are of two sorts, wherein their circumstances very much differ, the exercise of their power is also much different.

It is to be considered that all mankind (very few or none excepted) are combined into civil societies in various forms, as force, chance, agreement, or other accidents have happened to contrive them. There are very few also that have not some religion. And hence it comes to pass, that very few men but are members both of some church and of some commonwealth. And hence it comes to pass:

1. That in some places the civil and religious societies are co-extended, i.e., both the magistrate and every subject of the same commonwealth is also member of the same church; and thus it is in Muscovy, where they have all the same civil laws, and the same opinions and religious worship.

2. In some places the commonwealth, though all of one religion, is but a part of the church or religious society which acts and is acknowledged to be one entire society; and so it is in Spain and the principalities of Italy.

3. In some places the religion of the commonwealth, i.e., the public established religion, is not received by all the subjects of the commonwealth; and thus the Protestant religion in England, the Reformed in Brandenburg,[27] the Lutheran in Sweden.

4. In some places the religion of part of the people is different from the governing part of the civil society; and thus the Presbyterian, Independent, Anabaptist,[28] Quaker, Papist, and Jewish in England, the Lutheran and Popish in Cleve, etc.;[29] and in these two last the religious society is part of the civil.

---

27. The Electors of Brandenburg were Calvinist, but many of their subjects were Lutheran.

28. *Anabaptist:* Baptist.

29. Locke had visited Cleves (Kleve), part of the duchy of Brandenburg, in 1665–66 and had been impressed that religious pluralism and civil peace could subsist together.

There are also three things to be considered in each religion, as the matter of their communion. (i) Opinions or speculations or *credenda*. (ii) *Cultus religiosus*. (iii) *Mores*. Which are all to be considered in the exercise of church power, which I conceive does properly extend no farther than excommunication, which is to remove a scandalous or turbulent member.

1. In the first case there is no need of excommunication for immorality, because the civil law hath or may sufficiently provide against that by penal laws, enough to suppress it; for the civil magistrate hath moral actions under the dominion of his sword, and therefore 'tis not like[ly] he will turn away a subject out of his country for a fault which he can compel him to reform. But if anyone differ from the church in *fide aut cultu*,[30] I think first the civil magistrate may punish him for it, where he is fully persuaded that it is likely to disturb the civil peace, otherwise not. But the religious society may certainly excommunicate him, the peace whereof may by this means be preserved; but no other evil ought to follow him upon that excommunication as such, but only upon the consideration of the public peace, for if he will silently conceal his opinion or carry away his opinion or differing worship out of the verge[31] of that government, I know not by what right he can be hindered.

2. In the second case, I think the church may excommunicate for faults in faith and worship, but not those faults in manners which the magistrate has annexed penalties to, for the preservation of civil society and happiness.

3. The same also I think ought to be the rule in the third case.

4. In the fourth case, I think the church has power to excommunicate for matters of faith, worship, or manners, though the magistrate punish the same immoralities with his sword, because the church cannot otherwise remove the scandal which is necessary for its preservation and the propagation of its doctrine. And this power of being judges who are fit to be of their society, the magistrate cannot deny to any religious society which is permitted within his dominions. This was the state of the church till Constantine.[32]

But in none of the former cases is excommunication capable to be

30. *fide aut cultu:* faith or worship.
31. *verge:* sphere, domain.
32. The first Christian emperor, who converted ca. 313.

denounced by any church upon anyone but the members of that church, it being absurd to cut off that which is no part. Neither ought the civil magistrate to inflict any punishment upon the score of excommunication, but to punish the fact[33] or forbear, just as he finds it convenient for the preservation of the civil peace and prosperity of the commonwealth (within which his power is confined), without any regard to the excommunication at all.

Philanthropy

Mankind is supported in the ways of virtue, or vice, by the society he is of, and the conversation he keeps, example and fashion being the great governors of this world. The first question every man ought to ask in all things he doth or undertakes is, how is this acceptable to God? But the first question most men ask, is, how will this render me to my company, and those whose esteem I value? He that asks neither of these questions is a melancholy rogue, and always of the most dangerous and worst of men. This is the foundation of all the sects and orders, either of religion or philosophy, that have been in the world. Men are supported and delighted with the friendship and protection they enjoy from all the rest of the same way; and as these are more or less really performed amongst them, so the party increaseth or diminisheth. The Protestant religion, whilst it was a sect and a party, cherished and favoured each other; [and] increased strangely, against all the power and persecution of the Church of Rome. But since the warmth of that is over, and 'tis embraced only as a truer doctrine, this last forty years hath hardly produced as many converts from the Romish fopperies;[34] the greater clergy plainly inclining to go back to their interest, which is highest exalted in that religion; but the greater part of the laity, having an abhorrence to their cruelty and ambition, as well as their interests contrary, have divided themselves into sects and churches, of new and different names and ways; that they may keep up some warmth and heat, in opposition to the common enemy, who other-

33. *fact:* deed.
34. There was a widespread fear among Protestants in the late seventeenth century that, Europe-wide, their religion was contracting in the face of Catholic advances.

wise was like[ly] to find us all asleep.[35] The Quakers are a great instance, how little truth and reason operates upon mankind, and how great force, society, and conversation hath amongst those that maintain an inviolable friendship and concern, for all of their way.[36]

'Tis a true proverb, what is every man's business, is no man's. This befalls truth, she hath no sect, no corporation, 'tis made no man's interest to own her: there is no body of men, no council sitting, that should take care of him that suffers for her; the clergy have pretended to that care, for many hundreds of years past, but how well they have performed it the world knows; they have found a mistress, called the present power, that pays them much better than truth can. Whatever idol she enjoins, they offer us to be worshipped as this great goddess; and their impudence hath been so great that, though they vary it as often as the present power itself changeth, yet they affirm it still to be the same goddess, truth. Neither is it possible that the greatest part of that sort of men should not either flatter the magistrate, or the people: in both, truth suffers. Learning is a trade that most men apply themselves to with pains and charge, that they may hereafter live and make advantage by it: 'tis natural for trade to go to the best market: truth and money, truth and hire, did never yet long agree. These thoughts moved us to endeavour to associate ourselves with such as are lovers of truth and virtue; that we may encourage, assist, and support each other, in the ways of them; and may possibly become some help in the preserving truth, religion, and virtue amongst us; whatever deluge of misery and mischief may overrun this part of the world. We intermeddle not with anything that concerns the just and legal power of the civil magistrate; the government and laws of our country cannot be injured by such as love truth, virtue, and justice; we think ourselves obliged to lay down our lives and fortunes in the defence of it. No man can say he loves God that loves not his neighbour; no man can love his neighbour that loves

35. Locke reverses a common argument among Anglicans hostile to toleration that the fragmentation of Protestantism into diverse denominations weakened the common cause against popery and that such fragmentation was promoted by Catholics on the "divide and rule" principle.

36. Locke's tolerationism was no bar to disdain for what he saw as the wilder shores of Christianity.

not his country. 'Tis the greatest charity to preserve the laws and rights of the nation, whereof we are. A good man, and a charitable man, is to give to every man his due. From the king upon the throne, to the beggar in the street.

Infallibility Revisited

1.[37] Whether there be any infallible judge on earth.

2. Whether any church be that judge.

3. Whether the Roman Church be that church.

4. If it be, what capacity, whether the infallibility be in the pope as the head, or in the body of the church, and then whether in the whole body diffusive or in the collective in a council,[38] and if a council be infallible, then whether it be so only with the pope's confirmation, or without it.

5. How shall we certainly know who must be members of it, clergy and laics, or only clergy; or only bishops, presbyters too and deacons, or chorepiscopy[39] at least, for we find all these usually subscribing.

6. Or let the council be as they would have it; how shall I be sure they are infallible, for are they so absolutely infallible as they cannot determine falsely *in rebus fidei,*[40] do what they will.

7. How shall I know when they determine aright, and what is required to a synodical constitution; must all concur in the votes, or will the major part serve the turn.

8. What makes a council general; must all the bishops of the Christian world be called.

9. When they are all called must they all come, or else it is no general council.

37. This text is set out as a series of queries.

38. Before the nineteenth century, many Catholics believed that infallibility lay in the general council of the church rather than personally in the pope. During the late Middle Ages, the conciliar movement involved a debate whether Catholic truth lay in the collective body of the church and not in councils at all ("the church diffusive") and whether councils should have priests as well as bishops present.

39. *chorepiscopy:* a country bishop in the early church; a suffragan bishop serving the hinterland of a city.

40. *in rebus fidei:* in matters of faith.

10. Who must call the general council, the pope or the Christian kings and emperors, and how shall I be assured which of them must.

11. How far are those determinations infallible, whether in matters of fact as well as faith.

12. And if in matters of faith then whether in fundamentals only or in superstructures.

13. How shall I infallibly know which points are fundamental, which not.

14. But admit all these were determined, and our infallible judge were a general council with the pope, yet in a time of schism where there are two or three popes at once: Clement III, Gregory VII; Gelasius II, Gregory VIII; Celestine II, Honorius II; Anacletus II, Innocent II; Victor IV, Alexander III; Clement VII, Urban VI; Eugene IV, Felix V.[41] you may see [in] Gautier the Jesuit's book[42] a large catalogue more, and these warring one against another for forty or fifty years together: so that the learnedest clergymen alive know not which was St. Peter's true successor, and thus, saith reason, there may be again, then I ask how I shall know which is the infallible judge or by what rule a Romanist may tell when a truth is defined and when not, since Sixtus V defined one Bible to be true *anno* 1590, and Clement VIII another two years after, and each of them prohibited and condemned all but his own;[43] and these two Bibles contain many contradictions each to other, and certainly contradictory propositions cannot both be gospel, and if not then either one of these two was not really (whence inconveniency enough will follow) or they were both true popes, and so both these definitions true, and so no true papist hath any true Bible.

15. But suppose there be no schism and all agreed on the pope and a general council met, how shall I be sure that he that is reputed pope is so indeed, seeing by their own principles, secret simony makes him none, so

41. One of each of these pairs (whose names I have anglicized) is deemed by the Catholic Church to be an antipope; these popes reigned between the eleventh and fifteenth centuries.

42. Jacques Gaultier, *Table chronographique de l'estat du Christianisme* (Lyon, 1609).

43. Both were editions of the Vulgate (Latin) Bible, which alone was authorized for use in the Catholic Church, but the 1590 text was found to be faulty.

[says] the Bull of Pope Julius II *Super simoniaca papae electione si conti-gerit,*[44] and that he was not simoniacal it is impossible for me to know; the election of Sixtus V[45] was notoriously simoniacal, for Cardinal D'Essy,[46] whom he bribed and promised to obey and defend against any opposite faction etc., sent all these obligations subscribed by Sixtus V [in] his own hand to Philip then king of Spain, who in the year 1599[47] sent to Rome to bid the cardinals who had been elected before Sixtus V come to the see, to come to a council at Seville in Spain where the original writing was produced and the crime was evidently proved, and, if so, all the cardinals which were made by this Sixtus were in reality no cardinals, and then all the popes which have been really are no popes.

16. But admit the pope were certainly known to be such, that neither he nor any of his predecessors came in by simony, yet how shall I know whether those bishops, who with him make up a council are bishops. Indeed, for if they be no bishops then it is no council. And that they are true bishops it is for ever impossible for any papist certainly to know, for if he that did ordain them did not intend it when he gave orders[48] (and whether he did or no, God only knows), then by their own principles, they are no bishops and by consequence no council.

17. How shall I know that the pope and bishops so met (at Trent for example)[49] are Christians, for, if not, then they are no legislative council or church representative, and that they are Christians it is impossible for any Catholic to know with any infallible certainty, for if they be not baptised then I am sure with them they are no Christians, and if the priest that baptised them did not intend to do it then by the canon of the Trent Council's they are not baptised. Now what the priest intended

44. *Concerning the Simoniacal Election of the Pope* (1505).

45. Reigned 1585–90.

46. Louis D'Este (1538–86).

47. Philip III (r. 1598–1621) was king of Spain in 1599; it is not clear if the account here is accurate.

48. Here and in the next paragraph Locke alludes to the Catholic principle of "defect of intention," whereby an action may be deemed null if the agent did not intend what was outwardly done. (Annulments of marriage today are often made on this ground.) Protestants regarded the notion as a slippery and dangerous piece of casuistry.

49. The Council of Trent (1545–63) launched the Counter-Reformation.

when he administered that sacrament 'tis impossible that any (save God that knows the heart) should certainly know without immediate revelation, which they pretend not to, and consequently 'tis impossible that any of them should certainly know that ever there was a pope or a bishop or a priest since our Saviour's days; nay impossible that they should know whether there be now one Christian in their church, and therefore much less that there is or hath been a lawful council.

18. But admit all these doubts were clearly resolved and a council (in their own sense lawful) sitting and determining matters in controversy, yet how shall we know certainly that these are their determinations, specially since the Greek Church near 300 years since accused the Roman for forcing a canon into the Nicene Councils in behalf of the pope's being head of the universal church, which could never be found in the authentic copies, though the African bishops sent to Constantinople, Alexandria, and Antioch to search for them, Codex Can. Eccles. Afri. Iustel p. 39, 40.[50] We must rely on the honesty of the amanuensis, or of those persons that convey them to us, and those are certainly not infallible, and we know there are Indices Expurgatory,[51] [and] foisting in and blotting out of manuscripts.[52]

19. But admit all this cleared, yet when I have indeed the genuine canons and am sure of it, how shall I be assured of the true meaning of them, for we know that Vega and Soto (two famous and learned men in the Council of Trent)[53] writ and defended contradictory opinions, yet each thinketh the canon of the council to determine on his side; now, of necessity, one of them must mistake the doctrine of the council, unless you will say the council determined contradictions and then the council is not infallible itself, and if either of them mistook the council, then it was not an infallible guide to him; now if learned men who were members of the

50. Henri Justel, *Bibliotheca juris canonici veteris* (Paris, 1661).

51. The Roman Inquisition compiled an index of banned books. In due course, Locke's books were placed on it.

52. A standard charge was that Catholics forged and altered manuscript evidence. The most famous case was the "Donation of Constantine," a document in which the emperor Constantine had allegedly conferred imperial authority on the papacy. In the fifteenth century Lorenzo Valla demonstrated it to be a forgery.

53. Andrés de Vega (1498–1549) and Domingo de Soto (ca. 1495–1560).

council (such as disputed much in it) could not infallibly know the meaning of it, how can I who am neither.

20. What necessity of an infallible judge at all; the Christian world had no such judge for 325 years, for the Nicene Council was the first general [council] and if they understood Scripture and were saved then, when they had no such thing, why may not we now; and if they were not saved, the Church of Rome must blot out many hundreds and thousands of saints and martyrs out of her martyrology.

Till these twenty questions be infallibly resolved it seems impossible that any man should have any infallible knowledge of the Church of Rome's infallibility.

Religion in France

Nîmes, 3 January 1676. At Nîmes they have now but one temple (the other by the king's order being pulled down about four years since), its roof supported on an arch like that at Orange.[54] Two of their consuls[55] are Protestants, two papists, but are not permitted to receive the sacrament in their robes as formerly. The Protestants had built them here too a hospital for their sick, but that is taken from them. A chamber in it is left for their sick, but never used, because the priests trouble them when there, but notwithstanding their discouragement, I do not find that many of them go over.[56] One of them told me, when I asked him the question, that the papists did nothing but by force or money.

Montpellier, 31 January 1676. Uzès, a town in this province, not far from Nîmes, was wont to send every year a Protestant deputy to the assembly of the States[57] here at Montpellier, the greatest part being Protestants, but they were forbid to do it this year.[58] And this week the Protestants there

54. Locke had been at Orange in December; the city gave its name to the Dutch princes of Orange but was seized by France in 1660. The second Protestant church at Nîmes was demolished in 1664.

55. Officials of the local *parlement*.

56. *go over:* convert to Catholicism. Locke elsewhere argues that persecution generally fails in its aim of conversion.

57. *States:* the provincial assembly of Estates.

58. Protestant deputies had in fact long been excluded.

have an order from the king to choose no more consuls of the town of the religion, and their temple is ordered to be pulled down, the only one they had left there, though three-quarters of the town be Protestants. The pretence given is that their temple being too near the papish church, their singing of psalms disturbed the service.

Montpellier, 7 February 1676. The States every morning go to Notre Dame to prayers, where mass is sung. All the while the priest who says mass is at the altar saying the office, you cannot hear him [say] a word, and indeed the music is the pleasanter of the two. The cardinal[59] and bishops are all on the right hand [of] the choir [...] and all the lay barons on the left or south side. The cardinal sat uppermost, nearest the altar, and had a velvet cushion, richly laced with broad silver and gold lace; the bishops had none at all. He also had his book and repeated his office apart very genteelly with an unconcerned look, talking ever[y] now and then, and laughing with the bishops next him. He keeps a very fine mistress[60] in the town, which some of the very papists complain of, and hath some very fine boys in his train.[61]

Montpellier, 12 February 1676. If anyone [among the Protestant pastors] hold tenets contrary to their articles of faith, the king punishes him, so that you must be here either of the Romish or their church; for not long since it happened to one here, who was inclining to and vented[62] some Arian[63] doctrines, the governor complained to the king. He sent order he should be tried, and so was sent to Toulouse where upon trial, he denying it utterly, he was permitted to scape out of prison; but had he owned[64] it, he had been burnt as a heretic.

Montpellier, 17 February 1676. The consistory[65] manage their church censures thus. If anyone live scandalously, they first reprove him in private. If he mends not, he is called before the consistory and admonished there. If that works not, the same is done in the public congregation, and if after

59. Pierre de Bonzi (1631–1703), archbishop of Narbonne, president of the Estates.
60. Joanne de Gévaudan, who later married the comte de Ganges.
61. Most of the final two sentences are written in shorthand.
62. *vented:* gave outlet or expression to.
63. *Arian:* see note 68, p. 30.
64. *owned:* acknowledged, confessed.
65. *consistory:* in Calvinist churches, a court of presbyters.

that he stands incorrigible, he is excluded from the eucharist. This is the utmost of their power.

Montpellier, 19 February 1676. Public admonitions of their consistory happen seldom. The last two instances were, one for striking a cuff on the ear in the church on a communion day, for which he was hindered from receiving. The other for marrying his daughter to a papist, for which he stood excommunicate six months, but their excommunication reaches no farther than exclusion from the eucharist, not from the church and sermons.[66]

Avignon, 22 April 1676. At Villeneuve over against Avignon on the other side [of] the Rhone we saw the charterhouse where are sixty friars.[67] Their chapel well adorned, their plate, copes and relics very rich, amongst the rest a chalice of gold, given by René, the last king of Naples of the Anjou race.[68] I was going to take it in my hand, but the Carthusian withdrew it till he had put a cloth about the handle and so gave it into my hand, nobody being suffered to touch these holy things but a priest. In their chapel Pope Innocent the 6th lies interred; he died 1362, and in a little chapel in their convent stands a plain, old chair wherein he was infallible. I sat too little awhile in it to get that privilege. In their devotions they use much prostrations and kissing the ground. [...] The Carthusian that showed us the convent seemed not very melancholy. He enquired after their houses and lands in England, and asked whether, when we came to be papists, they should not have them again. I told him yes, without doubt, for there could be no reconciliation to their church without restitution. He told me I was a very good divine and very much in the right.[69] They have in their chapel several pictures of the execution of some of their order in England in Henry 8's reign.[70]

66. Compare these remarks on excommunication with those Locke makes in the *Letter Concerning Toleration,* p. 19.

67. Monks of the Carthusian order, whose monasteries are called charterhouses.

68. René d'Anjou (d. 1480), king of Sicily and count of Provence.

69. A standard element in Protestant fears of a Catholic restoration in England was that all medieval monastic and church lands, now in the hands of the laity, would be forcibly returned to the church. At his accession in 1685, James II specifically repudiated any such plan.

70. Three Carthusian monks were martyred in 1535.

Montpellier, 9 August 1676. This fortnight Protestant ministers [were] forbid to teach above two scholars at once.[71]

Castelnaudary, 5 March 1677. An advocate we met at supper who is judge of the place where we lived, being asked, could not tell what was the Second Commandment, and confessed he had never read the Scripture.[72]

Angers, 23 August 1678. We saw also at St. Maurice, the cathedral of Angers, abundance of relics, the tooth of one saint, the bone of another, etc. [. . .] but the things of most veneration were a thorn of the crown of Our Saviour, some wood of his cross which I believe was there, though I saw nothing but the gold and silver that covered it. There was also some of the hair, a piece of the petticoat and some of the milk of the Virgin, but the milk was out of sight; and one of the water pots wherein Our Saviour turned water into wine.[73] [. . .] I could not but wish for the pot because of its admirable effects to cure diseases, for once a year they put wine into it, consecrate it and distribute it to believers, who therewith cure fevers and other diseases.

Niort, 1 September 1678. Here a poor bookseller's wife, which by the largeness and furniture of her shop seemed not to have either much stock or trade, told me that, there being last winter 1,200 soldiers quartered in the town, two were appointed for their share (for they were Protestants), which, considering that they were to have three meals a day of flesh, breakfast, dinner and supper, besides a collation in the afternoon, all which was better to give them, and a fifth meal too if they desired it, rather than displease them, these two soldiers, for the three and a half months they were there, cost them at least forty écus.[74]

Paris, 25 April 1679. The Protestants within these twenty years have had above three hundred churches demolished, and within these two months fifteen more condemned.

71. The restriction was initially decreed in 1669. This entry is in shorthand.

72. Catholic ignorance of Scripture was a Protestant commonplace. The entry is in shorthand.

73. John 2.

74. Compulsory quartering of soldiers on private citizens was a familiar form of intimidation and a prime signifier of tyrannous state power. This report presages the *dragonnades*, by which troops were used to enforce conversion. See note 17, p. 11. *Écu:* a silver coin worth three francs.

The Obligation of Penal Laws

There are virtues and vices antecedent to, and abstract from, society, e.g., love of God, unnatural lust: other virtues and vices there are that suppose society and laws, as obedience to magistrates, or dispossessing a man of his heritage. In both these the rule and obligation is antecedent to human laws, though the matter about which that rule is, may be consequent to them, as property in land, distinction and power of persons, etc.

All things not commanded or forbidden by the law of God are indifferent, nor is it in the power of man to alter their nature; and so no human law can lay any new obligation on the conscience, and therefore all human laws are purely penal, i.e., have no other obligation but to make the transgressors liable to punishment in this life. All divine laws oblige the conscience, i.e., render the transgressors liable to answer at God's tribunal, and receive punishment at his hands. But because very frequently both these obligations concur, and the same action comes to be commanded or forbidden by both laws together, and so in these cases men's consciences are obliged, men have thought that civil laws oblige their consciences to entire obedience; whereas, in things in their own nature indifferent, the conscience is obliged only to active or passive obedience, and that not by virtue of that human law which the man either practises or is punished by, but by that law of God which forbids disturbance or dissolution of governments. The Gospel alters, not in the least, civil affairs, but leaves husband and wife, master and servant, magistrate and subject, every one of them, with the very same power and privileges that it found them, neither more nor less. And therefore when the New Testament says, obey your superiors in all things, etc.,[75] it cannot be thought that it laid any new obligation upon the Christians after their conversion, other than what they were under before; nor that the magistrate had any other extent of jurisdiction over them than over his heathen subjects: so that the magistrate has the same power still over his Christian as he had [over] his heathen subjects; so that, when he had power to command,

75. Colossians 3:18–22.

they had still, notwithstanding the liberty and privileges of the Gospel, obligation to obey.

Now, to heathen politics (which cannot be supposed to be instituted by God for the preservation and propagation of true religion) there can be no other end assigned but the preservation of the members of that society in peace and safety together. This being found to be the end will give us the rule of civil obedience. For if the end of civil societies be civil peace, the immediate obligation of every subject must be to preserve that society or government which was ordained to produce it; and no member of any society can possibly have any obligation of conscience beyond this. So that he that obeys the magistrate to that degree as not to endanger or disturb the government, under what form of government soever he lives, fulfils all the law of God concerning government, i.e., obeys to the utmost [all] that the magistrate or society can oblige his conscience, which can be supposed to have no other rule set it by God in this matter but this. The end of the institution being always the measure of operation.

The obligation of conscience then upon every subject being to preserve the government, 'tis plain that where any law is made with a penalty, is submitted to, i.e., the penalty is quietly undergone without other obedience, the government cannot be disturbed or endangered. For whilst the magistrate has power to increase the penalty, even to loss of life, and the subject submits patiently to the penalty, which he in conscience is obliged to do, the government can never be in danger, nor can the public want active obedience in any case where it hath power to require it under pain of death. For no man can be supposed to refuse his active obedience in a lawful or indifferent thing, when the refusal will cost him his life, and lose all his civil rights at once, for want of performing one civil action; for civil laws have only to do with civil actions.

This, thus stated, clears a man from that infinite number of sins that otherwise he must unavoidably be guilty of, if all penal laws oblige the conscience further than this.

One thing further is to be considered, that all human laws are penal, for where the penalty is not expressed, it is by the judge to be proportioned to the consequence and circumstances of the fault. See the practice of the

King's Bench. Penalties are so necessary to civil laws, that God found it necessary to annex them even to the civil laws he gave the Jews.

Toleration and Error

Penal laws, made about matters of religion in a country where there is already a diversity of opinions, can hardly avoid that common injustice which is condemned in all laws whatsoever, *viz.*, in retrospect. It would be thought a hard case, if by a law, now made, all would have to be fined that should wear French hats for the future, and those also who had worn them at any time in the year past. It is the same case to forbid a man to be a Quaker, Anabaptist, Presbyterian, for it is as easy for me not to have had on the hat yesterday, which I then wore, as it is in many cases not to have the same opinions, the same thought, in my head as I had yesterday, both being impossible. The great dispute in all this diversity of opinions is where the truth is. But let us suppose at present that it is wholly and certainly on the state's side, though it will be pretty hard to suppose it so in England, in France, Sweden, and Denmark at the same time; and yet in all these places they have an equal power to make laws about religion. But let us suppose yet that all dissenters are in error, are out of their wits: but your law found them in this delirium, and will you make a law that will hang all that are beside themselves? "But we fear their rage and violence."[76] If you fear them only because they are capable of a raging fit, you may as well fear all other men, who are liable to the same distemper. If you fear it because you treat them ill, and that produces some symptom of it, you ought to change your method, and not punish them for what you fear because you go the way to produce it. If a distemper itself has a tendency to rage, it must be watched and fit remedies applied. If they are perfect innocents, only a little crazed, why cannot they be let alone, since, though perhaps their brains are a little out of order, their hands work well enough? "But they will infect others." If those others are infected but by

---

76. Quotation marks have been added to remarks that Locke attributes to an imaginary interlocutor.

their own consent, and that to cure another disease that they think they have, why should they be hindered any more than a man is that might make an issue[77] to cure palsy, or might willingly have haemorrhoids to prevent an apoplexy? "But then all people will run into this error." This supposes either that it is true and so prevails, or that the teachers of truth are very negligent and let it, and that they are to blame; or that people are more inclined to error than truth: if so, then, error being manifold, they will be as distant one from another as from you, and so no fear of their uniting, unless you force them by making yourself an enemy to all by ill-treatment.

To settle the peace of places where there are different opinions in religion, two things are to be perfectly distinguished: religion and government, and their two sorts of officers, magistrates and ministers, and their provinces, to be kept well distinct (the not doing whereof was perhaps a great cause of distraction); a magistrate only to look at the peace and security of a city; ministers only [concerned] with the saving of the soul, and if they were forbidden meddling with making or executing laws in their preaching, we should be perhaps much more quiet.

Toleration in Israel

However people imagine that the Jews had a strict church discipline without any toleration yet it is to be observed besides that it was a law immediately given by God Almighty;

1. That there were no articles of faith that they were required to subscribe to, or at least that there was but one God and that Jehovah [was] their God;

2. That there were several laws given for excluding people [such] as bastards and eunuchs [and] Ammonites,[78] etc., out of their congregation but none for forcing anybody in.

---

77. *issue:* surgical incision.
78. *Ammonites:* an ancient people in conflict with the Israelites.

Toleration and Sincerity

No man has power to prescribe to another what he should believe or do in order to the saving of his own soul, because it is only his own private interest, and concerns not another man. God has nowhere given such power to any man or society, nor can man possibly be supposed to give it [to] another absolutely over him.

First, because man in all states being liable to error, as well governors as those under them, doctors as [well as] scholars, it would be unreasonable to be put under the absolute direction of those who may err in a matter of that concernment, eternal concernment, wherein if they misguide us they can make us no reparation.

Second, because such a power can by no means serve to the end for which only it can be supposed to be given, *viz.*, to keep men in the right way to salvation. For supposing all the different pretenders to this power were nearer agreed in the matters they prescribe, or could consent to resign all their pretensions to this power to one certain guide, neither of which is ever like[ly] to happen, yet the power of using force to bring men [to believe] in faith and opinions and uniformity in worship could not serve to secure men's salvation, even though that power were in itself infallible, because no compulsion can make a man believe against his present light and persuasion, be it what it will, though it may make him profess indeed. But profession without sincerity will little set a man forwards in his way to any place but that where he is to have his share with hypocrites, and to do anything in the worship of God which a man judges in his own conscience not to be that worship he requires and will accept, is so far from serving or pleasing God in it, that such a worshipper affronts God only to please men. For even the circumstances of the worship of God cannot be indifferent to him that thinks them not so, nor can the time, habit, posture, etc., be at pleasure used or omitted by one who thinks either acceptable or displeasing to the God he worships.

But though nobody can have a right to force men to receive such doctrines or to practise such ways of worship, yet this will not hinder the power of every society or profession of religion to establish within themselves confessions of faith, and rules of decency and order,[79] which yet are not to be imposed on anyone with constraint. It only forbids that men should be compelled into that communion, or anyone be hindered from withdrawing from it, whenever anything comes to be established in it which he judges contrary to the end for which he enters into such a communion or religious society, i.e., the believing and owning certain truths which are taught and professed there, and the worshipping of God in a way acceptable to him. *Sic argumentatus est Atticus: de quo videndum.*[80]

Latitude

Several Protestants not of the Church of England resident at Constantinople, had leave of Sir J. Finch,[81] the English ambassador there, to have a room in his house to meet to pray in, they being most[ly] of the French church. But at last it was thought fit that if they would continue in that privilege they should come and receive the sacrament in his chapel administered there by his chaplain to the discipline of the Church of England. Of which they having notice they accordingly came. But presented themselves to receive it according to the several fashions of their churches or persuasions of their own minds, some sitting and some standing, though the ambassador and all the usual congregation of the English there had received it kneeling. However, the chaplain thought he could not refuse it [to] anyone that came solemnly and seriously to receive it for any posture he presented himself in, and therefore administered the bread to them all. Which significant declaration that kneeling was no essential part of receiving the Lord's supper and no necessary part of worship, had so powerful an effect upon them, that when he came afterwards to give them the cup, they of their own accords received it every one kneeling.

79. John 21:16. The phrase occurs again in texts below.
80. "Thus Atticus has argued, concerning which see." Locke refers to his *Essay Concerning Toleration,* signed "Atticus."
81. Sir John Finch (1626–82), ambassador at Constantinople, 1672–82. His nephew, Daniel Finch, later second Earl of Nottingham, was a promoter of comprehension, i.e., reform of the Church of England in order to readmit moderate dissenters.

This way, if it were a little more practised, would perhaps be found not only the most Christian but the most effectual way to bring men to conformity. Mr. Covell.[82]

The Origin of Religious Societies

The light of nature discovering[83] to man that he is under the government and disposal of an invisible and supreme being, teaches him also that he was concerned so to behave himself as not to offend, or, if he did, to find means to reconcile and recover again the favour of that being, which over rules all human affairs and sovereignly dispenses good and evil in this world, and on whom depends eternal happiness and misery in another. This knowledge of a God and his absolute power over them put all men everywhere upon thoughts of religion who have but reflected on their own original, or the constitution of the visible things of nature, to any degree beyond brutes, and though morality be acknowledged by them all to be a great part of that wherein God may be offended or pleased with us, yet morality being that law which God hath implanted in the nature of man to preserve the being and welfare of himself and other men in this world, a great part of it has fallen under the magistrate's care, to whom the government of civil societies is committed, as the greatest means of the preservation of mankind in this world; and though men are persuaded that the observance of that law is a means also of pleasing, or displeasing God, and so a means too of procuring happiness or misery in another world, yet it has not passed under the name of religion, which has been appropriated to those actions only which are referred wholly to the pleasing or displeasing God without concerning at all my neighbour, civil society, or my own preservation in this life. For my praying to God in this or that fashion, or using any other ceremony in religion, or speculative opinions concerning things of another life, entrenches not at all upon the health or possession, good name, or any other right of my neighbour which serves to his well-being or preservation in this world. Religion being, then, those

82. John Covel (1638–1722), Church of England chaplain at Constantinople, later Master of Christ's College, Cambridge, Locke's source for this story.
83. *discovering:* revealing.

opinions and actions done, which I entertain and perform only to please God, and such as have no concernment at all with my neighbour, or the interest or affairs of this world, though many of these are outward and visible to others, are not within the civil magistrate's inspection and care, whose proper province is only civil society, in order to men's well being in this world.

This being the notion that men have had of religion as a transaction immediately betwixt God and them for the procuring his favour without concerning civil society at all, it has yet put men upon the necessity of uniting into societies about it, there being many parts of it that could not be performed in the solitary recesses of a retired man. For men, finding it their duty to honour and worship the God they served, were to do it by public acts of devotion, owning to the world thereby that deity by solemn acts of worship to whom they paid the internal acts of veneration in their hearts. And 'twas for this that men were obliged to enter into societies for religion, with those who were of the same belief and way of worship with themselves. The Christian religion, when it came into the world, proceeded upon the same grounds, and laid on its followers a necessity of public worship upon the same account, adding others which other religions did not so manifestly concern themselves in: and those were the particular edification of the members, and the preservation and propagation of its truth. But though Christian religion made it the duty of its followers to unite into societies for public worship, profession, and propagation of its doctrines, and edification of one another, yet it nowhere required or concerned the assistance or power of the civil magistrate in making or regulating those societies, not only because force and the sword and the proper instruments of the magistrate are altogether uncapable to convince men's minds, and bring them to the belief of the truth of any religion, but because it was like[ly] to go very ill with the true religion in the world, if it had been put into the power of the magistrate to determine what religion men should be of; and therefore our Saviour and the apostles in the first institution and propagation took great care of this, to keep theirs within the strict limits of religion, and to have nothing at all to do with secular affairs, or civil societies, and therefore left particular and peremptory commands to all that entered into it, to think themselves still under, and carefully pay all, the duties they owed their fathers, mas-ters, and magistrates and all other relations that they did before, not so much as prescribing to its followers a set form of government in their reli-gious societies but leaving them to that latitude therein, that they might be at liberty to make use of their prudence to accommodate it so as they should judge might best suit with the circumstances they are in.

This then being the present state of religion in the world, man is still as he ever was at liberty in reference to the civil magistrate to choose what religion he judges the likeliest for the salvation of his soul, and so to unite into religious (or as they are called) church societies about it. (For religious societies in contradistinction to the civil, are called churches, as the others are called states), it not being in the magistrate's power to force any man to be of this or that religion, or to choose for him whether his way to please God and be saved be to be a Christian, Mahumetan, Jew, or Gaurr.[84] And as little can a Christian magistrate prescribe to him that is a Christian whether he shall be a Papist, Lutheran, or Calvinist, or com-mand him to be of any other particular distinct Christian society, it being the privilege of every Christian as well as every man to choose of what religious societies he will be for the salvation of his soul.

These religious societies (at least among Christians) are called churches, which are only voluntary societies which men by their own consent enter into for the ends of religion above mentioned; [they] can have no other government than that which the society itself shall agree of over its own members, it being necessary to every society that has anything to do to have some order, and some distinction of offices amongst them and some laws to govern the members of that society. But these can reach none but those that are actual members of that society, which, if they will not submit to [it], the utmost power they have is [to] turn them out of the society, and to deny them the privileges of communicating with it. And, on the other side, as he entered freely into the society for the professing of the truth, the worshipping of God, and his edification, [so he] may quit again, when he thinks the constitution of that society serves not to

84. *Gaurr:* probably a variant of *Giaour,* a Turkish word for infidels.

those ends, or not so well as that of some other. For if I had the liberty to choose into what religious society I would at first enter into for the salvation of my own soul, I am for the same reason always at liberty to quit it again, when I judge it serves not to those ends, or not so well as another; nor let any man say that this is a principle that will make men change their religious societies, or religion, upon every fancy and slight occasion, for if we consider what difficulty it is for a man to quit the conversation and esteem of those he hath lived in society with, to be abandoned and cast out by his friends, relations and party, the credit a man has among them being that which is observed to be the thing which governs mankind more than any other; and, on the other side, with what suspicions a new convert is received into the church he enters into; and the reputation he meets with on all hands of an unsteady if not irreligious person, and an affecter of novelty and change; these, and a thousand inconveniences, do so necessarily attend men in the changing their religion or churches (even where the authority of the magistrate imposes not), have so great an influence upon men that I think those alone keep a very great part of men so fixed to their church communion; and we see the Jews in all countries, Christians in Asia and Africa, Mahumetan slaves in Christendom, Protestants in Papist, and Papists in Protestant countries do not so slightly change their religions, though they have not only the free leave of the magistrate but his encouragement to do it; and yet many of these, if their true reasons were known, would be found to be restrained by those outward considerations, and 'tis certain that those who are in earnest governed by the salvation of their souls and hopes of heaven would be much less given to change.

Enthusiasm

A strong and firm persuasion of any proposition relating to religion for which a man hath either no or not sufficient proofs from reason but receives them as truths wrought in the mind extraordinarily by God himself and influences coming immediately from him, seems to me to be enthusiasm, which can be no evidence or ground of assurance at all nor can by any means be taken for knowledge. [85](If such groundless thoughts as these concern ordinary matters, and not religion, possess the mind strongly, we call it raving, and everyone thinks it a degree of madness, but in religion men accustomed to the thoughts of revelation make a greater allowance to it, though indeed it be a more dangerous madness, but men are apt to think that in religion they may and ought to quit their reason.)[86] For I find that Christians, Mahumetans, and Bramins[87] all pretend to it (and I am told the Chineses too). But 'tis certain that contradictions and falsehoods cannot come from God, nor can anyone that is of the true religion be assured of anything by a way whereby those of a false religion may be and are equally confirmed in theirs. [88](Enthusiasm is a fault in the mind opposite to brutish sensuality,[89] as far in the other extreme, exceeding the just measures of reason as thoughts grovelling only in matter and things of sense come short of it.) For the Turkish dervises[90] pretend to revelations, ecstasies, vision, rapture, to be swallowed up and transported with illuminations of God, discoursing with God, seeing the face of God, *vide* Ricaut 216 (i.e., Of the Ottoman Empire, folio, London [16]70, 1. 2, c. 13, etc.)[91] and the jaugis[92] amongst the Hindous talk of being illuminated

85. The passage in parentheses was originally an addition in the margin of the manuscript.

86. Damaris Masham (1658–1708), who was brought up among the Cambridge Platonists, and to whom Locke sent these remarks on enthusiasm, responded in defense of spiritual experience. While, she said, it is true "that the proud and fantastic pretences of the conceited melancholists of this age to divine communion had indeed prejudiced many very intelligent persons against the belief of any such thing, they looking upon it but as a high-flown notion of warm imagination," yet it remains possible to believe that God "affords his intimacies and converses to the better souls" and that "the divine spirit does afford its sensible presence and immediate beatific touch to some persons." Letter to Locke, 20 April 1682.

87. Locke elides Brahmins with Hindus.

88. The passage in parentheses was originally an addition in the margin of the manuscript.

89. Contemporary religious psychology posited a polarity between, at one extreme, ascetic mysticism, and at the other, sensual superstition; the true Christian was admonished to seek a middle way.

90. *Dervises:* dervishes, Muslim mendicants, fakirs.

91. Sir Paul Rycaut, *Present State of the Ottoman Empire* (1667; 3rd ed., 1670).

92. *Jaugis:* yogis, Hindu ascetics.

and entirely united to God: Bernier 173 (i.e., Memoires, Tome 3, 8vo, London [16]72) p. 36,[93] as well as the most spiritualised Christians.[94]

It is to be observed concerning these illuminations that, how clear soever they may seem, they carry no knowledge nor certainty any farther than there are proofs of the truth of those things that are discovered by them and so far they are parts of reason and have the same foundation with other persuasions in a man's mind and whereof his reason judges, and if there be no proofs of them they can pass for nothing but mere imaginations of the fancy, how clearly soever they appear to, or acceptable they may be to, the mind, for 'tis not the clearness of the fancy, but the evidence of the truth of the thing which makes the certainty. He that should pretend to have a clear sight of a Turkish paradise and of an angel sent to direct him thither might perhaps have a very lively imagination of all this, but it altogether no more proved that either there were such a place or that an angel had the conduct of him thither than if he saw all this in colours well drawn by a painter, these two pictures being no more different (as to the assurance of anything resembled by them) than that one is a fleeting draught in the imagination, the other a lasting one on a sensible body.

That which makes all these pretences to supernatural illumination farther to be suspected to be merely the effect and operation of the fancy is that all the preparation and ways used to dispose the mind to these illuminations and make it capable of them are such as are apt to disturb and depress the rational power of the mind, but to advance and set on work the fancy, such are fasting, solitude, intense and long meditation on the same thing, opium, intoxicating liquors, long and vehement turning round, etc., all which are used by some or other of those who would attain to those extraordinary discoveries as fit preparations of the mind to receive them, all which do naturally weaken or disturb the rational faculty and thereby let loose the imagination and thereby make the mind

93. François Bernier, *The History of the Late Revolution of the Empire of the Great Mogul* (1671).

94. In response, Masham insists that there are "sincere and devout lovers of God and virtue ... amongst the most barbarous nations and professors of the wildest religions in the world."

less steady in distinguishing betwixt truth and fancy, but [rather] mistake [them] as crazy, weak, drunken or mad men do, one for the other.

I do not remember that I have read of any enthusiasts amongst the Americans[95] or any who have not pretended to a revealed religion, as all those before mentioned do; which if so it naturally suggests this inquiry: whether those that found their religion upon revelation do not from thence take occasion to imagine that since God has been pleased by revelation to discover to them the general precepts of their religion, they that have a particular interest in his favour have reason to expect that he will reveal himself to them if they take the right way to seek it, in those things that concern them in particular in reference to their conduct, state, or comfort. But of this I shall conclude nothing till I shall be more fully assured in matter of fact.

Ecclesia

Hooker's description of the church, lib. I, §15,[96] amounts to this: that it is a supernatural but voluntary society wherein a man associates himself to God, angels, and holy men. The original of it, he says, is the same as of other societies, *viz.*, an inclination unto sociable life, and a consent to the bond of association, which is the law and order they are associated in. That which makes it supernatural is that part of the bond of their association [which] is a law revealed concerning what worship God would have done unto him, which natural reason could not have discovered. So that the worship of God, so far forth as it hath anything in it more than the law of reason doth teach, may not be invented of men. From whence I think it will follow:

First, that the church being a supernatural society, and a society by consent, the secular power, which is purely natural, nor any other power, can compel one to be of any particular church society, there being many such to be found.

Second, that the end of entering into such society being only to obtain

95. *Americans:* Native Americans.
96. Richard Hooker, *Of the Laws of Ecclesiastical Politie* (1594–97), I.xv.2. Compare Locke's use of Hooker to bolster his arguments in *Two Treatises of Government*.

the favour of God by offering him an acceptable worship, nobody can impose any ceremonies unless positively and clearly by revelation enjoined, any farther than everyone who joins in the use of them is persuaded in his conscience they are acceptable to God; for if his conscience condemns any part of unrevealed worship, he cannot by any sanction of men be obliged to it.

Third, that since a part only of the bond of this association is a revealed law, this part alone is unalterable, and the other, which is human, depends wholly upon consent, and so is alterable, and a man is held by such laws, or to such a particular society, no longer than he himself doth consent.

Fourth, I imagine that the original of this society is not from our inclination, as he says, to a sociable life, for that may be fully satisfied in other societies, but from the obligation man, by the light of reason, finds himself under, to own and worship God publicly in the world.

Tradition

The Jews, the Romanists and the Turks,[97] who all three pretend to guide themselves by a law revealed from heaven which shows them the way to happiness, do yet all of them have recourse very frequently to tradition as a rule of no less authority than their written law. Whereby they seem to allow, that the divine law (however God be willing to reveal it) is not capable to be conveyed by writing to mankind distant in place, time, languages, and customs, and so through the defect of language, no positive law of righteousness can be that way conveyed sufficiently and with exactness to all the inhabitants of the earth in remote generations, and so must resolve all into natural religion, and that light which every man has born with him.[98] Or else they give occasion to enquiring men to suspect the integrity of their priests and teachers, who unwilling that the people should have a standing known rule of faith and manners, have for the

97. *Turks:* Muslims.
98. Locke echoes a common criticism of Catholicism, that, paradoxically, its very reliance on tradition and the infallible teaching of the church, as being necessary to sustain the authority and coherence of Scripture, readily collapses Christianity into deism once those props are doubted.

maintenance of their own authority foisted in another of tradition, which will always be in their own power to be varied and suited to their own interest and occasions.

Pennsylvania Laws

[WP] And if any person shall abuse or deride any other for his different persuasion and practice in matters of religion, such shall be looked on as a disturber of the peace and be punished accordingly.[99]

[JL] Matter of perpetual prosecution and animosity.

[WP] Whosoever shall speak loosely and profanely of Almighty God, Christ Jesus, the Holy Spirit, and the scriptures of truth, shall pay five shillings or five days imprisonment.

[JL] Q. What is loosely or profanely?

[WP] Adultery to be punished with twelve months imprisonment in the house of correction, and longer if the chief magistrate think meet.

[JL] Arbitrary power.

[. . .]

[WP] Erect and order all public schools.

[JL] The surest check upon liberty of consciences, suppressing all displeasing opinions in the end.

Pacific Christians

1. We think nothing necessary to be known or believed for salvation but what God hath revealed.

2. We therefore embrace all those who in sincerity receive the word of truth revealed in the Scripture and obey the light which enlightens every man that comes into the world.

3. We judge no man in meats, or drinks, or habits, or days, or any other outward observances, but leave everyone to his freedom in the use of those outward things which he thinks can most contribute to build up the inward man in righteousness, holiness, and the true love of God and his neighbour in Christ Jesus.

99. Locke is responding to William Penn's Frame of Government.

4. If anyone find any doctrinal part of Scripture difficult to be understood, we recommend him: (i) the study of the Scripture in humility and singleness of heart; (ii) prayer to the Father of lights to enlighten him; (iii) obedience to what is already revealed to him, remembering that the practice of what we do know is the surest way to more knowledge, our infallible guide having told us, if any man will do the will of him that sent me, he shall know of the doctrine (John 7:17); (iv) we leave him to the advice and assistance of those whom he thinks best able to instruct him. No men, or society of men, having any authority to impose their opinions or interpretations on any other, [even] the meanest Christian; since in matters of religion everyone must know and believe, and give an account for himself.

5. We hold it to be an indispensable duty for all Christians to maintain love and charity in the diversity of contrary opinions. By which charity we do not mean an empty sound, but an effectual forbearance and good will, carrying men to communion, friendship and mutual assistance one of another, in outward as well as spiritual things. And by dehorting[100] all magistrates from making use of their authority, much less their sword (which was put into their hands only against evil doers) in matters of faith or worship.

6. Since the Christian religion we profess is not a notional science, to furnish speculation to the brain or discourse to the tongue, but a rule of righteousness to influence our lives, Christ having given himself to redeem us from all iniquity and purify unto himself a people zealous of good works (Titus 2:14), we profess the only business of our public assemblies to be to exhort, thereunto, and laying aside all controversy and speculative questions, instruct and encourage one another in the duty of a good life, which is acknowledged to be the great business of true religion, and to pray God for the assistance of his spirit for the enlightening of our understanding and subduing our corruptions, that so we may perform unto him a reasonable and acceptable service and show our faith by our works. Proposing to ourselves and others the example of our Lord and Saviour Jesus Christ, as the great pattern for our imitation.

100. *dehorting:* dissuading.

7. One alone being our master, even[101] Christ, we acknowledge no masters of our assembly; but if any man in the spirit of love, peace, and meekness, has a word of exhortation we hear him.

8. Nothing being so opposite, or having proved so fatal to unity, love and charity, the first and great characteristical duties of Christianity, as men's fondness of their own opinions, and their endeavours to set them up and have them followed, instead of the Gospel of peace; to prevent these seeds of dissention and division, and maintain unity in the difference of opinions which we know cannot be avoided, if anyone appear contentious, abounding in his own sense rather than in love, and desirous to draw followers after himself, with destruction or opposition to others, we judge him not to have learned Christ as he ought, and therefore not fit to be a teacher of others.

9. Decency and order in our assemblies being directed, as they ought, only to edification, can need but very few and plain rules. Time and place of meeting being settled, if anything else, need regulation; the assembly itself, or four of the ancientest, soberest and discreetest of the brethren, chosen for that occasion, shall regulate it.

10. From every brother that after admonition walketh disorderly, we withdraw ourselves.

11. We each of us think it our duty to propagate the doctrine and practice of universal charity, good will, and obedience in all places, and on all occasions, as God shall give us opportunity.

Sacerdos

There were two sorts of teachers amongst the ancients. [First,] those who professed to teach them the arts of propitiation and atonement, and these were properly their priests, who for the most part made themselves the mediators betwixt the gods and men, wherein they performed all or the principal part, at least nothing was done without them. The laity had but a small part in the performance, unless it were in the charge[102] of it, and

---

101. *even:* namely.
102. *charge:* cost.

that was wholly theirs. The chief, at least the essential, and sanctifying part of the ceremony, was always the priests', and the people could do nothing without them. The ancients had another sort of teachers, who were called philosophers. These led their schools, and professed to instruct those who would apply to them in the knowledge of things and the rules of virtue. These meddled not with the public religion, worship, or ceremonies, but left them entirely to the priests, as the priests left the instruction of men in natural and moral knowledge wholly to the philosophers. These two parts or provinces of knowledge, thus under the government of two distinct sorts of men, seem to be founded upon the supposition of two clearly distinct originals, *viz.*, revelation and reason. For the priests never for any of their ceremonies or forms of worship pleaded reason; but always urged their sacred observances from the pleasure of the gods, antiquity, and tradition, which at last resolves all their established rites into nothing but revelation.[103] The philosophers, on the other side, pretended to nothing but reason in all that they said, and from thence owned[104] to fetch all their doctrines; though how little their lives answered their own rules, whilst they studied ostentation and vanity rather than solid virtue, Cicero tells us, *Tusc. Quest.*, 1. 2, c. 4.[105]

Jesus Christ, bringing by revelation from heaven the true religion to mankind, reunited these two again, religion and morality, as the inseparable parts of the worship of God, which ought never to have been separated, wherein for the obtaining the favour and forgiveness of the deity, the chief part of what man could do consisted in a holy life, and little or nothing at all was left to outward ceremony, which was therefore almost wholly cashiered[106] out of this true religion, and only two very plain and simple institutions introduced,[107] all pompous rites being wholly abolished,

103. In a footnote Locke reproduces a quotation from Cicero, *De natura deorum,* bk. 3, taken from Pierre Bayle, *Pensées diverses* (1683), §127.

104. *owned:* claimed.

105. Cicero, *Tusculan Disputations,* ii.4.

106. *cashiered:* dismissed with disgrace.

107. In the *Reasonableness of Christianity* (1695), chap. 11, Locke says that two things only are required of Christians, faith and repentance, i.e., believing Jesus is the Messiah, and conducting a virtuous life. In the *Third Letter for Toleration* he refers to the "plain simple truths of the Gospel"; see p. 80, above.

and no more of outward performances commanded but just so much as decency and order required in the actions of public assemblies. This being the state of this true religion coming immediately from God himself, the ministers of it, who also call themselves priests, have assumed to themselves the parts both of the heathen priests and philosophers, and claim a right not only to perform all the outward acts of the Christian religion in public, and to regulate the ceremonies to be used there, but also to teach men their duties of morality towards one another and towards themselves, and to prescribe to them in the conduct of their lives.

Error

The great division amongst Christians is about opinions. Every sect has its set of them, and that is called orthodoxy. And he who professes his assent to them, though with an implicit faith and without examining, he is orthodox and in the way to salvation. But if he examines, and thereupon questions any one of them, he is presently suspected of heresy, and if he oppose them or hold the contrary, he is presently condemned as in a damnable error, and [in] the sure way to perdition. Of this, one may say that there is, nor can be, nothing more wrong. For he that examines and upon a fair examination embraces an error for a truth, has done his duty, more than he who embraces the profession (for the truths themselves he does not embrace) of the truth without having examined whether it be true or no. And he that has done his duty, according to the best of his ability, is certainly more in the way to heaven than he who has done nothing of it. For if it be our duty to search after truth, he certainly that has searched after it, though he has not found it in some points, has paid a more acceptable obedience to the will of his maker, than he that has not searched at all, but professes to have found truth when he has neither searched nor found it. For he that takes up the opinions of any church in the lump, without examining them, has truly neither searched after, nor found, truth, but has only found those that he thinks have found truth, and so receives what they say with an implicit faith, and so pays them the homage that is due only to God, who cannot be deceived, nor deceive.[108]

---

108. Paragraph breaks have been added; they are not in the manuscript.

In this way the several churches (in which, as one may observe, opinions are preferred to life,[109] and orthodoxy is that which they are concerned for, and not morals) put the terms of salvation in that which the author of our salvation does not put them in. The believing of a collection of certain propositions, which are called and esteemed fundamental articles, because it has pleased the compilers to put them into their confession of faith, is made the condition of salvation. But this believing is not, in truth, believing, but a profession to believe; for it is enough to join with those who make the same profession; and ignorance or disbelief of some of those articles is well enough borne, and a man is orthodox enough and without any suspicion, till he begins to examine. As soon as it is perceived that he quits the implicit faith expected though disowned by the church, his orthodoxy is presently questioned and he is marked out for a heretic. In this way of an implicit faith, I do not deny but a man who believes in God the Father Almighty and that Jesus Christ is his only Son our Lord, may be saved, because many of the articles of every sect are such as a man may be saved without the explicit belief of. But how the several churches who place salvation in no less than a knowledge and belief of their several confessions, can content themselves with such an implicit faith in any of their members, I must own I do not see. The truth is, we cannot be saved without performing something which is the explicit believing of what God in the Gospel has made absolutely necessary to salvation to be explicitly believed, and sincerely to obey what he has there commanded. To a man who believes in Jesus Christ, that he is sent from God to be the saviour of the world, the first step to orthodoxy is a sincere obedience to his law.

Objection: But 'tis an ignorant day-labourer, that cannot so much as read, and how can he study the Gospel and become orthodox that way?[110] Answer: a ploughman that cannot read is not so ignorant but he has a conscience, and knows in those few cases which concern his own actions, what is right and what is wrong. Let him sincerely obey this light of nature, it is the transcript of the moral law in the Gospel; and this, even though there be errors in it, will lead him into all the truths in the Gospel

109. *life:* conduct of life, morals.
110. In the *Reasonableness,* chap. 14, Locke insists that the Christian religion must be plain enough for "day-labourers" and "dairy-maids."

that are necessary for him to know. For he that in earnest believes Jesus Christ to be sent from God, to be his Lord and ruler, and does sincerely and unfeignedly set upon a good life as far as he knows his duty; and where he is in doubt in any matter that concerns himself he cannot fail to enquire of those better skilled in Christ's law, to tell him what his Lord and master has commanded in the case, and desires to have his law read to him concerning that duty which he finds himself concerned in, for the regulation of his own actions. For as for other men's actions, what is right or wrong as to them, that he is not concerned to know; his business is to live well himself and do what is his particular duty. This is knowledge and orthodoxy enough for him, which will be sure to bring him to salvation, an orthodoxy which nobody can miss who in earnest resolves to lead a good life. And, therefore, I lay it down as a principle of Christianity that the right and only way to saving orthodoxy is the sincere and steady purpose of a good life.

Ignorant of many things contained in the Holy Scriptures we are all. Errors also concerning doctrines delivered in Scripture, we have all of us not a few. These, therefore, cannot be damnable, if any shall be saved. And if they are dangerous, 'tis certain the ignorant and illiterate are safest, for they have the fewest errors that trouble not themselves with speculations above their capacities, or beside their concern. A good life in obedience to the law of Christ their Lord is their indispensable business, and if they inform themselves concerning that, as far as their particular duties lead them to enquire and oblige them to know, they have orthodoxy enough, and will not be condemned for ignorance in those speculations which they had neither parts,[111] opportunity, nor leisure to know. Here we may see the difference between the orthodoxy required by Christianity, and the orthodoxy required by the several sects, or as they are called, churches of Christians. The one is explicitly to believe what is indispensably required to be believed as absolutely necessary to salvation, and to know and believe in the other doctrines of faith delivered in the word of God, as a man has opportunity, helps and parts; but[112] to inform himself in the rules and

111. *parts:* abilities.
112. *but:* the sense requires "and" here.

measures of his own duty as far as his actions are concerned, and to pay a sincere obedience to them. But the other, *viz.,* the orthodoxy required by the several sects, is a profession of believing the whole bundle of their respective articles set down in each church's system, without knowing the rules of everyone's particular duty, or requiring a sincere or strict obedience to them. For they are speculative opinions, confessions of faith that are insisted on in the several communions; they must be owned and subscribed to, but the precepts and rules of morality and the observance of them, I do not remember there is much notice taken of, or any great stir made about a collection or observance of them, in any of the terms of church communion. But it is also to be observed, that this is much better fitted to get and retain church members than the other way, and is much more suited to that end, as much as it is easier to make profession of believing a certain collection of opinions that one never perhaps so much as reads, and several whereof one could not perhaps understand if one did read and study; (for no more is required than a profession to believe them, expressed in an acquiescence that suffers one not to question or contradict any of them), than it is to practise the duties of a good life in a sincere obedience to those precepts of the Gospel wherein his actions are concerned: precepts not hard to be known by those who are willing and ready to obey them.

Scriptures for Toleration

Tolerantia Pro. Matthew 5:43–8, 7:24–7, Luke 6:27–8; Romans 12:14, 20–1; 1 Peter 3:9, Luke 23:34; Acts 7:60; 1 Corinthians 4:12–13; Galatians 5:9–10; Deuteronomy 14:21, 15:3, 23:19–20, 28:43, Exodus 22:21, 33:9; Leviticus 19:10; Jeremiah 7:6, 22:3, Zachariah 7:10, Malachi 3:5, Deuteronomy 10:18, 21:14.[113]

---

113. A motif in several of these verses is the treatment of "strangers" (migrants); for instance, Exodus 22:21: "Thou shalt neither vex a stranger, nor oppress him: for ye were strangers in the land of Egypt." The England and Netherlands of Locke's time were full of religious refugees.

INDEX

"absolute liberty," xxxi, 4

Acontius, Jacopo, xi

Act of Union (1707), 82n35

Acts of the Apostles: 7:60, 189; 19, 18n38

adiaphora. *See* "things indifferent" to salvation

"Against Samuel Parker" (1669–70; Locke), xxxv–xxxvi, 148–52

Ahab (biblical king), 110

ale-sellers, reception of Eucharist to maintain licenses, 88–89

Alexander III (pope), 161

alms to beggars, giving, 116

America: colonial settlement and expropriation of land, Locke on, 40n100; *Constitutions of Carolina* (1669–70), xiv, xxxv, 39n95, 128n58, 146–48; Harvard, Thomas Hollis Library at, vii–viii, xxii–xxiii; influence of Locke in, xxii–xxiii; intolerance in, ix; nonconformists fleeing to, ix, x; "Pennsylvania Laws" (1686; Locke), xl, 182; separation of church and state in, xiv; *Virginia Statute for Religious Freedom* (1779), xiv. *See also* Native Americans

Ammonites (biblical people), 171

Anabaptists, ix, 58, 59n57, 66, 78, 156, 170. *See also* Baptists; Protestant dissenters

Anacletus II (pope), 161

Analogy of Faith, 65

Angers, France, Locke on religion in, 167

Anglicans. *See* Church of England

Anne (queen of England), 88n48

Answer to Stillingfleet (1681; Baxter), 56n150

Anti-Remonstrants, 21n43, 58n157

anti-Trinitarianism, xvii, 4n3, 30n66, 58n157, 132n67

Antichrist, 136

anticlericalism: apostolic succession, clerical claims to, 17n34, 136–39; conspiracy between clergy and princes, 61n163, 138–39; in *Essay Concerning Toleration*, 134–35, 136–39; in "Infallibility," 141–42; in *Letter Concerning Toleration*, 22n46, 30n65,

anticlericalism (*continued*)
30n67, 61n163; Locke's tendency
toward, xiv, xxi–xxii; pastoral fail-
ures of clergy, 95; in "Philanthropy,"
158; preaching, ineffectualness of,
134–35; "priestcraft," concept of, xxii,
24n51; religion and morality, relationship between, 184–86; against
Roman Catholic clergy, 165; in
Third Letter for Toleration, 95
antinomianism: in *Essay Concerning
Toleration,* 117–18, 122–27, 133, 138; in
Letter Concerning Toleration, 23n50,
49–53; Locke on, xix–xx, xxi
antipodes, 107
apostolic succession, 17n34, 136–39, 162
Aquinas, Thomas. *See* Thomas
Aquinas
Argument for Toleration (1681; Whitaker), 56n150
*The Argument of The Letter Concern-
ing Toleration Briefly Consider'd
and Answer'd* (1690; Proast), 69n2,
94n56
Arianism, 30n68, 165
Aristotelians (Peripatetics), 73
Aristotle, 114n25, 116n31
Arminians, ix, 21n43, 58, 63nn165–66
Arminius, Jacob, 21n43
Art of Poetry (Horace), 66n171
articles of faith or religion, toleration
of, 44–48
Ashley, Lord (later Earl of Shaftesbury): *Constitutions of Carolina* and,
xxxv; *Essay* and, xxi, xxxiii, 122n45;
influence on Locke, xx; toleration,
efforts to obtain, xxxvi
assemblies: in *Constitutions of Carolina,* 148; Conventicles Act against
assembly for non-Anglican worship, 53–57
atheism: in *Constitutions of Caro-

lina,* 146, 147; doctrinal argument
leading to, 132; exclusion from
tolerance by Locke, xi, xviii–xix,
52–53; Proast's charges regarding,
Locke's answers to, 91–94; speculative opinion, belief in a deity not
regarded as, 132
Atticus, as pseudonym for Locke, 132,
173
Augustine of Hippo, x, xv
Aurangzeb (Mughal emperor), 39n93
Avignon, France, Locke on religion
in, 166

Baal (deity), 30, 98
banned books, index of (Roman
Catholic), 163
Baptists, x, 58n157, 125n52, 156n28.
See also Anabaptists; Protestant
dissenters
Baxter, Richard, 56n150
Bayle, Pierre, xi, xix, xl, 53n138, 185n103
beggars, giving alms to, 116
Bernier, François, 179
Bible. *See* Scripture
Bibliotheca juris canonici veteris (1661;
Justel), 163n50
Blount, Charles, 18n38
Bonzi, Pierre de, 165n59
Brandenburg (Cleves), religious plu-
ralism in, xxi, 156
Brounower, Sylvester, xxxviii
Brutum Fulmen (1585; Hotman),
51n128
Bunyan, John, x
Burnet, Gilbert, 95n60, 103n66
The Burthen of Issachar (1646; Max-
well), 139n82
Butler, Samuel, 90

Cadmus (king of Thebes), 98
Calvin, Jean, ix, 39n92

Calvinism: Arminians, persecution of, 21n43, 63n165–66; church government, system of, 16n32; Cleves, religious pluralism of, xxi; Locke's hostility toward, 58n154; parallels seen by Locke between Calvinism and Catholicism, 39n92; references to Geneva indicating, 27n56; religious vestments of, 27n61, 109; resistance theory, 75n15; on right of subjects to reform religion, 121n42; "rule of the saints" in, xix; *sola scriptura* (Rule of Faith) for, 64, 66

Carolina, Constitutions of (1669–70), xiv, xxxv, 39n95, 128n58, 146–48

Carthusians, 166

Castellio, Sebastian, xi

Castelnaudary, France, Locke on religion in, 167

Catholicism. *See* Roman Catholicism

Catiline (Cicero), 37n88

Cecrops (king of Attica), 98

Celestine II (pope), 161

censorship, 112

charity, xxxvi, 116, 158–60

Charles II (king of England), xx–xxi, 4n3

Chillingworth, William, xxxv

Christian belief, religious tolerance as mark of, 7–12, 134–35

Christian unity, creed-making inimical to, 80–83

Church of England: on apostolic succession, 17n34; during Civil Wars, x, 51n132, 57n154, 126n54; in *Constitutions of Carolina*, 146n8, 147; as established Church, xiii–xiv; heretics and schismatics, *Letter* postscript on, 63n166; intolerance by, ix, x; as party written for by Proast, 102–4; Protestant dissenters, attitudes toward, 23n47; public offices

and licenses, reception of Eucharist to maintain, 88–89; recusancy laws established by Elizabeth I, 86n44

Churches: changing, 176–77; communion with, terms of, 146–48, 153, 154; in *Constitutions of Carolina*, 146–48; duty of toleration, 19–23; end or purpose of religious society, 153, 154; examination of opinions of, 186–89; excommunication by (*see* excommunication); laws, proper matter of, 153, 154, 172–73; obedience to laws, means of procuring, 153–54, 155–56, 173; origins of, as religious societies, xxxviii–xxxix, 174–77, 180, 181; orthodoxy of every Church to itself, 7, 21; parallel civil and ecclesiastical powers, 152–58; Petrine versus apostolic succession, 16n33, 17n34; powers and laws of, 16–19; religious tolerance as mark of true Christian Church and belief, 7–12; state, coextensiveness of membership with, 156; state, relationship to, 29–31; state toleration of, 31–40; as voluntary and free religious societies, 15–17, 32, 156, 176–77, 180–81. *See also* separation of church and state

Churchill, Awnsham, xxxii

Cicero, xxxii, xl, 37n88, 114n25, 132n68, 185

"Civil and Ecclesiastical Power" (1674; Locke), xxxvi, 152–58

civil disobedience, 48–49, 113–14, 169

civil society. *See* state

Civil Wars (Julius Caesar), 37n88

Civil Wars, English: Church of England during, x, 51n132, 57n154, 126n54; intolerance by Protestant dissenters during, 118n35; Locke affected by, ix, x, xi, xx, xli

Clement III (pope), 161
Clement VII (pope), 161
Clement VIII (pope), 161
clergy: apostolic succession and
  claims of, 17n34, 136–39; as Christian ambassadors, 134–35; duty of
  toleration, 23–26; monarchs and
  magistrates, influence on, 137–
  39; pastoral care, duty of, 94–95;
  paternal power as origin of, 149,
  151–52; religion and morality, relationship between, 184–86. *See also*
  anticlericalism
Cleves, religious pluralism in, xxi, 156
clubs for claret, 56
coercion. *See* force and coercion
Colleton, Sir Peter, xxxv
colonial settlement and expropriation
  of land, Locke on, 40n100
Commandments, second table of,
  114–17
commonwealth. *See* state
compelle intrare, x, xi
comprehension (liberalizing terms of
  membership in national church),
  xiv, xxxvii, 4, 132n66, 173n81
conciliar movement, 160–64
conformists, corrupt, problem of,
  94–95
Congregationalists (Independents),
  58, 78, 125n52, 156. *See also* Protestant dissenters
Connecticut Colony, influence of
  Locke in, xxii
conscience of private person, laws
  inimical to, 48–49, 113–14
Constance, Council of (1415), 50n127
Constantine I the Great (Roman
  emperor), 157, 163n52
Constantine II (Roman emperor),
  30n68
Constantinople, xxxviii, 21–22, 52,
  173–74

Constitutions of Carolina (1669–70),
  xiv, xxxiv, xxxv, 39n95, 128n58, 146–48
consubstantiation, 83
Conventicle Acts (1664, 1670),
  53n140, 89
conventicles or assemblies for non-
  Anglican worship, 53–57
conversion: difficulties entailed in,
  177; freedom to convert, 176–
  77; French *dragonnades* used to
  enforce, 11n17, 167n74; intolerance
  encouraging rather than weaken-
  ing opinions, 123–24, 164; of non-
  Christians, hopes for, 59n158, 77, 80;
  of St. Paul, xv
Cooper, Anthony Ashley. *See* Ashley,
  Lord
Copernican cosmology, 107n8
1 Corinthians: 4:12–13, 189; 5:12–13, 59;
  11:14, 144n4; 14:26, 40, 36n82; 14:40,
  135n74, 144n5
2 Corinthians: 10:4, 11n16
Corporation Act (1661), 88–89
corporations, 134
corrupt conformists, problem of,
  94–95
corruption of human nature, 96, 99,
  100, 101
councils of the church: Constance
  (1415), 50n127; infallibility of, 160–
  64; Nicene Councils (325/787), 163,
  164; Trent (1545–63), 162, 163
Covel, John, 174
creed-makers, sectarianism imposed
  by, 80–83
Cromwell, Oliver, ix, 34n78, 133n71
cryptogram on title page of *Letter*,
  xxxi–xxxii
cultus religiosus. See worship

Dagon (deity), 97
Danaus (king of the Argives), 98
David (biblical king), 43, 100

De legibus Hebraeorum (1685; Spencer), 41n101

De natura deorum (Cicero), 185n103

De Officiis (Cicero), xxxii

Declarations of Indulgence, 4

defect of intention, 162–63

deism, reliance on tradition leading to, 181

demographics, Locke's preoccupation with, 122n44

dervishes, 178

Descartes, René, 87

Des Maizeaux (Desmaizeaux), Pierre, 146n8

Deuteronomy: 2, 43; 2:9, 43n105; 5.1, 41n103; 7:1, 43n105; 10:18, 189; 14:21, 189; 15:3, 189; 21:14, 189; 23:19–20, 189; 28:43, 189

Diana of the Ephesians, 18

Discourse of Ecclesiastical Politie (1669; Parker), xxxv–xxxvi, 148n15

Discourse of the Pastoral Care (1692; Burnet), 95n60, 103

Discourse on Method (1637; Descartes), 87

disorder, intolerance as means of preventing: conventicles or assemblies for non-Anglican worship, 53–57; impossibility of completely suppressing disorder, 133–34; persecution, encouragement of opinions by, 123–24, 134

distinctive groups, suppression of, 118–21, 134

divine right of kings (*jure divino*), 106, 138

divine worship. *See* worship

divorce and polygamy, as "things indifferent," 110

dominion founded in grace, doctrine of, 23, 40n100, 51

Donation of Constantine, 163n52

dragonnades, 11n17, 167n74

"Ecclesia" (1682; Locke), xxxix, 180–81

Eclogues (Virgil), 37n87

Edict of Nantes, Revocation of, x, xi, xxxvii

Edward VI (king of England), 31

Egyptians, idolatry of, 97–99

Elizabeth I (queen of England), ix, 31, 50–51n128, 85–86

Emims (biblical people), 43

England: Carthusians, martyrdom of, 166; Civil Wars (*see* Civil Wars, English); conventicles or assemblies for non-Anglican worship, 53–57; France and Spain, fears regarding, 133n71; history of state control of Church in, 30–31; intolerance in, ix, x; Jews readmitted to, 34n78, 156; in North America, 39n96; Papal excommunication and deposition of Elizabeth I, 50–51n128; religious pluralism in, 156; religious refugees in, x, 189n113; Roman Catholic restoration, fears of return of monastic and church lands following, 166; separation of church and state in, xiii–xiv; state and Church, coextensiveness between, 156

English statute law: Act of Union with Scotland (1707), 82n35; Conventicle Acts (1664, 1670), 53n140, 89; Corporation Act (1661), 88–89; penal laws, xxxvii–xxxviii, 85–87, 168–70; Roman Catholicism, statutory toleration of, 49n126; Test Act (1673), xiii–xiv, 88–89; Toleration Act (1689), xi, xiii, xv, 4n3, 4n5, 23n47, 54n144, 57–58n154, 58n157, 85n41, 95n59; Uniformity Act (1662), 89

enthusiasm: chapter added to *Essay Concerning Human Understanding* on, 124n50; defined, 124n50;

enthusiasm (*continued*)
"Enthusiasm" (1682; Locke), xxxix,
177–80; human tendency to pursue,
124; interpretation of Scripture and,
145; Masham's rebuttal of Locke
on, xxxix, 178n86, 179n94
Ephesian cult of Diana, 18
Epicureanism, accusations against
Locke of, 91–94
Epicurus, 91n55
Episcopalians. *See* Church of
England
equality of rights as basis for toleration, 57–61
error: human liability to, 172; right to
argue against, xviii, 46, 147–48; tolerance for, xxxviii, 170–71 (*see also*
toleration)
"Error" (1698; Locke), xl, 186–89
Esau (biblical figure), 43
*Essay Concerning Human Understand-
ing* (1671/1689; Locke), xvii, xxxvi,
xxxix, 124n50
Essay Concerning Toleration (1667;
Locke), 105–39; additional passages, xxxiv, 132–39; anticlericalism
in, 134–35, 136–39; Ashley, Lord,
and, xxi, xxxiii, 122n45; development of Locke's thought in, xxi;
distinctive groups, suppression
of, 118–21, 134; effectiveness and
Christian character of toleration,
134–35; end or purpose of state,
105–7; *Letter Concerning Toleration*
and, xxi, 115n27; practical opinions,
as "things indifferent," 110–14; on
Protestant dissenters, 125–30; on
Roman Catholics and other antinomians, 117–18, 122–25, 133; on
separation of church and state, 135–
39; speculative opinions, 107–10,
132; textual notes, xxxiii–xxxiv; on
"things indifferent," 65n170, 107–10,

132–33, 135–36; uniformity, danger
of establishing, 131–32; uniformity,
only producible by extreme severity, 125, 129–31; worship, 107–10
Essays on the Law of Nature (1663–64;
Locke), xxxv, xxxviii, 116n31
*Essential Rights and Liberties of Prot-
estants* (1744; Williams), xxii
established religion (National Religion), 74, 76, 81, 85, 90, 94, 99–101,
102, 103, 136
Estates, French provincial assembly
of, 164, 165
Eucharist: kneeling for, 38n90, 109,
173–74; public offices and licenses,
reception of Eucharist to maintain,
88–89
Eugene IV (pope), 161
evangelical tolerance, xi–xii, 7–12, 24–
26, 134–35
examination of ecclesiastical opinions, necessity of, 186–89
excommunication: ecclesiastical right
of, 19–20, 157–58; Locke's beliefs
regarding, xxxvi; monarchs, excommunication and deposition of,
50–51; by Montpelier Protestants,
165–66
Exodus: 20:12–17, 114n24; 22:20–21,
41n101, 42; 22:21, 189; 33:9, 189

faith: Analogy of Faith, 65; examination of opinions necessary to, 187;
Rule of Faith (*sola scriptura*), xxxv,
xxxix, 64–67, 82–83; toleration of
articles of, 44–48
fanaticism/phanaticism, 78, 122, 125,
152. *See also* Protestant dissenters
fatherly power as origin of both monarchy and priesthood, 149, 151–52
Felix V (pope), 161
fiduciary or trust, government as,
105n1

Finch, Daniel, 2nd Earl of Nottingham, 173n81
Finch, Sir John, 173
First Letter Concerning Toleration
(Locke). *See Letter Concerning
Toleration*
force and coercion: distinctive groups,
means used to suppress, 120–21;
end or purpose of civil society
not constituted for suppression of
religious belief by, 69–76; inward
judgment not affected by, 13–15,
74n11, 89–91, 112, 125–27, 172; not to
be used to enforce religion, 19–23,
153–54, 155–56, 172–73; penal laws
of England, 85–87; prejudice not
removed by, 87–88; reasons for
avoiding use of, 120–21; uniformity
only producible by extreme severity in, 125, 129–31. *See also* disorder,
intolerance as means of preventing;
ineffectiveness of intolerance
Fourth Letter for Toleration (1706;
Locke), xv
"Fragments on Toleration" (Locke),
xxi, xxxiv; "Against Samuel Parker"
(1669–70), xxxv–xxxvi, 148–52;
"Civil and Ecclesiastical Power"
(1674), xxxvi, 152–58; *Constitutions
of Carolina* (1669–70), xiv, xxxv,
39n95, 128n58, 146–48; "Ecclesia"
(1682), xxxix, 180–81; "Enthusiasm" (1682), xxxix, 177–80; "Error"
(1698), xl, 186–89; "Infallibility"
(1661), xxxiv–xxxv, 141–45; "Infallibility Revisited" (1675), xxxvii,
160–64; "Latitude" (1679), xxxviii,
173–74; "The Obligation of Penal
Laws" (1676), xxxvii–xxxviii, 168–
70; "The Origin of Religious Societies" (1681), xxxviii–xxxix, 174–77;
"Pacific Christians" (1688), xl, 182–
84; "Pennsylvania Laws" (1686),
xl, 182; "Philanthropy" (1675),
xxxvi, 158–60; "Religion in France"
(1676–79), xxxvii, 164–67; "Sacerdos" (1698), xl, 184–86; "Scriptures
for Toleration" (ca. 1676–90), xl,
189; "Toleration and Error" (1676),
xxxviii, 170–71; "Toleration and
Sincerity" (1679), xxxviii, 172–
73; "Toleration in Israel" (1678),
xxxviii, 171; "Tradition" (1682),
xxxix, 181–82
France: *dragonnades* used to enforce
conversion, 11n17, 167n74; English
fears regarding, 133n71; influence
of Locke in, xxii, 3; intolerance in,
ix, x; "Religion in France" (1676–
79; Locke), xxxvii, 164–67; secular republican tradition in, xiv; St.
Bartholomew's Day Massacre, ix,
130. *See also* Huguenots

Galatians: 2:11, 80; 5, 10; 5:6, 8n9; 5:9–
10, 189
Galileo, 107n8
galley slaves, 55n146, 126
Gaultier, Jacques, 161
Gaurr/Giaour, 176
Gelasius II (pope), 161
general councils of the church, infal-
libility of, 160–64
Geneva, as term for Calvinism, 27n56.
See also Calvinism
Germany: Cleves/Brandenburg, reli-
gious pluralism in, xxi, 156; influ-
ence of Locke in, xxii; intolerance
in, ix
Gévaudan, Joanne de, 165n60
Giaour/Gaurr, 176
Gibeonites (biblical people), 43
God: as party written for, 102–4;
speculative opinion, belief in a
deity not regarded as, 132
government. *See* state

grace, doctrine of dominion founded
  in, 23, 40n100, 51
Great is Diana of the Ephesians (1680;
  Blount), 18n38
Greeks, idolatry of, 98–99
Gregory I the Great (pope), 130n64
Gregory VII (pope), 161
Gregory VIII (pope), 161
Gunpowder Plot, 50n128

Ham (biblical figure), 98
Harvard, Thomas Hollis Library at,
  vii–viii, xxii–xxiii
"hat honor," Quaker refusal of, 118
Hebrews 7:23–25, 10:11–12, 137n79
Henry VIII (king of England), 31, 166
Henry of Navarre, later Henry IV
  (king of France), 51n128
heretics and schismatics: distinction
  between, 63n166; heresy defined,
  64–66; keeping faith with, 50, 121;
  popes, schismatic, 161; postscript,
  Letter Concerning Toleration, 63–67;
  same religion required for, 63–64;
  schism defined, 66; sola scriptura
  (Rule of Faith), 64–67
Hinduism, 178–79
Hobbes, Thomas, 50n128, 117n32, 152
Hollis, Thomas, and Thomas Hollis
  Library, vii–viii, xxii–xxiii
Honorius II (pope), 161
Hooker, Richard, xxxix, 41n101, 74, 75,
  180
Horace, 40n99, 66n171
Horims (biblical people), 43
Hotman, François, 51n128
Hudibras (1663; Butler), 90
Huguenots: England, fleeing to, x;
  French persecution of, 9n10, 55n146,
  56n149, 164–67; quartering of sol-
  diers in households of, 11n17, 167;
  "stranger" communities, toleration
  of, 42n104

human nature, corruption of, 96, 99,
  100, 101
Hus, Jan, 50n127

idolatry: biblical inclination of Jews
  toward, 79; history of, 97–101; in
  Mosaic Law, 38–44
"ignorance is the mother of devotion," as aphorism, 130n64
Independents (Congregationalists),
  58, 78, 125n52, 156. See also Protestant dissenters
index of banned books (Roman
  Catholic), 163
Indians, American. See Native
  Americans
"indifferent things." See "things indifferent" to salvation
ineffectiveness of intolerance: Alpine
  or reciprocity argument, xv–xvi;
  in Essay Concerning Toleration,
  112, 125–28; inward judgment not
  affected by force or persecution,
  13–15, 74n11, 89–91, 112, 125–28; in
  Letter Concerning Toleration, xv–
  xvi, 13–15; Locke's views on, xiv–
  xvi; persecution, encouragement of
  opinions by, 123–24, 134; in Third
  Letter for Toleration, 74n11, 89–91
infallibility: chair of Innocent VI,
  not conferred by, 166; "Infallibility"
  (1661; Locke), on papal infallibility, xxxiv–xxxv, 141–45; "Infallibility
  Revisited" (1675; Locke), on conciliar infallibility, xxxvii, 160–64
Innocent II (pope), 161
Innocent VI (pope), 166
intolerance: encouragement of opinions by, 123–24, 164; inward judgment not affected by, 13–15, 74n11,
  89–91, 112, 125–27, 172; Locke's
  argument from patterns of, xvi;
  Scriptural basis for, x, xi, xii, xv,

xl; in 17th century, ix–x; tolerance
denied to the intolerant, 51n132, 118,
123; uniformity only producible by
extreme severity of, 125, 129–31. *See
also* disorder, intolerance as means
of preventing; ineffectiveness of
intolerance; toleration
Ireland: Cromwell in, ix; Locke's
silence about Catholicism of,
82n35
Isis (Egyptian ruler/deity), 97
Islam: antinomianism, 52; Christian
galley slaves under, 126; Christian unity, effects of lack of, 80, 82;
Christians practicing under, xxxviii,
21–22, 173–74; civil rights accorded
to, 58–59, 77–79; conversion of
Muslims, hopes for, 77, 80; dervishes, 178; enthusiasm in, 178, 179;
heretics and schismatics, Muslims
not regarded as, 63–64; separation
of church and state, as example of,
135; tradition in, 181–82
Italy, coextensiveness between state
and Church in, 156

James II (king of England), 4n3,
23n47, 124n51, 166n69
Japan, suppression of Roman Catholicism in, 130–31
jaugis/yogis, 178–79
Jefferson, Thomas, xiv
Jeremiah 7:6, 22:3, 189
Jews and Judaism: Christian unity,
effects of lack of, 80, 82; civil rights
accorded to, 77–79; conversion of,
hopes for, 59n158, 77, 80; in England, 34n78, 156; Mosaic Law, 41–
44, 170; philosemitism, 17th century, 59n158; toleration in biblical
Israel, xxxviii, 171; toleration of, 34,
44, 59, 133; tradition, role of, 181–82;
worship of, 36

John: 3:1–2, 147n13; 14:2, 31n71; 17:3, 80;
18:36, 139n81; 21:16, 135n73, 173n79
Joshua (biblical figure), 43
Joshua 2:9, 43n107
Julius Caesar, 37n88
Julius II (pope), 162
Jupiter Belus (deity), 97, 98
Jupiter Hammon (deity), 97, 98
jure divino (divine right of kings),
106, 138
Jurieu, Pierre, 51n132
Justel, Henri, 163n50

kings. *See* monarchs
1 Kings 21:1–16, 110n14
kneeling for Eucharist, 38n90, 109,
173–74
Knights of St. John of Malta, 64

"Latitude" (1679; Locke), xxxviii, 173–
74
latitudinarianism, xvii–xviii, 33n75,
95n59, 131–32, 173–74
Laud, William, 129n61
law: charity in preservation of, 160;
of Churches, 153–54, 155–56, 172–73;
English statutes (*see* English statute
law); interpretation of, 141; obedience to, means of procuring, 153–56;
penal laws of England, xxxvii–
xxxviii, 85–87, 168–70; proper matter
of, 153, 154; sin and, 41, 114–17
Le Clerc, Jean, xxxii
Letter Concerning Toleration (1685/
1689; Locke), 1–67; anticlericalism in, 22n46, 30n65, 30n67, 61n163;
articles of faith or religion, 44–48;
Churches, duty of toleration by,
19–23; Churches, toleration by state
of, 31–40; clergy, duty of toleration
by, 23–26; conscience of private
person, laws inimical to, 48–49,
113–14; conventicles or assemblies

Letter Concerning Toleration (*continued*)
for non-Anglican worship, 53–57;
cryptogram, xxxi–xxxii; editions
and translations of, xxii, xxix–xxxi,
3; equality of rights as basis for
toleration, 57–61; *Essay Concerning
Toleration* and, xxi, 115n27; evangelical tolerance proclaimed by,
xi–xii, 7–12, 24–26; exclusions from
tolerance, 49–53; on ineffectiveness
of intolerance, xiv–xvi, 13–15; influence of, xxii–xxiii; magistrates, duty
of toleration by, 26–32; original title
page, 1; Popple's preface, xxxi, 3–5;
postscript on heretics and schismatics, 63–67; private persons, duty
of toleration by, 20–23; on separation of church and state, xii–xiv,
12–19, 24, 34, 38, 59–61; skepticism,
limited role of, xvi–xviii; speculative opinions, 44; textual notes,
xxix–xxxii; worship, 33–44, 132–33
Letter to a Person of Quality (1675),
61n163
Leviathan (Hobbes), 50n128, 152n21
Leviticus 19:10, 189
liberalism, Locke associated with, xi
libertinism (Epicureanism), accusations against Locke of, 91–94
liberty: human pursuit of, 124, 126–27;
religious societies, voluntary and
free nature of, 15–17, 32, 156, 176–77,
180–81; tolerance and, 25, 46–47, 53
Liberty of Prophesying (1647; Taylor),
xxxv, 51n132
licenses, reception of Eucharist to
maintain, 88–89
Life of Lycurgus (Plutarch), 116n31
Limborch, Philip van, xi, xxxi–xxxii
Locke, John: anti-Trinitarian charges
against, xvii, 132n67; anticlericalism
of, xiv, xxi–xxii; Atticus as pseudonym for, 132, 173; chronology of life
of, xli–xlvi; development of views
of, xx–xxi; English Civil Wars
affecting, ix, x, xi, xx, xli; Epicureanism and skepticism, accusations
against Locke of, 91–94; evangelical
tolerance of, xi–xii; liberalism, association with, xi; portrait of, ii, xxiii;
on separation of church and state,
xii–xiv; on skepticism, xvi–xviii
Locke, John, writings of, xxvi; *Essay
Concerning Human Understanding*
(1671/1689), xvii, xxxvi, xxxix, 124n50;
Essays on the Law of Nature (1663–
64), xxxv, xxxviii, 116n31; *Fourth
Letter for Toleration* (1706), xv; on
index of banned books (Roman
Catholic), 163n51; *Letter to a Person
of Quality* (1675), possible involve-
ment in, 61n163; *Oeuvres diverses
de Monsieur Jean Locke* (1710), xxii;
Reasonableness of Christianity (1695),
xvii, xxii, 24n51, 185n107; "Rules of
the Dry Club" (1692), xl; *Two Tracts
on Government* (1660–62), xx, xxi,
xxxiii, xxxvi, 33n75, 139n82; *Works*
(1714 and subsequent), xxii, xxx,
xxxiii, xl. *See also Essay Concerning
Toleration;* "Fragments on Toleration"; *Letter Concerning Toleration;
Second Letter Concerning Toleration; Third Letter for Toleration; Two
Treatises of Government*
Lot (biblical figure), 43
Lough, John, xxxvii
Louis XIV (king of France), x, 9n10
Luke: 6:27–28, 189; 14:23, x, xi; 22:25, 8;
22:32, 8; 23:34, 189
Luther, Martin, ix
Lutherans, xxi, 58n154, 59n157, 64, 66,
156, 176
Lycurgus, Life of (Plutarch), 116n31

magistrate. *See* monarchs; state

Magna Charta, 106

Maizeaux, Pierre Des. *See* Des Maizeaux, Pierre.

Malachi 3:5, 189

Manners, Reformation of, 10n14, 83–84, 96–97

Marvell, Andrew, xxxvi

Mary I (queen of England), 31

Masham, Damaris, xxxix, 178n86, 179n94

Massachusetts Colony, intolerance in, ix

Matthew: 5:43–48, 189; 7:13–14, 100n64; 7:14, 15n29; 7:44, 27, 189; 8:23–27, 142n2; 13:25, 136n77, 16:18–19, 16n33; 16:18–22, 142n3; 18:20, 17; 18:22, 25n52

Maxwell, John, 139n82

Melibaeus, 37

Melville, Andrew, 139n82

Metamorphoses (Ovid), 61n154

Mile-End (London), 76

Mill, John Stuart, xi

Milo, 37n88

Milton, J. R. and Philip, xxxiii

The Mischief of Separation (1680; Stillingfleet), xxxix

monarchs: clergy, conspiring with, 61n163, 138–39; divine right of (*jure divino*), 106, 138; excommunication and deposition of, 50–51; paternal power as origin of, 149, 151–52

Montpelier, France, Locke on religion in, 163–67

moral virtue and vice, 41, 84, 114–17, 184–86

Mosaic Law, 41–44, 170

Muscovy, 156

Muslims. *See* Islam

mysteries, divine, 132, 143–44

mysticism. *See* enthusiasm

Naboth's vineyard, 110

Nantes, Revocation of Edict of, x, xi, xxxvii

nation-state. *See* state

National Religion (established religion), 74, 76, 81, 85, 90, 94, 99–101, 102, 103, 136

Native Americans: colonialization of and expropriation of land from, Locke on, 40n100; in *Constitutions of Carolina,* 146; ends of civil society among, 76; enthusiasm among, 180; Spanish treatment of, 39n96, 128n58; toleration of beliefs of, 39–40

natural religion, reliance on tradition leading to, 181

Netherlands: influence of Locke in, xxii, 3; intolerance in, ix; Jews tolerated in, 34n78; *Letter* postscript on heretics and schismatics and, 63n165–66; Lutheranism in, 58n154; nonconformists fleeing to, ix; religious refugees in, 189n113

Nicene Councils (325/787), 163, 164

Nicodemism, 147n13

Nîmes, France, Locke on religion in, 163

Niort, France, Locke on religion in, 167

non-Christians, extension of tolerance to: Christian unity, effects of lack of, 80, 82; conversion, hopes for, 59n158, 77, 80; in *Letter Concerning Toleration,* 8, 11, 34, 39–40, 58–59, 63; Locke's categorical acceptance of, xiii, 59n158; in *Third Letter for Toleration,* 77–79. *See also* Islam; Jews and Judaism; Native Americans

Nottingham, Daniel Finch, 2nd Earl of, 173n81

Numbers 33:50–52, 43n105

Oath of Allegiance (1606), 51n128
"The Obligation of Penal Laws" (1676; Locke), xxxvii–xxxviii, 168–70
Occasional Conformity Controversy, 88–89
Oeuvres diverses de Monsieur Jean Locke (1710), xxii
Of the Laws of Ecclesiastical Politie (1593–97; Hooker), xxxix, 74n13, 180n96
On Liberty (Mill), xi
Orange, France, Locke on religion in, 163
"The Origin of Religious Societies" (1681; Locke), xxxviii–xxxix, 174–77
orthodoxy: of every Church to itself, 7, 21; examination of ecclesiastical opinions and, 186–89
Osiris (Egyptian ruler/deity), 97
outward worship. *See* worship
Ovid, 61n154
Owen, John, xxxvi

"Pacific Christians" (1688; Locke), xl, 182–84
pagans. *See* non-Christians, extension of tolerance to
Palatine Library, destruction of, 130n64
papacy and papists. *See* Roman Catholicism
parallel civil and ecclesiastical powers, 152–58
Paris, France, Locke on religion in, 167
Parker, Samuel, xxxv–xxxvi, 148–52
party, writing for, 102–4
pastoral care, 94–95
paternal power as origin of both monarchy and priesthood, 149, 151–52

peace, intolerance as means of preserving. *See* disorder, intolerance as means of preventing
penal laws of England, xxxvii–xxxviii, 85–87, 168–70
Penn, William, x, xi, xl, 182n99
"Pennsylvania Laws" (1686; Locke), xl, 182
Pensées diverses (1683; Bayle), xl, 185n103
people, power and authority of state derived from, 106
Peripatetics, 73
persecution. *See* force and coercion; intolerance
1 Peter: 2:13, 74, 75n15; 3:9, 189; 5:2–3, 81
Petrine succession, 16n33, 17n34, 162
phanaticism/fanaticism, 78, 122, 125, 152. *See also* Protestant dissenters
"Philanthropy" (1675; Locke), xxxvi, 158–60
Philip II (king of Spain), 162
philosophers and priests, pre-Christian, separation of religion and morality by, 184–86
Philosophical Commentary on the Words of Our Lord, "Compel them to Come in" (1686; Bayle), xi
Phoroneus (king of the Argives), 98
Pius V (pope), 50n128
pluralism, religious, xxi, 156
Plutarch, 116n31
Politics (Aristotle), 116n31
polygamy and divorce, as "things indifferent," 110
Popple, William, xxix–xxxi, xxxii, 3–5, 56n150, 58n157
population: Locke's preoccupation with, 122n44; Protestant dissenters and Catholics as proportion of, 128n59

practical opinions, as "things indifferent," 110–14
preaching, ineffectiveness of, 134–35
prejudice, force and coercion not removing, 87–88
Presbyterians, ix, 51n132, 57–58n154, 58, 78, 82n35, 125n52, 139, 156, 170. *See also* Protestant dissenters
Presbytery Displayed (1663; Maxwell), 139n82
"priestcraft," xxii, 24n51. *See also* anticlericalism
priests. *See* clergy
princes. *See* monarchs
private interest, salvation as matter of, 172
private persons: conscience of, laws inimical to, 48–49, 113–14; duty of toleration, 20–23
Proast, Jonas, xv, xxx, xxxii–xxxiii, 69n2. *See also Argument of The Letter Concerning Toleration . . .; Third Letter Concerning Toleration*
property rights: colonialization of and expropriation of land from Native Americans, Locke on, 40n100; state regulation of, 116n31
Protestant dissenters: accused of intolerance, 51n132, 118; antinomianism of, xix, xxi; *Essay Concerning Toleration* on treatment of, 125–30; fragmentation of Protestantism by, fears regarding, 158–59; France, Locke on religion in, 165; "friendly debate" with (1666–1674), xxxvi; on kneeling for Eucharist, 38n90, 109, 173–74; Locke's versus Popple's list of tolerated sects, 58; Nicodemism, 147n13; phanatics/fanatics as term for, 78, 122, 125, 152; as proportion of English population, 128n59; recu-

sancy laws applicable to, 86n44; Roman Catholics and, James II seeking alliance between, 124n51; sects of, 125n52 (*see also* specific sects, e.g., Quakers); in *Third Letter for Toleration,* 78; Toleration Act (1689, England), xi, xiii, xv, 4n3, 4n5, 23n47. *See also* Puritans
Protestantism: fears of contraction and fragmentation of, 158–59; France, Locke on religion in, 164–67; intolerance of, in 17th century, ix, x; as middle way between Catholic superstition and sectarian enthusiasm, 124n50; penal laws versus Roman Catholic persecutions, 85n40. *See also* specific sects and denominations
Psalm 14:3, 100n63
public offices, reception of Eucharist to maintain, 88–89
Puritans: Civil Wars, hegemony during, 126n54; grace, doctrine of dominion founded on, 23n50; on "indifferent things," xvii; kneeling for Eucharist, objections to, 38n90, 109n12; radicalism of, ix, xi, xix; on religious vestments, 27n61, 109n13; on right of subjects to reform religion, 121n42; suppression under Archbishop Laud, 129

Quakers, x, 58, 78, 119, 125n52, 156, 159, 170. *See also* Protestant dissenters
quartering of soldiers in Huguenot households, 11n17, 167

Rahab (biblical figure), 43
Real Presence, 83
"reason of state" arguments for toleration, 57n153, 122n43–44

Reasonableness of Christianity (1695; Locke), xvii, xxii, 24n51, 185n107, 187n110

reciprocity argument on ineffectiveness of intolerance, xv–xvi

recusancy laws established by Elizabeth I, 86n44

Reformation of Manners, 10n14, 83–84, 96–97

relics, 166, 167

"Religion in France" (1676–79; Locke), xxxvii, 164–67

Religion of Protestants (1638; Chillingworth), xxxv

religious pluralism, xxi, 156

religious societies: origins of, xxxviii–xxxix, 174–77, 180, 181; "Pacific Christians" (1688; Locke) as guidelines for, xl, 182–84; voluntary and free nature of, 15–17, 32, 156, 176–77, 180–81. *See also* Churches

religious tolerance. *See* toleration

religious vestments, 27n61, 109

Remonstrants, 21n43, 58n157, 66. *See also* Arminians

René d'Anjou (king of Sicily), 166

resistance, right of, xxxvii, 75n15, 113n21, 169

respect for beliefs of others, xviii

Revocation of Edict of Nantes, x, xi, xxxvii

rights, equality of, 57–61

Roman Catholicism: allegiance to papacy, 52, 124; in Cleves, Germany, xxi; defect of intention, principle of, 162–63; exclusion from tolerance, xi, xix–xx, 49–52, 117–18, 122–25, 133; fears of return of monastic and church lands following restoration in England, 166; "Fragments on Toleration" concerning, xxi; France, Locke on religion in,

164–67; grace, doctrine of dominion founded in, 23n50, 51; "ignorance is the mother of devotion," as aphorism of, 130n64; index of banned books, 163; infallibility, papal and conciliar (*see* infallibility); intolerance of, in 17th century, ix, x; in Ireland, Locke's silence about, 82n35; in Japan, 130–31; keeping faith with heretics, 50, 121; monarchs, excommunication and deposition of, 50–51; Nicodemism, 147n13; Parker's *Discourse on Ecclesiastical Politie*, Locke's arguments against, 150–51; Petrine succession, 16n33, 17n34, 162; population of England, as proportion of, 128n59; possibility of tolerance of, xx, 44, 52n137, 118n33; Protestant dissenters and, James II seeking alliance between, 124n51; Protestant fears of reversion to, 158; Protestant penal laws versus persecutions of, 85n40; recusancy laws applicable to, 86n44; religious pluralism in England and, 156; schismatic popes, 161; Scripture, ignorance of, 167; secular power, pope regarded as, 124, 139; statutory toleration in England, 49n126; in *Third Letter for Toleration*, 78; tradition in, 64, 181–82; transubstantiation, doctrine of, xix, 38n90, 44, 83, 107; Vatican, references to, 27

Romans: 12:6, 65n170; 12:14, 20–21, 189; 13:1, 75n15; 13:4, x

Rule of Faith (*sola scriptura*), xxxv, xxxix, 64–67, 82–83

"rule of the saints" in Calvinism, xix

rulers. *See* monarchs

"Rules of the Dry Club" (1692; Locke), xl

Russia, 156
Rycaut, Sir Paul, 178

sabbatarians, 37n83
"Sacerdos" (1698; Locke), xl, 184–86
sacrifices, 37–38
St. Bartholomew's Day Massacre, ix, 130
St. John of Malta, Knights of, 64
St. Paul, conversion of, xv
salvation: examination of ecclesiastical opinions and, 187; as matter of private interest, 172; "things indifferent" to (see "things indifferent" to salvation)
Satires (Horace), 40n99
Saturn (deity), 97
schismatic popes, 161
schismatics generally. See heretics and schismatics
Scotland, Act of Union between England and (1707), 82n35
Scottish Presbyterianism, 57–58n154, 82n35, 139
Scripture: Analogy of Faith, 65; divine mysteries of, 132, 143–44; importance of studying, 186–89; interpretation of, 141–45; intolerance/intolerance, basis for, x, xi, xii, xv, xl, 189; Mosaic Law, 41–44, 170; papal authorizations of different editions of, 161; Roman Catholic ignorance of, 167; sola scriptura (Rule of Faith), xxxv, xxxix, 64–67, 82–83; "stranger" communities, toleration of, 42–44, 189n113; toleration in biblical Israel, xxxviii, 171. See also specific books, e.g., Exodus
"Scriptures for Toleration" (ca. 1676–90; Locke), xl, 189
Second Letter Concerning Toleration (1690; Locke), xv; fiction of author

as third party defending First Letter, 70n3; hope for conversion of Muslims, Jews, and pagans in, 59n158; on Native American civil societies, 76–77n118; public offices, reception of Eucharist to maintain, 88n48; Third Letter citing, 69n1, 77n19, 83n38, 89n49
second table (of Ten Commandments), duties of, 114–17
secrecy in religious belief and observance, 147
sectarianism: dangers of, 158–59; imposed by creed-makers, 80–83; Protestant fears of contraction and fragmentation, 158–59. See also Protestant dissenters
Select Discourses (1660; John Smith), xxxix
separation of church and state: dangers of confounding, 59–61; in Essay Concerning Toleration, 135–39; in Letter Concerning Toleration, xii–xiv, 12–19, 24, 34, 38, 59–61; Locke's arguments for, xii–xiv; in "The Origin of Religious Societies," xxxviii–xxxix, 174–77; parallel civil and ecclesiastical powers, 152–58; Parker's Discourse on Ecclesiastical Politie, Locke's arguments against, 148–52; Stillingfleet's arguments against, xxxix
Servetus, Michael, ix, 39n92
sexual irregularities, Catholic clergy accused of, 165
Shaftesbury, Earl of. See Ashley, Lord
Sheldon, Gilbert, xxxvi, 148n15
simony, 161–62
sin and law, relationship between, 41, 114–17
sincere seeking after truth, 87–88
Sixtus V (pope), 51n128, 161, 162

skepticism: of Bayle and Spinoza
compared to Locke, xi; *First Letter,*
limited role in, xvi–xviii; Proast's
charges regarding, Locke's answers
to, 91–94

slavery, in *Constitutions of Carolina,*
148

Smith, John, xxxix, 38n96

social order and rectitude, state's
responsibility for ensuring, 45–48,
96–97, 112–13

Socinians, xvii, 30n66, 59n157, 78

sola scriptura (Rule of Faith), xxxv,
xxxix, 64–67, 82–83

soldiers quartered in Huguenot
households, 11n17, 167

Solomon (biblical king), 43

Soto, Domingo de, 163

souls of men, as party written for,
102–4

Sozzini, Fausto (Faustus Socinus),
30n66

Spain: in Central and South America,
39n96, 128n58; English fears regarding, 133n71; state and Church, coextensiveness between, 156

Spanish Armada, 50n128

Sparta, 116

speculative opinions: belief in a deity
not regarded as, 132; in "Civil and
Ecclesiastical Powers," 153, 157; in
Constitutions of Carolina, 148; in
Essay Concerning Toleration, 107–10,
132; importance of examination of,
189; in *Letter Concerning Toleration,*
44–45; Locke's insistence on freedom of, xvii

Spencer, John, 41n101

Spinoza, Baruch, xi, xix, 53n138

spiritual experience. *See* enthusiasm

Stanton, Timothy, xxxix

state: antinomian threat to, xix–xx;
charity in preservation of, 159–
60; Churches, coextensiveness of
membership with, 156; Churches,
relationship to, 29–31; Churches,
toleration of, 31–40; "Civil and
Ecclesiastical Power" (1674; Locke),
xxxvi; civil interests, constituted
only for advancement of, 12–15;
clergy, influences of, 137–39; communion with, 153, 154; conscience
of private person, laws inimical to,
48–49, 113–14; duty of toleration,
26–32; end or purpose of, 69–76,
105–7, 153, 154, 169; as fiduciary or
trust, 105n1; Locke's developing
thought on role of, xx; membership in, nonvoluntary nature of,
156; moral virtue and vice, respon-
sibilities regarding, 41, 84, 114–17;
parallel civil and ecclesiastical
powers, 152–58; Parker's *Discourse
on Ecclesiastical Politie,* Locke's
arguments against, 148–52; penal
laws, use of, xxxvii–xxxviii, 85–87,
168–70; people, power and authority derived from, 106; resistance,
right of, xxxvii, 75n15, 113n21; social
order and rectitude, responsibility
for ensuring, 45–48, 96–97, 112–13;
"things indifferent," power of magistrate to compel, 133, 135. *See also*
force and coercion; law; monarchs;
separation of church and state

States, French provincial assembly of.
See Estates, French provincial assembly of

Stillingfleet, Edward, xxxviii–xxxix

"stranger" communities, toleration of,
42–44, 189n113

Stuart kings of England, ix

Sweden, coextensiveness between
state and Church in, 156

Table chronographique de l'estat du Christianisme (1609; Gaultier), 161

Taylor, Jeremy, xxxv, 51n132

Ten Commandments, second table of, 114–17

Test Act (1673), xiii–xiv; 88–89

Theseus (king of Attica), 98

"things indifferent" to salvation (adiaphora), xvi–xvii; divorce and polygamy as, 110; in *Essay Concerning Toleration*, 65n170, 107–10, 132–33, 135–36; interpretation of Scripture regarding, 145; kneeling for Eucharist, 38n90, 109, 173–74; in *Letter Concerning Toleration*, xvi–xvii, 33 36, 65n170; practical opinions as, 110–14; Puritans on, xvii; state power to compel, 133, 135; in *Third Letter for Toleration*, 110–14; vestments, religious, 27n61, 109; worship, circumstances of, 133, 135–36

Third Letter Concerning Toleration (1691; Proast), 69n2, 78n19, 80n28, 83n38, 85n39, 87n45, 91n55, 94n56, 96n61, 97n62, 102n65

Third Letter for Toleration (1692; Locke), 69–104; on accusations of Epicureanism, skepticism, and atheism, 91–94; corrupt conformists, problem of, 94–95; on corruption of human nature, 96, 99, 100, 101; creed-makers, sectarianism imposed by, 80–83; on end or purpose of civil society, 69–76; fiction of author as third party defending *First Letter*, 70n3; on history of idolatry and historical absence of toleration, 97–101; inward judgment not affected by force or coercion, 89–91; on non-Christians' civil rights, 77–79; on penal laws of England, 85–87; on prejudice and

sincere seeking after truth, 87–88; Proast, refutation of, xv, xxxii–xxxiii, 69n2; public offices and licenses, reception of Eucharist to maintain, 88–89; on Reformation of Manners, 83–84, 96–97; "Sacerdos" and, 185n107; textual notes, xxxii–xxxiii; on writing for party, 102–4

Thirty-Nine Articles, xiii–xiv, 90

Thomas Aquinas, 41n102

Thoth (Egyptian ruler/deity), 97–98

2 Timothy: 2:19, 8n8; 4:2, 95n57

Titus 2:14, 183

toleration, ix–xxiii; antinomianism and (*see* antinomianism); of atheists (*see* atheists); in context of 17th century intolerance, ix–x; denied to the intolerant, 51n132, 118, 123; development of Locke's views on, xx–xxi, 33n75; effectiveness of, 128–29, 134–35; equality of rights as basis for, 57–61; of error, xxxviii, 170–71; historical absence of, 97–101; liberty and, 25, 46–47, 53; precursors and contemporaries of Locke writing on, xi; of Protestant dissenters (*see* Protestant dissenters); "reason of state" arguments for, 57n153, 122n43–44; of Roman Catholics (*see* Roman Catholicism); Scriptural arguments regarding, x, xi, xii, xl, 189; separation of church and state (*see* separation of church and state); weak sects, as ruse of, 39–40, 51n132. *See also* intolerance, and specific works by Locke, e.g., *Letter Concerning Toleration*

Toleration Act (1689, England), xi, xiii, xv, 4n3, 4n5, 23n47, 54n144, 57–58n154, 58n157, 85n41, 95n59

"Toleration and Error" (1676; Locke), xxxviii, 170–71

"Toleration and Sincerity" (1679; Locke), xxxviii, 172–73
"Toleration in Israel" (1678; Locke), xxxviii, 171
town charters, 134
tradition: in Roman Catholicism, 64, 181–82
"Tradition" (1682; Locke), xxxix, 181–82
Traité sur la tolerance (1764; Voltaire), xxii
transubstantiation, xix, 38n90, 44, 83, 107
Trent, Council of (1545–63), 162, 163
Trinity, as divine mystery, 132, 143–44. *See also* anti-Trinitarianism
true Christian Church and belief, religious tolerance as mark of, 7–12
trust or fiduciary, government as, 105n1
truth, 87–88, 159, 186–89
Turks. *See* Islam
Tusculan Disputations (Cicero), 185
Two Tracts on Government (1660–62; Locke), xx, xxi, xxxiii, xxxvi, 33n75, 139n82
Two Treatises of Government (1679–83/1689; Locke): *Essay Concerning Toleration* and, 105n1, 108n10, 110n18, 116n31, 122n45, 124n49; Hooker, Locke's use of, 180n96; *Letter Concerning Toleration* and, xiii, xxxii, 34n76, 39n100, 47n117–19, 49n123, 49n125, 52n133, 61n163; "The Obligation of Penal Laws" (1676) and, xxxvii; religious tolerance arguments not present in, xiii; *Third Letter for Toleration* and, 70n4, 74n13, 76n16, 86n44
Tyrrell, James, xxxviii

uniformity: danger of establishing, 131–32; extreme severity, only producible by, 125, 129–31

Uniformity Act (1662), 89
Union of England and Scotland (1707), 82n35
unity, Christian, creed-making inimical to, 80–83
The Unreasonableness of Separation (1681; Stillingfleet), xxxix
Urban VI (pope), 161
Uzès, France, Locke on religion in, 163–64

Valens (Roman emperor), 30n68
Valla, Lorenzo, 163n52
Vega, Andrés de, 163
vestments, religious, 27n61, 109
vice and virtue, 41, 84, 114–17, 184–86
Victor IV (pope), 161
Villeneuve, France, Locke on religion in, 166
Virgil, 37n87
Virginia Statute for Religious Freedom (1779), xiv
virtue and vice, 41, 84, 114–17, 184–86
Voltaire, xxii

Walwyn, William, xi
Whitaker, Edward, 56n150
Williams, Elisha, xxii
Williams, Roger, xi
Works (1714 and subsequent; Locke), xxii, xxx, xxxiii, xl
worship: in "Civil and Ecclesiastical Powers," 153, 157; in *Essay Concerning Toleration,* 107–10, 132–33, 135–36; kneeling for Eucharist, 38n90, 109, 173–74; in *Letter Concerning Toleration,* 33–44; "things indifferent," 133, 135–36
writing for party, 102–4

yogis/jaugis, 178–79

Zachariah 7:10, 189

This book is set in Adobe Caslon Pro, a modern adaptation by Carol Twombly of faces cut by William Caslon, London, in the 1730s. Caslon's types were based on seventeenth-century Dutch old-style designs and became very popular throughout Europe and the American colonies.

This book is printed on paper that is acid-free and meets the requirements of the American National Standard for Permanence of Paper for Printed Library Materials, z39.48–1992. ∞

Book design by Louise OFarrell
Gainesville, Florida
Typography by Graphic Composition, Inc.
Bogart, Georgia
Printed and bound by Worzalla Publishing Company
Stevens Point, Wisconsin